LIVERPOOL
JOHN MOORES UNIVERSITY
AVRIL ROBARTS LRC
TEL. 0151 231 4022

WITHDRAWN

LIVERPOOL JMU LIBRARY

3 1111 00766 6454

JR. : NEBRASKA
BOOK : STUDIO 708

LIVERPOOL
JOHN MOORES UNIVERSITY
AVRIL ROBARTS LRC
TEL. 0151 231 4022

GENDER IN THE
SECONDARY CURRICULUM

The 'gender gap' in schooling, as manifested by the current disparity in boys' and girls' achievement at GCSE, continues to create problems for teachers. In this volume a team of contributors considers the gender issues particular to a range of subjects in the secondary curriculum. They discuss effective strategies – supported by their research and practice – and offer some ways forward for teachers.

The book begins with an overview of contemporary social and cultural approaches to schooling and gender, focusing particularly on the contribution of feminist scholars to the debate. It further examines key aspects of the secondary school curriculum and the implications for learners of their gendered identity. The final section moves beyond the classroom to discuss the influence of current theoretical perspectives on the complex interrelationship between the curriculum and young people's gendered identities, and its implications for their future development and career destinations.

In discussing the nature of boys' and girls' achievements in a range of school subjects, the authors seek to 'balance the books' by debating the different, if sometimes competing, needs of boys and girls.

Ann Clark and **Elaine Millard** are both lecturers in education at the University of Sheffield. Both of them have research interests in the effects of gender on attitudes and performance in the curriculum and have published widely in journals.

LIVERPOOL
JOHN MOORES UNIVERSITY
AVRIL ROBARTS LRC
TEL. 0151 231 4022

GENDER IN THE SECONDARY CURRICULUM

Balancing the books

*Edited by Ann Clark
and Elaine Millard*

London and New York

First published 1998
by Routledge
11 New Fetter Lane, London EC4P 4EE

© 1998 Ann Clark and Elaine Millard, selection and editorial matter;
individual contributors, their chapters

Typeset in Goudy by
J&L Composition Ltd, Filey, North Yorkshire
Printed and bound in Great Britain by
TJ International Ltd, Padstow, Cornwall

All rights reserved. No part of this book may be reprinted or
reproduced or utilised in any form or by any electronic,
mechanical, or other means, now known or hereafter
invented, including photocopying and recording, or in any
information storage or retrieval system, without permission in
writing from the publishers.

British Library Cataloguing in Publication Data
A catalogue record for this book is available
from the British Library

Library of Congress Cataloging in Publication Data
Gender in the secondary curriculum:
balancing the books/edited by Ann Clark and Elaine Millard.
Includes bibliographical references and index.
1. Sex differences in education–Great Britain.
2. Education, Secondary–Great Britain–Curricula.
3. Feminism and education–Great Britain.
4. Educational equalization–Great Britain.
I. Clark, Ann, 1961– . II. Millard, Elaine.
LC212.93.G7G46 1998
306. 43–dc21   97-32353
CIP

ISBN 0-415-16701-9 (hbk)
ISBN 0-415-16702-7 (pbk)

FOR WILLIAM AND HANNAH

CONTENTS

CONTENTS

CONTENTS

ILLUSTRATIONS

FIGURES

TABLES

ILLUSTRATIONS

CONTRIBUTORS

Jacky Brine has taught in post-16/adult education for many years. She is a lecturer in post-16 in the Division of Education at the University of Sheffield. She has been researching gender and post-16 education for ten years and has recently completed a project for the EC on this subject.

Ann Clark is a lecturer in the Division of Education, University of Sheffield (Modern Languages) and teaches on ITE courses. She has previously taught French, German and Spanish in comprehensive schools and in FE. Her current research interests lie in the influence of gender on pupils' attitudes towards language learning.

Julia Davies has taught English in comprehensive schools for thirteen years. Her current research as lecturer at the University of Sheffield is into talk, learning and the differential speech patterns of boys and girls. She teaches on the PGCE Educational and Professional Studies programme, as well as tutoring on the MEd Distance Learning Programme for English Language Teaching.

Carolyn Dixon is currently completing a PhD at the University of Sheffield based on an interactional study of the construction of sexuality, gender and class identity in school. She was previously Head of Department in a comprehensive school for ten years.

Chris Haywood was employed as a research fellow in the Division of Education at the University of Sheffield. He is currently working with Professor Máirtín Mac an Ghaill on a project focusing on the sexual politics of schooling.

David Jesson is currently Professor of Economics in the Centre for Performance Evaluation and Resource Management at the University of York. He is also a director of research in the Division of Education at the University of Sheffield.

Máirtín Mac an Ghaill is Professor of Education at the University of Sheffield. He is currently researching around issues of working class masculinities, changing work and family forms, funded by the Leverhulme Trust.

Elaine Millard is Co-Director of Sheffield University's Master's Degree in Literacy. She previously worked as an English teacher in a wide variety of 11–18 comprehensive schools and from 1989 to 1990 was employed as an advisory teacher by Nottingham LEA.

Clive Opie is a lecturer in the Division of Education, University of Sheffield, and has specific responsibility for IT developments within the Division as a whole. His teaching involves being an Initial Teacher Education Science tutor and working on the Division's Distance Learning MEd IT course.

Hilary Povey is Head of the Mathematics Education Centre at Sheffield Hallam University, where she lectures in mathematics and mathematics education. In her teaching, research and writing she is concerned with social justice issues in and through the mathematics curriculum.

John Quicke is Professor of Education and Head of Continuing Professional Development (CPD) in the Division of Education at the University of Sheffield. He is a qualified educational psychologist and has worked as a teacher in primary and secondary schools.

Jon Scaife is a lecturer in education at the University of Sheffield. He has taught physics, maths, IT, science and technology at secondary and tertiary level and also undergraduate physics.

Alan Skelton trained as a teacher in physical education and then taught in secondary schools. Currently he works at the University of Sheffield where he is developing his interest in masculinities in academia.

Lorna Unwin is a senior lecturer and the Director of the Centre for Research in Post-compulsory Education and Training in the Division of Education at the University of Sheffield. Her particular interests are the workplace as a site for learning and research into modern apprenticeships.

Jerry Wellington taught science in Tower Hamlets, London, before joining the Division of Education at the University of Sheffield, where he is now a Reader in education. For several years he has been running a soccer club for girls.

INTRODUCTION

Ann Clark and Elaine Millard

Since the re-emergence of feminism and the arrival of the Women's Movement in the late 1960s, with its historic coupling of the personal and the political, two generations of feminist academics have succeeded in calling into question the way in which the social and cultural relationships of men and women in the home and the workplace can be conceptualised and researched. By the 1970s, feminist scholarship, which had its beginnings in literary, sociological and linguistic theories, reflected in the work of Millett, Mitchell and Spender, created the conditions for the introduction of both new areas of study and alternative methods of researching existing disciplines such as the sociology of education. Several books were published in the 1970s and early 1980s by well-established writers such as Arnot, Byrne, David, Deem, Delamont and Spender, and the obvious interest in this new area of scholarship led to the inception of the journal *Gender and Education* in 1989 (see Acker, 1994). At the same time, the Sex Discrimination Act (1975), whilst difficult to enforce, provided an impetus in the 1980s for equal opportunities initiatives in school and the workplace, focused on improving the status and employment opportunities of women.

Similarly, feminist scholarship contributed to the growth of Women's Studies courses, which, in conjunction with the work of a wide number of feminists engaged in education, have focused specifically on the gendered nature of schooling and documented the effect of gender difference in a wide range of classroom and playground settings. Beginning from simple notions of sexual stereotyping and role modelling, researchers have moved to more complex models of analysis, such as gender regime and gendered identity. The cumulative effect of this work has been two-fold. Firstly, there is now a general acceptance in educational contexts that schools tend to confirm pupils in their gendered identities, and secondly, there is a recognition that the effect of schooling, at every level of education, from pre-school to post-16, works to increase rather than reconcile difference. Marland (1983) articulated this viewpoint in the now often-quoted pronouncement that schools act merely as 'amplifiers for society's stereotypes'.

From the earliest years, girls and boys in the same classroom have been observed to create quite different educational experiences for themselves (Weiner, 1985; Walkerdine, 1989; Delamont, 1990). In observing very young children, Licht and

Dweck (1987) found that girls had less confidence in their ability to succeed in intellectually challenging tasks. They noted that this pattern emerges in the pre-school and early school years, despite the fact that girls consistently performed as well as, if not better than, boys. Researchers have also repeatedly shown that in both formal and informal settings boys dominate physical space (Scott, 1980; Mahoney, 1985; Thorne, 1992) linguistic space, (Spender, 1980; Stanworth, 1983), and use these gains also to monopolise teacher attention. Girls perform well in school because many of them readily acquiesce to the 'good girl role' (Maccoby and Jacklin, 1975). This role makes them neat and tidy, more tolerant of boring tasks and more compliant than their male counterparts (Scott, 1980). By contrast, the sex role socialisation of boys encourages them to interact in larger groups, to engage in rough and tumble play or mock fighting, to be involved in team sports and to a certain extent to underachieve at school (Thorne, 1992; Mickelson, 1992). In their study of attitudes towards work, Harris et al. (1993) found that girls devoted considerably more time to homework than boys and were more likely to make an effort to improve their grades, whereas 'for boys, if there were problems of self-motivation or self-discipline, there tended to be less of a struggle to overcome them' (1993: 7). Ironically, girls' lack of self-confidence often leads to increased conscientiousness. Girls may work harder because they experience a degree of anxiety about 'doing the right thing' (Kelly, 1985).

In addition to the divergence in attitudes towards school work, it has been argued that the curriculum itself is gendered, with the discourses of particular disciplines signalling to learners, from the outset, their greater relevance to one sex than the other. Kelly (1981) pointed to the preponderance of male teachers in the science curriculum, particularly in physics and chemistry, and to the exclusion of girls from top science groups. Walkerdine and Walden demonstrated how boys' and girls' behaviour patterns are interpreted to suggest that boys 'understand' mathematics better than girls and, how even when girls do significantly better in class work, their behaviour is interpreted as rule governed and derived from a desire to please through hard work, in contrast to the real understanding of more disruptive boys who are placed in higher examination sets on the basis of their potential (Walden and Walkerdine, 1985).

In mixed schools, just as in the workplace, women and girls are subjected to sexual insult from both men and boys. This has been characterised by researchers as 'slagging off' (Lees, 1986; Walkerdine, 1981). Even very young boys reject girls as work partners (Goodenough, 1987; D'Arcy, 1991) and employ sexual insults to refer to both their classmates and the women teachers who supervise them (Clarricoates, 1978).

In the early 1980s, in response to the perceived inequalities of contemporary schooling and the singular failure of the Sex Discrimination Act (1975) to challenge structural inequalities, a number of projects, funded both locally and centrally, were focused on specific ways of changing teachers' classroom practices to accommodate the needs of both sexes. These have largely been targeted at the performance of girls in mathematics, science and technology, although TVEI projects, such as that which produced Genderwatch (Myers, 1987, 1992) and the work of sub-committees of subject associations, such as NATE's Language and Gender Committee, have provided classroom teachers with strategies for working towards a less gender-biased education for all pupils. The findings in the early 1980s by the APU that girls were falling behind in mathematics, for example, resulted in a series of projects to render the subject more 'girl friendly' (Joffe et al. 1988; Walden and Walkerdine, 1985; Walkerdine, 1989) and some textbooks and mathematical tasks were successfully redrafted to reflect girls' interests. Similarly, the GIST project (Girls into Science and Technology project), a joint venture between the former Manchester Polytechnic and the University of Manchester, worked from a hypothesis that female underachievement in science and technology was socially constructed both by the curriculum itself and setting procedures of the school. Further initiatives such as WISE (Women into Science and Engineering) and GATE (Girls and Technology Education) sought to rectify the imbalance between the two sexes in the sciences and to encourage girls to consider careers in this typically male domain (see Measor and Sikes, 1992).

Despite the increased awareness of the need to afford pupils equal opportunities and equal access to the curriculum, the wealth of accumulated evidence demonstrates the persistence of difference in the opportunities afforded to the sexes by contemporary schooling. Furthermore, the problem of how best to raise the issue within a school context remains a vexed one, because teachers may be wary of the feminist discourse itself or concerned about the risk of alienating colleagues (see Acker, 1994). One reason may be found in the fact that until very recently there has been no parallel focus on the relative underachievement of boys in the language curriculum. On the contrary, feminists have demonstrated that books chosen for reading with English classes in school are biased towards boys' lives, suggesting alternatives with positive role models for girls (Stones, 1983; Whyte, 1983; Baines, 1985), including the feminist rewriting of fairy stories (Lurie, 1980). It is of course perfectly understandable that feminists have focused on girls' needs, particularly as many women academics have experienced discrimination in the workplace, finding male academic institutions resistant to change (Rudduck, 1994: 9). There does not appear to be a corollary between the number of women entering further and higher education and their subsequent economic status. Indeed, despite legislation and the changing nature of employment, girls still tend to select from a narrower range of occupations than boys because of the preoccupation with thoughts of balancing the needs and demands of a family life with a career (see Griffin,1984). Thus fewer women are found in professional employment or in politics; despite the current influx of women into the new Labour government, they are still outnumbered three to one by men (EOC, 1997). Women traditionally work in service industries or in low status, stereotypically female locations such as secretarial or domestic work and are more likely to work part-time than men. Rates of pay clearly reflect this assumed inferior status: in 1990, women earned 76.6 per cent of men's gross weekly earnings (Davidson and Cooper, 1992).

Notwithstanding these facts, the concern to equalise the opportunities for girls in school has created its own difficulties by focusing on monocausal explanations for inequality in which one sex is represented as oppressed by the other in a perpetuation of sex role stereotyping. The movement in feminist thought recently has been away from oversimplified and reductive models of unified subjects located in social reproduction theories, towards a more complex understanding of the creation of subjectivity within the contradictory and fluctuating positions of power relationships. As Acker points out 'women are possessors of multiple subjectivities based on race, class, age, sexual orientation, religion, and so forth' (1994: 20). Clearly, certain groups of girls are at a greater disadvantage than others and are more likely to accept traditional, stereotypical female roles and to be resistant to feminist ideas and notions of equality.

Current theories of masculinity have also encouraged feminists to reconceptua-lise the formation of gendered identity by describing relations in which dominant forms of male behaviour are constructed as much by their difference from sub-ordinated forms of masculinity as from aspects of femininity (Connell, 1987; Mac an Ghaill, 1994; Jordan, 1995). There has been a perceptible break from a view of girls or boys, women or men, as single unifying categories towards a foregrounding of the context in which relationships are played out.

There are therefore two immediate concerns which inform this current collection of essays. The first stems from a growing awareness that a simple polarisation of male and female roles in schools, within an explanatory framework of patriarchal oppression, masks many other patterns of difference contingent on social status, race and class; the second from the increasing scepticism of committed feminist teachers about the efficacy of anti-sexist initiatives in changing patterns of beha-viour in schools. Ways of moving beyond anti-sexist programmes in schools have been most effectively developed by researchers in Australia (Davies, 1997). Through a Literacy Intervention Strategies for Boys project, teachers' attention has been directed towards helping boys to deconstruct masculinity, which she describes as 'a move towards multiple voices, multiple perspectives, multiple ways of seeing the world'. The focus is on encouraging a critical literacy which enables pupils to question all aspects of their reading rather than challenging sexism in texts head on.

In the following chapters each writer is committed not only to describing how particular areas of schooling are gendered, but also to suggesting ways in which practising teachers can attempt to 'balance the books' and render their classrooms and their curriculum open and accessible to both sexes in the hope that 'education can make a difference' (Acker, 1994: 19) and so that practitioners can work progressively to surmount the barriers to change.

The first section highlights specific subject concerns. Several authors consider boys' apparent disadvantage in the language curriculum which has led to a marked disparity in results between boys and girls at GCSE (*Statistical Bulletin*, HMSO). Clark argues that boys in the average and below average ability groups underper-form in modern languages because they find the subject matter and the teaching/learning styles employed often unappealing, and are demotivated by the difficulty of the subject.

4

Davies considers the gendered nature of oracy in the classroom. She suggests that girls' linguistic behaviour is less competitive and more collaborative than that of the majority of boys, noting that this supportive way of working, whilst seen as a positive element within assessment criteria, may not necessarily reap rewards beyond the classroom. Millard, focusing on the English curriculum, is concerned on the one hand that boys' disinterest in the literacy experiences provided for them in the early years disadvantages them in a school environment, where reading and writing are essential keys to the curriculum. However, she also expresses concern that girls are gaining less experience in the new forms of technological literacy which will be an important key to their future employment.

Opie focuses further on gender stereotyping in IT, noting that girls are still viewed as being technologically more inept than boys. This persistent 'computers are for boys' syndrome is a consequence of social stereotyping and has no support in how boys and girls actually perform. He argues that until IT activities move away from the competitive, individualistic, mode characteristic of males, to ones which encourage co-operation and more humanistic activities, this gender division will remain. Scaife argues that little has changed in terms of science education more than a decade after the GIST project, which sought to render the science curriculum more accessible to girls. He suggests that the apparent gains of girls in GCSE examinations in science are masking a consistent bias towards masculinist ways of categorising what is worth knowing in the subject.

Skelton's chapter reflects further on the male dominance of certain areas of the curriculum, arguing that PE is governed by a set of 'macho values' underpinned by competitiveness and aggression, which exclude many girls and 'non-macho' boys. He argues convincingly for an inclusive approach which allows for a gamut of attitudes towards PE and more adequately prepares pupils to make decisions about their current and future lifestyles. Wellington charts the history of girls' football from the late nineteenth century to the current day, demonstrating the obstacles and prejudices still encountered by those who wish to enter this male-dominated sport. He considers some of the pseudo-scientific, 'biological' arguments deployed in this area which are analogous to those used in the past in core areas of the curriculum such as science and mathematics. Wellington argues for more equal access to football both in and outside school, and for the promotion both of local girls' teams *and* new structures to allow girls entry to our so-called 'national game'.

Povey, in analysing the nature of school mathematics, echoes Scaife's concerns about male-patterned domination of the subject's epistemology. She argues that radical changes are required to create conditions in which non-hierarchical, co-operative methods of mathematical problem solving can be validated in the classroom.

Dixon's study takes a different perspective on the classroom, concentrating on pupils' physical embodiment within the context of the design and technology workshop. She argues that teachers often ignore the 'bodily' presence of their students. The episodes she describes demonstrate how pupils' growing awareness or denial of their own embodiment acts either to empower or to disadvantage them as learners.

The second section focuses on the post-16 curriculum. Unwin explores the extent to which girls and boys have different curricular opportunities and experiences in the post-compulsory stages of education. Drawing on quantitative data on destination patterns, achievement and participation, she considers whether girls and boys face the future on equal terms or whether they separate into traditional, stereotypical cul-de-sacs in the labour market, in education or as non-participators. Whilst qualitative evidence suggests that girls have been influenced by feminist thinking and want now to compete on equal terms, the labour market still erects considerable barriers for women who want to break out of the stereotypical mould. She argues that schools have a vital role to play in ensuring that girls develop appropriate interpersonal and assertiveness skills to carry forward their academic and vocational achievements into the world beyond the classroom and in opening routes and providing an appropriate curriculum for boys who want to embark on non-typical careers.

Brine discusses the training policy of the European Commission as interpreted by the UK government. Against a backdrop of changing patterns of work and access to training, she underlines the importance of understanding the nature of training opportunities, and the ways in which projects which initially have a gender focus can be manipulated by governments to undermine the basic premises on which they were founded.

The final section considers questions of equity across and beyond specific curriculum areas. Jesson gives the statistical basis for the arguments currently drawing attention to boys' underachievement across the curriculum at GCSE. Drawing on his pioneering work into 'value-added' considerations, he notes that even where these are included in the equation, girls' performance in most schools is better than that of boys, although the few exceptions give rise to optimism that patterns of underachievement may be challenged.

To counteract the current demand for simple panaceas to complex causalities, Mac an Ghaill and Haywood suggest a more complex reading of gender relations, exploring the interface between gender and other variables such as the family, peer groups, class and ethnicity and their impact on pupils' schooling experience. They argue forcibly that the growing concern about boys' underachievement may serve to mask new forms of class and racial institutional discrimination, experienced by both men and women.

Quicke seeks to explode the myth about underachieving boys and overachieving girls and the spurious definitions between 'hard work' and 'innate intelligence'. He points to the gendered nature of the curriculum, showing that although girls are now achieving success in traditional 'male' subjects, they do not perform as well as in other subject areas, nor do they select these given a free choice at 'A' level, thus excluding themselves from career opportunities in science and technology. He further notes how the pattern of performance of the sexes is not perpetuated post-16 and how the career aspirations of boys and girls differ. In seeking for solutions, he rejects tokenistic attempts to identify and work with students at risk of underachieving, advocating instead the establishment of mechanisms within the school which would encourage pupils to be self-reflective.

In the endnote, Millard considers the patterns of difference and disadvantage created by the National Curriculum, and looks to the future to suggest ways in which boys and girls can be helped to achieve their full potential in a more equitable curriculum.

REFERENCES

Acker, S. (1994) *Gendered Education: Sociological Reflections on Women, Teaching and Feminism*, Buckingham: Open University Press.

Baines, B. (1985) 'Literature and sex bias in the secondary school English curriculum in NATE Language and Gender working party', *Alice in Genderland*, Sheffield: NATE Publications.

Byrne, E. (1978) *Women and Education*, London: Tavistock.

Clarricoates, K. (1978) 'Dinosaurs in the classroom: the "hidden" curriculum in primary schools', in M. Arnot and G. Weiner (eds) *Gender and the Politics of Schooling*, London: Unwin Hyman.

Connell, R.W. (1987) *Gender and Power*, Oxford: Blackwell.

D'Arcy, S. (1991) 'Towards a non-sexist primary classroom', in E. Titchell (ed.) *Dolls and Dungarees: Gender Issues in the Primary Curriculum*, Milton Keynes: Open University Press.

David, M.E. (1980) *The State, the Family and Education*, London: Routledge and Kegan Paul.

Davidson, M.J. and Cooper, C.L. (1992) *Shattering the Glass Ceiling: The Woman Manager*, London: Paul Chapman.

Davies, B. (1997) 'Constructing and deconstructing masculinities through critical literacy', *Gender and Education* 9: 1.

Deem, R. (1980) *Schooling for Women's Work*, London: Routledge and Kegan Paul.

Delamont, S. (1980, 2nd edn 1990) *Sex Roles and the School*, London: Routledge.

EOC (1997) *Facts about Women and Men in Great Britain 1997*, Manchester: Overseas House.

Foxman, D., Ruddock, G., Joffe, L., Mason, K., Mitchell, P. and Sexton, P. (APU) (1985) *A Review of Monitoring in Mathematics 1978-1982*, London: HMSO.

Goodenough, R. (1987) 'Small group culture and the emergence of sexual behaviour: a comparative study of four children's groups', in G.L. Spindler (ed.) *Interpretive Ethnography of Education*, Hillsdale, NJ: Lawrence Erlbaum.

Griffin, C. (1984) *Typical Girls: Young Women from School to the Job Market*, London: Routledge and Kegan Paul.

Harris, S., Nixon, J. and Rudduck, J. (1993) 'Schoolwork, homework and gender', *Gender and Education* 5(1).

Joffe, L., Foxman, D. and Jordan, E. (1988) *Attitudes and Gender: Mathematics at Age 11 and 15*, London: HMSO.

Jordan, E. (1995) 'Fighting boys and fantasy play: the construction of masculinity in the early years of school', *Gender and Education* 7: 1.

Kelly, A. (1981) *The Missing Half*, Manchester: Manchester University Press.

—— (1985) 'The construction of masculine science', *British Journal of Sociology of Education* 6(2).

Lees, S. (1986) *Losing Out: Sexuality and Adolescent Girls*, London: Hutchinson.

Licht, B.G. and Dweck, C.S. (1987) 'Sex differences in achievement orientations', in M. Arnot and G. Weiner (eds) *Gender and the Politics of Schooling*, London: Unwin Hyman.

Lurie, A. (1980) *Clever Gretchen and Other Forgotten Folk Tales*, London: Heinemann.

Mac an Ghaill, M. (1994) *The Making of Men: Masculinities, Sexualities and Schooling*, Buckingham: Open University Press.

Maccoby, E. and Jacklin, C.N. (1975) *The Psychology of Sex Differences*, London: Stanford.

Mahoney, P. (1985) *Schools for the Boys: Co-education Re-assessed*, London: Hutchinson.

Marland, M. (ed.) (1983) *Sex Differentiation and Schooling*, London: Heinemann.

Measor, L. and Sikes, P.J. (1992) *Gender and Schools*, London: Cassell.

Mickelson, R.A. (1992) 'Why does Jane read and write so well? The anomaly of women's achievement', in J.Wrigley (ed.) *Education and Gender Equality*, London: Falmer.

Millett, K. (1971) *Sexual Politics*, London: Rupert Hart-Davis.

Mitchell, J. (1974) *Psychoanalysis and Feminism*, Harmondsworth: Penguin.

Myers, K. (ed.) (1987) *Genderwatch*, Cambridge: Cambridge University Press.

—— (1992) *Genderwatch! After the Education Reform Act*, Cambridge: Cambridge University Press.

Rudduck, J. (1994) *Developing a Gender Policy in Secondary Schools*, Buckingham: Open University Press.

Scott, M. (1980) 'Teach her a lesson: sexist curriculum in patriarchal education', in D. Spender and E. Sarah (eds) *Learning to Lose*, London: The Women's Press.

Spender, D. (1980) *Man-made Language*, London: Routledge and Kegan Paul.

—— (1982) *Invisible Women: the Schooling Scandal*, London: Writers' and Readers' Publishing.

Stanworth, M. (1983) *Gender and Schooling: A Study of Sexual Division in the Classroom*, London: Hutchinson.

Stones, R. (1983) *Pour out the Cocoa Janet: Sexism in Children's Books*, London: Longman.

Thorne, B. (1992) 'Girls and boys together . . . but mostly apart: gender arrangements in elementary schools', in J. Wrigley (ed.) *Education and Gender Equality*, London: Falmer.

Walden, R. and Walkerdine, V. (1985) *Girls and Mathematics: from Primary to Secondary Schooling*, London: Institute of Education.

Walkerdine, V. (1989) *Counting Girls Out*, London: Virago Education Series.

—— (1981) 'Sex, power and pedagogy', *Screen Education*, 38.

Weiner, G. (ed.) (1985) *Just a Bunch of Girls*, Milton Keynes: Open University Press.

Whyte, J. (1985) *Girl Friendly Schooling*, London: Methuen.

8

Part I

THE GENDERED CURRICULUM

1

TAKING RISKS OR PLAYING SAFE

Boys' and girls' talk

Julia Davies

INTRODUCTION

Current concerns about the comparative underachievement of boys span the whole school curriculum (Woodhead, 1996). In a quest to raise the achievement of boys, educationists and researchers have responded with an examination of both curriculum and pedagogy (SCAA, 1996), and of boys' attitudes and culture (Younger and Warrington, 1996). Issues regarding the differential achievement of boys and girls have been addressed by a wide variety of interest groups, such as parents, politicians, the media and academics. Ironically, those individuals who seem least worried are the boys themselves.

The data which forms the basis of this chapter was collected from small group discussions in English lessons. The linguistic confidence and loquacity of the boys exemplified in the data serve to undermine the concerns of the groups listed above. The findings presented in this chapter do, despite their roots within the English lesson, have implications for all those curriculum areas which use small group work as a vehicle for teaching and learning; the methods of analysis and the conclusions drawn can be applied equally to them.

BACKGROUND TO THE RESEARCH

Using data gathered from a variety of schools, this chapter will focus on the talk of boys and girls in an exploration of their differential linguistic performances in the classroom. The well-rehearsed arguments which link language and learning (Barnes *et al.*, 1969; DES, 1975; Wells, 1986) provide a rationale behind this focus. Consequently, the trends emerging from the linguistic data have reverberations across all subject areas. This is due in part to the proliferation of the use of small group work across the disciplines, such has been the response to research endorsing the

11

inextricable link between talk and learning. Moreover, as I shall indicate, even in lessons where small group working is not the norm, the general principles and conclusions regarding the strength of the relationship between language and learning, and the speech habits specific to boys and to girls, will still stand. This is because in whole class discussion, boys' and girls' linguistic behaviour retains many of those characteristics evident within the small group arena. Indeed, in whole class discussion, many gender-specific features seem to be exaggerated. This chapter will draw upon research about language and learning as well as upon the work of feminist linguistics in unravelling the strands of the spoken texts of girls' and boys' discourse. Subsequently, in focusing upon the language of pupils in school and upon the issue of boys' underachievement, three paradoxes emerge. Firstly, if, as some feminist linguists assert (Spender, 1980; Lakoff, 1975), female language is less powerful and language in general perpetuates the subordination of women, then how is it that girls gain better overall examination results than boys? Secondly, and clearly related to the first paradox, if boys speak so much more than girls in classrooms, why are they not achieving higher grades than girls? Does this suggest that the talk which is conducive to learning or which attracts positive assessment is less often used by boys? Finally, is there a hidden link which can explain the sustained domination of men's discourse in the world at large, if they are, apparently, the educational subordinates of women?

The three paradoxical issues outlined here all have an ultimate relevance to boys' underachievement in school. The issues raised have implications for the employment of appropriate teaching methods. Through the conclusions drawn from an analysis of specific features of transcribed spoken data of male and female pupils, this chapter evaluates and comments upon the salient characteristics of each gender's linguistic behaviour in classrooms. The paradoxes noted above will be addressed and suggestions for suitable pedagogical strategies for the classroom will be offered. The implementation of such strategies will potentially enhance and develop the verbal repertoires of both boys and girls in an attempt to adjust the imbalance within and beyond the parameters of the classroom.

LANGUAGE AND LEARNING

Many teachers no longer depend on whole class discussion as a learning medium through which they seek to 'deliver' a curriculum, or 'transmit' knowledge. The small discussion group is seen by many teachers as an ideal forum for the development of children's language and learning. The potential offered by small group talk is that pupils have more opportunities to speak and the reduced number of participants allows less confident interlocutors a greater sense of security to test out ideas. The predominant argument has been that each participant is able to speak more. This, as will be illustrated, has implications for the increased amount of time all pupils, but girls in particular, are allowed to offer their views and to ask questions of each other and themselves.

The process through which children engage with each other and with new topics in small group talk facilitates the opportunity to consolidate and reiterate existing knowledge as well as to experiment with new ideas and concepts in a relatively safe environment. The centrality of the spoken word in encouraging tentative, exploratory and interactive thinking is evident now in many class-rooms. Pupils are ideally allowed the scope to ponder and explore, via a circuitous route if necessary, in a manner which whole class discussion would inhibit. Pupils are allowed the space to produce the kind of exploratory and tentative talk which is difficult to sustain in a whole class setting, and I shall return to this issue later in the chapter.

The move by many practitioners away from whole class discussion as the predominant *modus operandi* for teaching has been prompted by the kind of arguments outlined above. A further catalyst for the instigation and proliferation of small group discussion has been the stipulation in some GCSE subject areas for the assessment of pupil talk or assessment of knowledge *through* talk. However, the progress implicit in the development of this kind of pedagogy is not without its problems. Some of the impediments to learning within whole class discussion are perpetuated within the small group. One of these impediments to learning, for both boys and girls, is the issue of gender.

Data from classrooms presented here, representing the talk of girls in small groups, exemplifies some of the tendencies described by the feminist linguistics of Lakoff (1975) who has suggested female interlocuters defer to men and frequently reduce the impact and power of their language. Yet such features are often strategically and effectively utilised in a way which enhances girls' talk. It is not the case that tag questions and hedges are intrinsically weak. Indeed these characteristics of girls' talk, as well as others I shall present, are features which contribute to the positive regard in which girls' talk is held by the education system and which so easily enables girls to fulfil the criteria laid down by the National Curriculum. Moreover, these characteristics enable girls to access the talk-related learning referred to above. Concomitantly, it may also be that the kind of risk taking talk which boys so readily exhibit in class and which frequently does them so much educational damage offers them greater power, allowing them to rehearse the manipulative verbal skills which serve them so well beyond the classroom.

The data presented here will indicate that effective talk in classrooms is of two varieties: the 'female' variety, which is positively regarded and rewarded; and the 'male' talk variety, which is often perceived as threatening, powerful, and as break-ing the smooth running of 'normal' classroom discipline. As I shall suggest later, the 'male' variety could be regarded as powerful, highly charismatic and effective talk. Neither variety of talk is superior to the other; each is appropriate in specific scenarios. Thus, skilful speakers will ideally possess, within their verbal repertoire, aspects of language which 'belong' to both gender 'varieties'.

WHOLE CLASS DISCUSSION ISSUES

Whole class discussion is often used as a strategy to orientate the interest of a class to a new subject area for study, as a check on pupil learning and knowledge, or to provoke pupils to consider new ideas and exchange views. However, as a pedagogical strategy, and as a classroom management issue, whole class discussion can often be highly problematic.

Management issues often come to the fore when pupils who are not involved in the verbal interchanges become bored or restless and impatient to take their turn in speaking. Furthermore, it is frequently a minority of pupils who are able to access the discussion space. In mixed-sex schools this privileged minority of pupils usually comprises boys. For example, one practitioner comments thus on her experiences:

> boys . . . had an almost complete monopoly on student talk and contributions. I discovered that what I thought of as "Whole Class Discussion" was in fact small group discussion with the teacher's participation. The rest of the class (twelve girls and the other five boys) became the audience for speakers in the discussion.
>
> (Bousted, 1989: 43)

Moreover, exchanges are often performance related rather than genuine moments of learning, with teachers frequently asking closed questions in a routine way and the same confident children often answering each time. There are probably only a few moments where developed thinking takes place (for a further explanation of these issues, see e.g. Barnes *et al.*, 1969; Coulthard, 1977; Davies, 1996). In a study of classroom interaction, Spender (1982) reports that in classroom discussion:

> for every four boys who participated, there was only one girl. When teachers asked questions they asked two boys to every one girl, and when teachers provided praise and encouragement three boys received it to every one girl. And in these classes there were more girls than boys.
>
> (Spender, 1982: 55)

Certainly, it has not been difficult to find supporting evidence for such claims about boys' oral domination in classrooms. In 1995, a group of PGCE students from the University of Sheffield undertook a small scale research project. In pairs, the students observed four English lessons in two schools and undertook a frequency count of pupils' verbal participation in teacher-led discussion. Their results confirmed that boys dominate teacher-centred discussion in English lessons. Table 1.1 gives the statistics the students gathered over the course of four English lessons.

Inevitably, perhaps, the students encountered methodological problems in categorising some of the contributions made by the pupils, for example distinguishing

Table 1.1 Comparison of boys' and girls' participation in English lesson discussion

	Boys	Girls
Total no. of oral contributions	254	83
Answers question	13	8
Shouts out	57	10
Comment on task	28	19
Comment off task	58	13
Asks question on task	82	31
Asks question off task	16	2

between on- and off-task questions, or on- and off-task comments. However, each lesson was observed by two student researchers and a consensus was reached after discussion. Disparity of opinions was insignificant, however, particularly in the light of the overwhelming evidence which demonstrates boys' domination of whole class discussion.

Clearly illustrated in the above data is the first of the paradoxes mentioned earlier. There is a tension in the arguments about the relationship between language and learning considering the dominance of male talk in classrooms and the under-achievement of boys. Boys' propensity for articulating their thoughts and ideas seems not to attract positive regard or reap tangible benefits by way of examination success. Many of the boys' contributions are perceived as negative. The bulk of male interlocutors' utterances are recorded as uninvited (e.g. calling out) or 'off task'. The exchanges being initiated by these boys do not follow the explicit rules of classroom discipline, thus representing the potential to disrupt management. The boys' contributions are frequently interpreted as irrelevant, unhelpful and not conducive to learning. The PGCE students' study commented that boys often asked questions which had already been answered, invented problems about understanding the work, and derided contributions made by others. Boys were frequently told to be quiet and to stop being 'silly'. These findings are supported by the research of OFSTED, which noted that:

> in many lessons boys dominated proceedings, answering more questions, offering more opinions and interrupting more frequently than girls.
>
> (OFSTED, 1993)

In these situations, girls do not use talk for learning in the same way as they do in small group discussion. Moreover, it appears that the kind of talk boys are producing in teacher-led discussion is perceived negatively, seeming to demonstrate their predisposition towards risk taking, rather than 'playing safe' like the girls. The element of risk taking by boys is, in itself, a feature which carries a significance which will be explored in greater depth later in this chapter. The gendered varieties of talk in these situations may indicate a gendered variety of learning. This is an area which requires further research.

GENDER ISSUES IN SMALL GROUP WORK: THE RISK TAKERS AND THE BET HEDGERS

The research represented here is drawn from two main data sets. The first data was gathered in 1987 when I was an English teacher in a Midlands comprehensive school and consisted of tape recordings of my Y9 (then third-year) class. The second collection was gathered in 1995 whilst working as a teacher/researcher in two other comprehensive schools in South Yorkshire. The data will, however, be presented together, since the method of collection did not differ fundamentally in nature; moreover, the gender-specific linguistic features have strong similarities.

The tasks assigned to pupils were designed to encourage a high degree of discursive interaction and were based entirely along the lines of 'ordinary English lessons'. The work formed part of ongoing English coursework, and as such was not artificial in nature or content. The data could therefore be described as authentic, in the sense that it elicited talk which might ordinarily occur in English lessons. Pupils worked in small groups, each group having been provided with a small cassette recorder to be operated by the pupils themselves. The tasks set included the interrogation of a poetry text, via questions and prompts provided on a worksheet; simulation or role play exercises, for example pupils took on roles as teachers in order to solve a bullying problem; questions were designed to trigger personal discussion and anecdotes about early school memories. Pupils were arranged in both mixed- and single-sex groupings, so that gender dynamics could be observed. Pupils were unaware of the gender issues under scrutiny.

GIRLS: THE 'SAFE BETTERS'

In this chapter girls are described as 'safe betters', since the transcriptions of their discussions revealed patterns which reflect their propensity for hedging their individuality, their avoidance of being overdominant and a tendency to reflect equality within the group.

The girls were able to assist each other in finding the right words. If a participant floundered over her words or paused to think, she was given time and help as shown in the following examples:

Example 1
VICKI: To get erm . . . (laughs).
DONNA: Go on then (quietly).
TRACEY: Detention? (Rising intonation)
JOANNE: The kids under control? (Rising intonation)

Example 2
MELANIE: Go on then . . . (laughs) you don't have to wait for me.
KATHRYN: Yeah but . . . (quietly).
SAMANTHA: I thought you were going to say something, sorry. What . . .

16

Example 3
SAMANTHA: Yeah why can't they build it at pack (*sic*) . . . pack of (*laughs*).
MELANIE: Back?
SARAH: Back of the town hall?
SAMANTHA: Mmmmm.

Here, in examples 1 and 3, the girls are given help with words, whilst in example 2, participants are keen to ensure that everyone has the right of participation.

The maintenance of good relations seemed vital within the groups and any disagreement with what was being said was frequently qualified by phrases of reassurance or an acknowledgement of other interlocutors' right to their own views. The texts took on a positive aspect, owing to the high level of confirmatory responses, even where there was disagreement. Challenges were frequently presented in the following ways:

Example 4
LOUISE: Yeah, I know but . . .

Example 5
SARAH: Yes but.

Example 6
LISA: I know, but . . .

The girls' discussions were chiefly characterised by a variety of *collaborative* strategies, a predisposition for agreement and mutual understanding. They more frequently attempted to find a unified approach to tasks set, demonstrated a sense of shared experience – manifest particularly in 'story-matching' and exchanges of personal disclosure, and the ability to speak 'as one voice'.

Example 7
SALLY: I got this trophy at Middle School and I was dead chuffed, I thought it
    was great.
DENISE: I got one of them, at the fourth year juniors, that's what I got.
SALLY: That you'd improved and you'd done right well.
ELAINE: Your attendance, you'd improved, there was all sorts.
SALLY: You'd done right well in your school work.
LAURA: You'd took part in sports day and everything.
SALLY: And you were friends with everybody and you'd got a nice personality.
LAURA: I got one of them.

Sometimes the girls' discussions manifest themselves as a series of compound sentences which allowed the development of a text that was seen as a whole, both cohesive and coherent. Each person's comments expanded upon and developed the previous person's remarks. The sense of shared understandings, in this example, of family values, is clear in the next extract:

Example 8
KATHRYN: There's the children. The children'll have to go, erm . . .
MELANIE: Across the busy main roads.
LISA: Mmm. The busy dangerous roads.
LOUISE: Plus who wants to live near a station?
MELANIE: Yes.
KATHRYN: And when if they're little children, and when they're asleep at night, it'll just wake 'em up.
SAMANTHA: And I mean, they're supposed to get eight hours sleep aren't they?

In the following example the conjunction 'and' is used in a way typical of girls' groups:

Example 9
JOANNE: It's about his behaviour all the time.
DONNA: And about scruffy kids and that.
JOANNE: And skiving at the back of the room.

Several girls' groups were able to tell a story or explain something together using a highly cohesive style, with symmetrical grammatical and lexical patterns. Their stories were often well constructed, detailed and designed to include other members of the group, either by direct reference or by implication:

Example 10
WENDY: When I went to school X first day I was about I don't know how big I were, I was about 6, no I were about 5, I came and had my red wellies on my raincoat on and my Mum walked me into school and she walked me into the class and saw my teacher and I saw Lisa. You know when they say ah does anyone want to look after Wendy and show her around? Lisa put her hand up. I was painting. We were doing finger painting. I grabbed all this paint and I just threw it at Lisa and we started to have a paint fight. And I thought it was really funny because I made a new friend. My first day at school. Lisa. I've just told em about first day at school when you and me had a paint fight, you were my best friend. There is one about friendship for you. Come on Dawn you've got to think of one now. Now when Dawn was supermodel she learned a very valuable lesson, she will not forget her friends. We were all poor and she was rich.
DAWN: Then we sat down and talked about it and I realised my friends were important.
WENDY: And she gave us all a million quid.

18

DAWN: Well not really a million but I gave them some money. Now I don't do modelling anymore so I am poor like them.
(Laughter)

The first speaker, Wendy, constructs a narrative of a length not to be found in any of the boys' or mixed groups; the detail creates an image: 'had my red wellies on, my raincoat on'. Wendy creates suspense and interest with a keen awareness of audience. A feeling of inclusivity is achieved through a naming of the other interlocutors, weaving them into her story. Finally, there is an implied invitation for Dawn to speak. Dawn recognises her cue and ends the moralistic tale, concluding Wendy's anecdote.

THE BOYS' DISCUSSION GROUPS: THE RISK TAKERS

The analysis of transcriptions gathered from the boys' groups reflected a highly competitive spirit within the discourse: participants seemed intent upon representing themselves as powerful speakers, keen to outwit and outmatch other interlocutors' daring and skill in the manipulation of language. Boys seemed to demonstrate their power by retaining their rights to speak, as well as in directing the discussion. Tactics included the use of repetition and increased volume:

Example 11
REECE: Gi o'er then, Gi o'er, Gi o'er, Gi o'er, Gi o'er, Gi o'er, Gi o'er, Gi o'er. Look we got to pretend we're one of these now. *(Reading)* Number five.

Reece spoke in strong dialect. 'Gi o'er' is the regional vernacular for 'Give over', meaning 'stop it', or 'shut up'. The use of dialect here gives his utterance a certain bombastic strength, which works alongside the repetition of the lexical item. It is language from the playground which connotes with physical activity and a strong sense of the young male peer group. This was a drastic but effective measure. The response from Matthew in this instance was, 'Right OK'. Similarly Jamie was successful elsewhere:

Example 12
JAMIE: No, no, no, no, no, no, no, no, we'll start with parent.
MATTHEW: OK. The parents then. All right.

And again:

Example 13
JAMIE: Right, Headteacher. *(Shouting)* SPEAK! SPEAK! SPEAK! SPEAK! SPEAK!
NICHOLAS: Well er, . . . it was er . . .

It was unusual that Jamie requested Nicholas to speak. He had not been called upon to participate prior to this point. Jamie's repetitions delayed the opportunity for Nicholas to speak. The only words Nicholas did speak are those cited above in an incomplete utterance.

Boys had much shorter turns than girls in the all-girl groups. The following example is taken from the beginning of a discussion. Length of turn directly contrasts to those taken by girls, shown in example 10 above.

Example 14
TOM: What should schools be for? *(In a mock authoritarian voice)*
ANDY: Schools should be learning and for getting an education. *(In a mock serious voice)*
(Laughter)
TOM: Socialising.
LEE: Sex. That's the truth, honest.
ANDY: What?
LEE: Schools should be for sex.
ANDY: What for learning or doing it?
LEE: Both!

Similarly, another all-male group began:

Example 15
ROB: Well the first question is what are . . . .
PETE: What should schools be for? Pulling birds obviously.
ANDY: Or for birds pulling us.
FRED: What are the most important experiences schools should offer?
ANDY: Pete, stop looking at *(name of female teacher)*'s arse.

The desire to perform dominated most male groups. Tactics which enabled boys to display a certain linguistic dexterity and prowess were frequently used to gain and retain the air space. Boys interrupted, joked, played games with language and frequently moved off task in order to fulfil an agenda not set by the teacher.

A boy in one school who had forgotten that he was being taped was concerned about what I would do with the transcripts. His comments revealed his own agenda as far as talk was concerned:

Example 16
ROGER: Miss we keep laughing.
RESEARCHER: It doesn't matter . . .
ROGER: No miss that's my comedy act, you can't nick my jokes.
RESEARCHER: Your comedy act? What do you mean by 'your comedy act'?
ROGER: My little stand up gig.

In a convincing statement about his work, Roger demonstrates with clarity the performance orientation of much of the boys' work. Boys vied with each other, sometimes aggressively, to have their utterances validated by laughter or further comment. The discussions involve a high degree of risk, since boys often break traditional classroom rules with their language or risk their reputations in using daring words, ideas and new jokes. Pupils sometimes made songs out of words used by others and could ridicule other boys' contributions in this way. For example, in one group the boys sang their own version of 'Glad to be gay' in response to one boy's use of the word 'glad'. The boy had been ostracised previously for being 'gay', this insult frequently used as a synonym for 'weak' or 'stupid'. The experimental, competitive nature of much of the boys' discussion seems to be concerned with the promotion of their own individuality. It is this which is risky and in direct contrast to what girls seem to be doing in their supportive, collaborative work where they so often speak 'with one voice'.

The boys display many skills, and careful listening was certainly required for the high velocity interchanges which typify much of the boys' work. A sense of belonging to the boys' groups requires quick wit and confidence. Quiet boys were thus frequently ostracised, ridiculed and silent. Outsiders to the boys' groups are clearly defined through the boys' language, which is often sexist (excluding girls) and iconoclastic (excluding adults). Membership of boys' groups often demands a show of vehement heterosexuality and enjoyment of the discussion of sexual topics, football and fights. The discussions would often swing towards the fantastical in an ever increasing spiral of daring, almost as if slapping cards on the games table.

Ironically, it is the boys' determination to create group solidarity and identity through these joint ventures, which is similar to the girls' work. It is the means by which this solidarity is achieved, as well as the implications for learning, which are different.

MIXED GROUPS

Within the mixed groups observed, there was frequently a modification of gendered speech styles. Girls' speaking turns became shorter, whilst boys were more able to produce longer stretches of talk.

The boys were more likely to relate personal information and express their more sensitive feelings:

Example 17

LUKE: I always remember when I first moved to XX. I didn't have any friends for the first year and I thought that everyone was snobby and stuck up, not one person tried to be nice.

However, some boys were still reticent; here, for example, a girl asks a boy to share his memories:

Example 18
JOHN: Errr no, I'm not sharing them. Next?

The same boy is later encouraged to comment on a peer's experience in a relevant way:

Example 19
JOHN: You know Pete up our road? He has a home tutor.

After a few of the girls comment on how they would feel about this, the boy gains confidence, adopts a more personal way of working and expands on how he would feel about his father teaching him:

Example 20
JOHN: I think it would be right funny. My Dad would get it across but in the wrong way.

In mixed-sex groups, girls' stories were not so elaborate in their betrayal of personal information. Quiet boys were offered opportunities to speak. Sometimes discussions deteriorated alarmingly in mixed groups and the gender divide sharpened. Boys had the upper hand in their use of aggressive tactics of sexist language and game playing.

Example 21
JAMES: Hello, my name's James Bell, if you didn't know.
SCOTT: I'm Scott.
MATTHEW: I'm Matthew.
SARAH: Sarah.
LOUISE: I'm Louise *(barely audible)*.
SAMANTHA: I'm Samantha *(more confident)*.
JAMES: Oh no! 'Oh I'm Samantha' *(imitates)*. I think we should get rid of these crap gay assemblies. And registers. I mean, what would you want an assembly for? All it gives you is news. You should have . . .
SAMANTHA: We have to have a register.

Taking on the genre of a television chat show by formally introducing themselves, the boys set the precedent to 'perform' for the tape. The girls were hesitant and quietly spoken, seeming uncomfortable with the notion of performance. Samantha spoke more loudly than the other two girls. James' imitated the girl who seemed more confident and his ensuing long utterance condemned the girls' work, used taboo vocabulary and included a question which he answered himself. In this manner he was able to establish himself as a powerful speaker, creating his own dialogue moving swiftly from one subject to another at great speed, making sweeping statements and decisions.

Some of the humour was entirely at the expense of girls and women. This meant that girls within the group were ostracised and made to feel deviant. When the boys derided femininity the girls became implicated in this because of their co-operative strategies and unwillingness to contradict overtly. They seemed to endorse and even encourage the very language which oppressed them and prevented their full involvement:

Example 22

JAMES: *(Scribbling loudly all over his timetable)* Louise is *so* big, *so* big and strong! *(Ironic intonation)*

LOUISE: Oh God! *(Loud and breathy)*

JAMES: Not big like a man. Like a woman. *(Draws exaggerated female form with his hands.)*

LOUISE: Shut up James. *(Quietly and laughing)*

JAMES: But you can't smack them. God! Girls make me sick.

In the mixed groups, the girls seemed to speak mainly in reaction to the boys' linguistic behaviour. They were sometimes put into a position of defence. Quiet girls became quieter. More confident girls sometimes became the target of humour and derision, although others managed to facilitate an atmosphere more conducive to learning than any found within the all-male groups. Quiet boys became more confident. The boys who gained dominant roles in mixed groups were more aggressive than in single-sex groups.

I make no suggestions about genetic, psychological or social predispositions for the tendency to prepare themselves for particular roles. I would say simply that the differential linguistic dexterity of girls and boys, men and women, may well equip them for different roles in society.

Despite the differences in language use, each gender appears to be working together, but separately, to establish group identity and solidarity. When the groups do come together, the assumption of each group seems to be that they, in speaking the same English language, have the same suppositions about its use. Thus boys will continue to play on the words girls (and boys) use, will joke, pun and deride. However, often because the girls continue to disclose personal detail and to give the floor to others, they can be seen as weak players in the competition to gain floor space and to manipulate the language. They seem not to have the same determination or inclination to push back the barriers and confines of the usual speech rules in the same way as the boys.

CONCLUSIONS

As noted in the introduction, there are concerns that girls seem more able to fulfil National Curriculum criteria than boys. In general their talk does not break traditional classroom discourse rules. They are 'sensitive', they seem to be 'showing understanding', are 'responsive to others' and offer 'exploratory tentative comments' (SCAA, 1996: 11, 26–7). The skills which boys reveal do not receive positive regard from teachers; their utterances, as noted earlier, in full class discussion are potentially disruptive and within the small group often block others' opportunities to speak. Thus, within male-only groups, there is a principle of 'survival of the fittest'. The most confident speakers control the dynamics and are able to set their own agendas. To gain air space in male groups is often a risk, since the competitive, rather than the supportive, spirit is embraced by the most powerful interlocutors.

It is interesting to note that statistics show that the Cambridge University students who gain the highest degree results in history are predominantly men. The research presents the argument that it is because male students are more willing to take risks than female students (reported in *The Times Higher Educational Supplement*, Targett, 1996). The conduct of boys in small groups reflects the necessity for successful speakers to be risk takers. It may well be that the skills displayed in the classroom are the embryonic form of the powerful speech practised by the mainly male leaders in politics, business and the professions. Girls' relative lack of experience in competitive talk which promotes the individual, rather than the success of the whole group, may go some way towards explaining their lower profile within leadership roles in the adult world.

Boys' lower achievement in examinations has been convincingly explained by the influence of peer group pressure not to work hard (e.g. Younger and Warrington, 1996; Willis, 1977) but another contributory factor is likely to be their style of speaking in classrooms. The socio-cultural context of schools is highly complex, and within that context it is difficult to discern how far speech patterns are a symptom, reflection or cause of some of the problems arising out of that complexity.

If powerful speakers set an agenda which is predominantly 'off task', then other boys are drawn into competitive 'off-task' talk. This clearly inhibits learning. Moreover, the fast pace of on-task talk, compared with girls' more ponderous exploratory work, which allows for tentative suggestions and hypothesis, does not offer boys so much time to be reflective about their work.

The evidence seems to weigh more and more towards the argument that boys and girls have an asymmetrical relationship in terms of power in discourse. The strategies which males use seem designed to block others' turns, whilst girls seem to search for ways of providing everyone with an equal share of the air space. The discourse rules the girls adopt are fated to fail in a competitive arena since they voluntarily relinquish individual power in favour of communal success, and this is deemed to be weakness in the boys' eyes.

PEDAGOGICAL IMPLICATIONS

There is a clear responsibility for teachers in schools to facilitate equal opportunities for all pupils. There are definite issues demonstrated by the data I have presented. Boys have shown their predisposition to be performance oriented in their talk. While this may serve some boys well out of school, it is evidently not benefiting the majority.

I have found in my teaching and research that boys can be helped by being offered the opportunity to work with girls as well as by taking on particular roles within groups. By offering boys roles to 'hide behind', they are often afforded more freedom to apply themselves specifically to the agenda offered by the teacher. Girls, however, do need to work in single-sex groups since in mixed groups their talk opportunities are often curbed. However, it is vital that they also are given the opportunity to work with boys in a discursive scenario.

Teaching pupils specifically about gender differences in language and language use has the potential to allow for linguistic development and expertise in acquiring skills which typify the speech habits of the opposite sex. The use of tape recordings, transcriptions and video tapes of themselves and their peers in discussion can be used as a way forward in developing such awareness.

Boys produce much more off-task talk when they are asked to discuss personal issues. They need to be given more support in expressing their views, perhaps working only in pairs when required to give a personal account of themselves. If boys are offered models for this kind of work, being shown how the girls are supportive of such stories, for example, this may pave the way for more confidence.

The creation of space for boys to talk during recreation times may be useful in providing an appropriate place for boys to talk informally with each other and develop moments for sharing personal stories and anecdotes. Boys need more provision than girls in this respect, since currently it is not the norm for boys to chat personally in school. Research has shown (Mahony, 1985) that boys tend to spend their recreation time in school playing sports in arenas unconducive to talk. Girls, however, have ample time to discuss personal issues in breaks devoted to 'grooming activities' in dining halls and girls' toilets. It is perhaps these 'hidden curriculum' moments which help foster some of the most enduring differences in male and female talk.

The three paradoxes mentioned in the opening paragraphs of this chapter can be addressed through teaching. Girls seem naturally to use the language which helps them to learn from each other. Such language makes them vulnerable in mixed-sex scenarios because it facilitates others. By contrast, boys frequently practise competitive ways of speaking, spending time developing skills which allow them to speak for longer than others, and to be assertive in challenging contexts. The use of highly sexist language is just one of these strategies and girls can be potentially disabled by the boys' implementation of such strategies. However, as outlined above, arguments of linguistic determinism are inappropriate and insupportable;

language is a vital social phenomenon and education can serve to inform and nurture the communicative strategies of each individual.

REFERENCES

Barnes, D., Britton J. and Rosen, H. (1969) *Language, the Learner and the School*, Harmondsworth: Penguin.

Bousted, M. (1989) 'Who talks? The position of girls in mixed sex classrooms', *NATE: English in Education* 23 (3).

Coulthard, M. (1977) *An Introduction to Discourse Analysis*, London: Longman.

Davies, J. (1996) 'Fighting talk', in A. J. Trafford (ed.) *Learning to Teach*, Sheffield: USDE.

Department for Education and Science (1975) *A Language for Life*, London: HMSO.

Lakoff, R. (1975) *Language and Woman's Place*, New York: Harper & Row.

Mahony, P. (1985) *Schools For the Boys?*, London: Hutchinson.

OFSTED (1993) *Boys and English*, London: HMSO.

SCAA Boys and English Working Group (1996) *Boys and English*, London: SCAA.

Spender, D. (1980) *Man-made Language*, London: Routledge and Kegan Paul.

—— (1982) *Invisible Women: the Schooling Scandal*, London: Writers' and Readers' Publishing.

Targett, S. (1996) 'Women told to take risks to get a first', *The Times Higher Education Supplement* 1 November.

Wells, G. (1986) *The Meaning Makers*, London: Hodder & Stoughton.

Willis, P. (1977) *Learning to Labour: Why Working Class Boys Get Working Class Jobs*, Aldershot: Saxton House.

Woodhead, C. (1996) 'Boys who learn to be losers', *The Guardian* 8 March.

Younger, M. and Warrington, M. (1996) 'Differential achievement of boys and girls at GCSE: some observations from the perspective of one school', *The British Journal of Sociology of Education* 17(3).

2

RESISTANT BOYS AND MODERN LANGUAGES

A case of underachievement

Ann Clark

INTRODUCTION

Following the 1944 Education Act and the setting up of a tripartite system of academic, technical and general education, the study of a modern foreign language was confined to an elite few, principally those at grammar school. Even under the comprehensive system, there remained a clear divide between the 'academic', who took an 'O' level qualification in a modern language and the majority who either took a CSE in the language or opted for the French/German Studies courses, which were recognised to be academically less taxing, focusing in a more general way on the country and its culture and less on the rigours required by a traditional language examination. By the same token, many voted with their feet and opted in large numbers to abandon their studies of a foreign language after the compulsory three years, in favour of courses deemed more interesting and more accessible. In 1983, the DES Consultative Paper *Foreign Languages in the School Curriculum* commented that whereas in 1965, slightly more than half the first-year secondary intake began a foreign language, the position almost twenty years later was that approximately 90 per cent of first-year (Y7) pupils learnt a foreign language. However, by the fourth year (Y10) the proportion of pupils studying a foreign language had dropped to about a third, barely higher than in 1965. The advent of GCSE extended the appeal of foreign languages and more pupils were encouraged to consider continuing their studies to 16. Furthermore, the introduction of the National Curriculum and its recommendation of a modern language for all to 16 has led several departments to opt for an inclusive policy in advance of the statutory requirements, which has brought about a further increase in GCSE entries. Thus the percentages of those taking GCSE in French has increased steadily (see Table 2.1) and, by 1995, 74 per cent of Y11 pupils took a modern language (and a small number took two languages) at GCSE with the breakdown

27

Table 2.1 Attempts and graded results at GCSE for boys and girls for French* as a percentage of 16-year-old pupils

	Boys attempting GCSE	Girls attempting GCSE	Total attempting GCSE	Boys gaining grade A–C	Girls gaining grade A–C	Total gaining grade A–C
1988–9	34	49	41	17	26	21
1989–90	35	50	43	16	25	20
1990–1	42	56	49	17	26	22
1991–2	45	58	51	17	28	22
1992–3	48	59	53	19	30	24
1993–4	49	59	54	20	32	25
1994–5	51	59	55	21	32	26
1995–6	49	58	53	20	32	26

Sources: Statistical Bulletin, 1990, 1991, 1992, 1993, 1994, 1995, 1996, DfEE

* Despite programmes to encourage diversification, French is still nationally by far the most commonly studied foreign language (see percentages for GCSE entries quoted below). I have quoted the GCSE statistics for French because the sample is biggest and because there is less likelihood of it being a second foreign language taken to a large extent by more able pupils, which would obviously have a bearing on the performance of pupils and potentially distort the statistics.

between languages as follows: 55 per cent French, 21 per cent German, 5 per cent Spanish, 3 per cent other modern languages (*Statistical Bulletin*, DfEE, 1996).

Table 2.1 also shows that, whilst the study of a modern language remained optional, there remained a significant difference in the uptake between boys and girls and in the percentage of boys and girls gaining grades A–C. In line with other curriculum areas, the performance of boys at GCSE in a modern language is disappointing when compared with that of girls, even where the study of a modern language is still an option and where the truly disaffected and demotivated can therefore opt out. Thus in 1996, whilst 32 per cent of girls nationally achieved grades A*–C in French, only 20 per cent of boys did so.

HMI (1985) suggested there were three principal reasons influencing boys to continue with their studies of a modern language. Firstly, if they had enjoyed the subject; secondly, if they thought it would be useful in their future career; and finally, if they had experienced success in the first three years of their studies. Powell and Littlewood (1983) suggest that the image of modern languages is that it is a subject for the 'brainy'. Given that more boys experience difficulties with language skills in the early years, it may follow that more boys may struggle in modern languages and that only the more able boys have hitherto opted to continue with the study of a foreign language to 16.

Alternatively, it may be the case that the curriculum is gendered and that boys perceive the study of a modern foreign language as more suitably the domain of the girls. MacDonald (1980: 29–50) maintains that gender is recontextualised within schools so that 'the notions of appropriate behaviour for each sex [are] converted into the appropriate academic disciplines'. She argues that some school subjects acquire a masculine image and some a feminine one and that once a subject has a

Table 2.2 The degree subject of graduate teachers analysed by sex (all with degrees which include the named subject working in secondary schools)

	Men	Women
French	3,228 (34%)	6,169 (66%)
Other modern languages	3,432 (40%)	5,239 (60%)

Source: Statistics of Education, Teachers in Service in England and Wales (DES, 1992)

Table 2.3 'A' level entries and success rates

	Males aged 17 and under* (any subject)	Males aged 17 and under* (French)	Success rate (%) (m)	Females aged 17 and under* (any subject)	Females aged 17 and under* (French)	Success rate (%)(f)
1991–2	84,261	6,982	88.4	94,234	17,279	85.4
1992–3	83,834	6,800	89.5	93,909	16,366	86.4
1993–4	102,706	7,023	88.0	114,622	17,087	85.8
1994–5	101,553	6,849	88.5	113,213	16,069	87.6

Source: Statistical Bulletin (DfEE, 1993, 1994)
* Age at the start of the academic year

masculine image, participation in it can be seen to enhance a boy's masculinity and diminish a girl's femininity. If this hypothesis is well founded, it clearly has implications for modern languages, where the message drawn from the disproportion of male and female staff must be that this is a feminine subject (see Table 2.2).

MacDonald's hypothesis would also seem to be substantiated by the disparity in uptake in modern languages at 'A' level between boys and girls, which inevitably leads to a disparity in the number of languages graduates and ultimately of languages teachers. The success rate of boys and girls is very similar, as can be seen in Table 2.3, but, to echo the words of Blackstone (1985) writing about girls and physics, the problem is not that boys do badly in French but that they have opted out of the subject altogether in such large numbers.

As the compulsory study of a foreign language for five years was coming to fruition with the first full cohort of Y10 pupils in 1996, I felt a degree of urgency to examine the underlying reasons for the often negative attitudes towards modern languages amongst all pupils, but particularly amongst boys.

RESEARCH BACKGROUND

With this in mind, I gave questionnaires to all Y11 pupils (396 respondents) and staff teaching Y11 pupils (eight respondents) in three comprehensive schools in a shire county, in the Easter term of 1996, and followed these up with a representative sample of pupil and staff interviews. The three schools were selected in consultation with the advisory teacher for that county as a representative sample of schools in that LEA. Pupil interviews were conducted according to sex and ability in groups of three to four pupils, divided into three broad groups: (i) able pupils; (ii) average pupils; (iii) low achieving pupils. The rationale behind separating girls and boys was to explore whether their attitudes differed regardless of their ability. Staff were asked to 'set' pupils interviewed according to ability, because of previous findings concerning the importance of success for engendering positive attitudes towards a subject (Oller and Perkins, 1978). Pupils were asked about the importance of studying a modern foreign language when compared with other areas of the curriculum; they were asked to describe a typical lesson, to explain which aspects of the lessons they enjoyed and which they disliked, and finally to suggest ways in which their language learning could be made more enjoyable and their learning facilitated. A cross-section of the modern languages department in each school was interviewed including, in each case, the Head of Department. Teachers were asked about pupil attitudes towards languages in the school in general, about teaching styles and resources and about any perceived differences in the performance of boys and girls. Interviews were recorded and transcribed. In all, sixty-one pupils and seven members of staff were interviewed. Whilst an attempt was made to interview a cross-section of staff in terms of age, experience and to ensure a mixture of male and female, it has to be said that the only two male interviewees were in fact Heads of Department and there were no new graduates in any of the three departments.

On analysing the data collected from these pupils, three prominent issues emerged: the notion of relevance, the problem of difficulty and the intrinsic appeal of the subject to a teenage audience. I shall consider these issues in turn, before examining the issue of boys' attitudes to work and underachievement generally, and finally broaden the perspective to consider the impact of different learning styles and of the pupil–teacher relationship.

NOTIONS OF (IR)RELEVANCE

The question of relevance appears to be an important issue in terms of pupil motivation in modern languages. In comparison with the other subjects which are 'core' for the five years of secondary education under the National Curriculum (namely, English, mathematics, science, technology), modern languages do not command the same degree of acceptance, and in some instances one senses an element of resistance to the compulsion to study a subject for which several pupils fail to see any relevance to their lives. When questioning Y11 pupils about the relative importance of various areas of the curriculum, two clear lines of thought emerged. Firstly, a clear link was made with future careers:

It depends what you want to do, doesn't it. If I wanted to be a translator or something in that kind of field where a language is necessary, or a travel agent or something, I'd say it would be important, but if you wanted to be a PE teacher then it wouldn't be as important.

(B)

Although some pupils looked beyond their immediate career plans to consider implications for business and commerce, generally pupils quoted stereotypical jobs, where they felt the study of a foreign language would be useful, such as a travel agent or air hostess, and if their interests did not lie in these fields, felt the subject was irrelevant. Powell and Littlewood found similar perceptions in their survey of third-year (Y9) pupils, when the options system was still in place. They felt that girls were possibly opting out of languages less than boys because of 'suggestions all around them that girls would find more opportunities to use a language in the sorts of jobs girls choose or are expected to do' and in contrast, boys 'appeared to envisage themselves either in professional careers where foreign language ability is clearly not a pre-requisite or . . . in unskilled jobs where the need to use a foreign language was most unlikely to occur' (Powell and Littlewood 1983: 37).

The other main justification perceived by the pupils for their study of a foreign language was that of holidays:

I wouldn't use it unless I went on holiday or something.

(G)

These insular, narrow attitudes contrast strongly with the perceived need and motivation of our European counterparts to learn English, which they perceive as a world language and as an essential part of their education. It is noteworthy that for many years now, the study of a modern language has formed a compulsory part of examinations in France and Germany at the age of 18. Clearly, one needs to raise the profile of the study of a modern language in this country, either by bringing it forward into Key Stage 2 along with all the other core subjects, or by making it compulsory in examinations at 18. As one teacher interviewed explained:

what would change the perceptions is if possibly languages were started in KS2, which would reinforce the idea that learning languages is a normality as opposed to a freak event which only happens in KS3 and 4.

Staff also commented on the influence parents brought to bear on their children's attitudes towards language learning, in some instances advising their children to concentrate on 'more useful subjects'. In addition to the possible long-term curricular changes suggested above, further steps need to be taken by schools, employers and government to underline the need for good linguists. Pupils need to see role models in government, industry and the media using languages as an essential part of their daily working lives to underline the potential future importance and relevance of this area of the curriculum to them. There is a stark contrast between the reluctance (or inability?) of prominent British figures to speak a foreign language and the expertise frequently displayed by their European counterparts, with politicians, trade unionists and sports personalities demonstrating a good command of English. Furthermore, the anti-European image presented by the popular press in headlines such as 'Up yours, Delors', and in the particularly anti-German 'hype' connected with World Cup football (see front page images in the *Mirror*, showing Pearce and Gascoigne wearing tin hats with the headline 'For you Fritz, ze World Cup is over', June 1996), does little to create empathy for our European counterparts and may contribute in part to the rather negative, insular attitudes found in some pupils as far as the learning of modern languages is concerned, particularly amongst the boys.

Further research could usefully examine pupils' attitudes towards language learning on the south coast where, arguably, the contact with the continent is much more immediate, to ascertain if the motivation were higher because the perceived need is much more evident.

NOTIONS OF DIFFICULTY

The questionnaire results showed that 36 per cent of pupils ranked modern languages their most difficult subject, 62 per cent placed it in their top three (out of ten) for difficulty. There was a very real sense that the study of a foreign language was distinctive, demanding different skills and a higher level of concentration. Interestingly, the DfEE's *Statistical Bulletin* (1996: 4) seems to corroborate this impression, noting that 'in the majority of subjects, the most common grade obtained by 15 year old candidates was grade C . . . whereas in French it was D'. It was certainly singled out as an area of difficulty for the great majority of pupils. In contrast with other areas of the curriculum, modern languages require pupils to memorise a lot of material, to work with a high degree of accuracy and to develop finely tuned listening skills.

> I think it's just learning all the vocabulary, there is so much it's impossible to have it all, there is always words and stuff that we do that you don't know and that makes you think you can't do it. I think that's what makes it difficult.
>
> (G)

Learning vocabulary, genders, spelling, grammar all seem to pose problems for pupils:

> I get all the spellings wrong.
>
> (B)

I find it difficult to learn lists of vocabulary and the order of sentences.

(B)

It's hard to know which tense you should be using.

(B)

The burden on memory was a recurrent theme in these and earlier interviews (see Clark and Trafford, 1995):

It's just basically remembering, that's the hard bit.

(G)

If you are good at learning then you tend to find languages easy.

(B)

Pupils are not often asked to memorise spellings or vocabulary in English and learning by rote is not expected in most subjects. In many ways, some of these skills are quite alien to them and do not receive support or practice apart from within the languages classroom, and may consequently be devalued. Indeed, in the pupil interviews, when asked about learning vocabulary and structure, pupils intimated that this was something they did if they had time, once they had done their other homework. Written homework was considered important, whereas learning homework was less easily quantifiable and could be more readily disregarded. Some pupils openly admitted to not even looking at the words set, others tried to articulate the problem of quantifying what they had done:

I think the problem with that as well you don't actually know when you have learnt them. Say for example you look at a list of ten words and you could remember them, and then you could come back in ten minutes and not remember them so it's difficult to know when to stop.

(B)

There were further indications that the study of a foreign language was distinctive. There was a sense that learning in other curriculum areas is easier because there is almost a narrative holding a topic together, whereas in languages pupils are presented with an enormous amount of disparate parts which do not hang together in the same way, and which are therefore much more difficult to recall.

I think with languages I don't actually feel I'm getting anywhere – at the end of the lessons I feel I've learnt another 10/15 words, but it doesn't feel I'm any closer to a goal, whereas with Science I've learnt a new section or something and it feels like I'm getting somewhere, with languages it just seems that there is so much I don't know.

(B)

I much prefer understanding than actually learning and with languages there is quite a lot of learning.

(B)

You can't grab the concept the way you can in science, you can't think of a French lesson the same way you think of a science lesson.

(B)

If you are learning something in French, you need a lot more time to learn it than say in Business Studies or whatever.

(G)

Given the perceived difficulty of learning new vocabulary and structure, many pupils articulated a need for strategies to be taught to assist them in their learning:

If they [teachers] can try and think of ways of making you remember things

(B)

I remember it by thinking of, by linking it to this . . . and not just saying that word means that.

(G)

Many pupils felt pressurised by the sheer volume of the GCSE curriculum; some suggested the need for additional lessons simply to consolidate work already covered. There is a strong argument for increasing the amount of contact time devoted to modern languages in Key Stage 3, as this is the only core subject which pupils have not had the opportunity to study in primary school, and yet the expectation is that by the end of Key Stage 4, their level of expertise will be approximately equal across all the core subjects. Ideally, one would like to see a daily contact with the foreign language to assist the pupils in their language acquisition.

Language learnt needs to be regrouped and reformulated in order to be used in different contexts, and again this was a skill not expected elsewhere in the curriculum and a skill most pupils found beyond them.

I think it's sometimes difficult because you can't reuse it, if you know a set phrase but you might not want to say exactly that, you might just want to know bits of it, but sometimes what word in the phrase means what . . . . It's OK learning set phrases but it doesn't really help you when you go abroad, because that is all you can say; it's OK for exams, but it's no good for proper use.

(G)

The impression that the study of a foreign language is difficult has an impact on pupils' enjoyment of the subject:

> If it's hard work you're not going to enjoy it are you, you don't want to be slogging through something that you don't want to do.
>
> (B)

The perceived lack of relevance, coupled with the difficulty of studying a foreign language, naturally have a detrimental effect on pupil motivation. The curriculum and approach to learning are in need of review certainly at Key Stage 4, where pupils are aware of a sudden increase in difficulty, where they more frequently experience failure and can consequently lose the enthusiasm that is undoubtedly sparked in the early years of language learning.

> My French teacher said I won't do very well, so I thought why bother with that when I can spend an extra ten minutes on another subject that I know I'm going to do well in, and I could just pick up another grade.
>
> (G)

> I'd love to go to another country and talk their language and stuff like that but . . . you don't feel you're achieving anything, like in Science you can think 'oh I understand that', or 'I've worked that out', or 'oh yeah I know how to do that bit', but in French there's none of that. You don't feel like you're getting anywhere.
>
> (G)

THE INTRINSIC APPEAL OF A MODERN LANGUAGE

In addition to the fact that many pupils questioned the need for the study of a foreign language at all, there was a sense that in terms of lesson content, modern languages lacked the intrinsic appeal that other subjects held. Several pupils referred to the repetitive nature of their languages curriculum and there was a sense of frustration at the lack of progress over the five years of the course:

> It tends to drag on because it's the same thing over and over again.
>
> (B)

> It seems like what we learned in Y7 and Y8 and we are just repeating all that now and not getting any further.
>
> (G)

Progress seemed to be more in terms of 'proliferation of language than growing sophistication and independence in the manipulation of language' (Clark and

Trafford, 1994: 17). The content of the syllabus for GCSE in a modern language was a disappointment to many pupils. Based loosely around the notion of a trip to the country as most syllabuses are, pupils articulated a feeling of disillusionment in the language taught:

> We are learning things that we'll probably never use, and we can't actually hold a conversation like chatting.
>
> (G)

Indeed, those pupils who had taken part in a school exchange felt ill-prepared to communicate with their partners, saying

> You couldn't chat with them informally. It was dead formal, like please would you pass the salt or whatever.
>
> (G)

There was a real sense that the curriculum is probably dated, concentrating too heavily on the transactional rather than allowing pupils the opportunity to perso-nalise language and use it in contexts relevant to their lives and their personalities. They wanted to know for example:

> more modern things, like music and stuff like that, we do a load on describing your school, how many pupils there are, if you are talking to someone that's not very interesting.
>
> (G)

Some of the gaps in their vocabulary in the foreign language were in areas crucially important to young people. One girl, for instance, commented that she did not know the word for boyfriend; another remarked that

> It would be nice to be able to talk about your friends.
>
> (G)

Powell's (1986) view that there is a mismatch between the intellectual and emo-tional sophistication of pupils and the anodyne, transactional nature of the sylla-buses seems to be borne out by the comments these pupils made. Since it has been shown by researchers (Scott, 1980) that girls are more tolerant of the 'boring' tasks, more malleable and wishing to please than boys, the inappropriacy of the languages curriculum could be deemed partially responsible for boys' underachievement and might lead one to consider whether the curriculum could be rendered more 'boy friendly' in a similar way to the approaches taken in the 1980s (Whyte, 1986) to make the science curriculum 'girl friendly', or less alienating for girls. As schemes of work are devised for the new GCSE, it seems essential to attempt to find a content which will have more appeal and greater relevance to these teenagers, to vary the approach within lessons and possibly to reduce the volume of vocabulary, concentrating more on reworking, manipulating and personalising language than on learning chunks of phrase-book French without any understanding of the workings of the language.

BOYS' UNDERACHIEVEMENT

The startling disparity in performance between boys and girls at GCSE in modern languages has a parallel in English, and as OFSTED states in its report (1993) *Boys and English*, the reasons are not easily identifiable. The report notes, however, that boys tend to have more negative attitudes towards reading and writing than girls, and have difficulty with the affective aspects of English (see also Millard in this volume). Similar tasks are required in the modern languages classroom and seem to meet with resistance. This could potentially be attributed, as one Head of Languages postulated, to the fact that girls are socialised differently, and feel more at home with the types of task expected in modern languages:

> Essentially languages is a communicative subject, and you are talking and expressing things, and I think there are very few 14, 15 year old boys in England who are very good at expressing themselves. . . . If they were the sort of lad who would do it in English, and do it very articulately, then when they are trying to do it in a foreign language, where they are stumbling and hesitating, I think it makes them feel extremely embarrassed and extremely put off and sometimes their reaction is to back out of it . . . . Lads at that age are much more into doing things with their hands and doing things with machines, rather than interacting with people very much.
>
> (Female Head of Department)

Many of the contexts chosen for GCSE not only fail to interest many boys, but in addition may make boys feel a certain embarrassment at being asked to talk in a personal way and to pronounce words in the foreign language with all the concomitant fear of ridicule from their peers.

There are many differences between boys and girls in the approaches towards work, which have been extensively documented elsewhere. Girls are typically more conscientious, present their work better (Clark and Trafford, 1994), spend longer on homework (Harris *et al.* 1993), are more compliant in class (Scott, 1980). Boys monopolise physical space, linguistic space and teacher attention (Scott, 1980; Stanworth, 1983; Mahoney, 1985) and feel under pressure to 'mess about' (Askew and Ross, 1988). The nature of foreign language learning and acquisition requires a consistent 'steady slog' approach, which girls are more willing to accept than boys. One of the teachers interviewed commented:

I think girls come to terms much more with the idea, 'I don't like this particularly but at the end of two years I want a decent grade, and I'm going to buckle down and I'm going to get on with it, and I'm going to work and do it.' Lads, I think, have a less mature attitude towards things generally and it's all a bit ad hoc.

Mickelson (1992) maintains that the high achievement of female students may be due to two separate sex role processes, with girls performing well because this is how they are socialised, and better than many boys because their sex role socialisation demands an element of academic underachievement.

The current position of summative assessment in modern languages may put boys at a disadvantage by setting goals which are much too distant and long term for the average and below average student, who do not commit the time to learning over five years so important in a sequential subject. By Y11, they consequently find themselves so far behind that they feel they cannot catch up, thus losing any motivation to work in modern languages, and feeling their time would be more usefully devoted to a subject where they may be able to improve their grade. It may be that one could assist boys' performance if more short term, attainable goals were built into the languages curriculum to give them a sense of achievement. Furthermore, it seems vital that all pupils should be given more regular contacts with the foreign language with a deliberate view to revisit, revise and consolidate, given their tendency to spend little time on homework and thus to allow so readily for the fade and decay factors, which inhibit their progress and obviously simply serve to demotivate.

THE IMPACT OF TEACHER PERSONALITY AND LEARNING STYLES

The pupils interviewed were themselves able to suggest ways in which they felt their language learning experience could be improved. Interestingly, the remarks made by pupils on both the teacher personality and the effect of different learning styles were not gender specific. Nonetheless, they provide useful insights into ways in which teachers may be able to make modern languages more enjoyable. One highly significant factor in terms of the pupils' attitudes and motivation, mirrored in earlier research (see Clark and Trafford, 1994), was without doubt the rapport the pupils enjoyed with their teacher. In many interviews, notions of pressure and failure emerged; pupils felt pressurised by the amount of work, by the burden on their memory, by the need for accuracy (alluding to the difficulty of verbs, genders, accents, pronunciation amongst other things); they also felt a sense of failure communicated in the teacher's remarks and said their ideal teacher would be:

someone who doesn't get annoyed with you if you can't do it the first time.

(B)

someone who isn't pushing you all the time. Because I just feel like saying, 'oh I'm not doing it', but you have to.

(B)

[someone who should] understand you're not as clever as everybody else.

(G)

They wanted a teacher who would be approachable, friendly, helpful, who would 'have a laugh', empathise, be more personal, treat them like young adults.

Apart from the question of teacher personality, a key factor mentioned by pupils was the need for more variety in lessons:

When you are writing all the time, it just seems a bit of a drag, you are just writing but not concentrating on what you are doing, it's just like copying down.

(G)

Suggestions made included the use of more television and video, more integration of IT, more games which served to involve them more, the element of competition motivating them to concentrate and therefore learn more, more visits and trips abroad or simply more contact with native speakers. Many suggested a greater need for pair and group work, stressing that peer learning was often more effective and certainly more enjoyable than individualised work.

It's helpful when you have someone else, because sometimes the thing you know, they don't and vice versa.

(G)

I like group work best, because you can have a bit of fun and it makes it easier to learn when everyone around you is trying to do it as well.

(B)

We used to make our own role plays on the subject we'd just been covering . . . we used to get a group together and sort it out, we used to mess around, but we did it and it was a good laugh, and then we'd do it in front of the class . . . . Practical work in French is important because you can't remember anything by just writing it down. I think when you are doing practical stuff you remember things better.

(G)

Batters found that self-image in foreign language learning seems to be linked to the embarrassment experienced by the pupils at speaking in front of the whole class, while still lacking confidence and getting things wrong. These feelings of embarrassment were less acute when the pupils were allowed to work in small groups. She concluded:

while language teachers continue to see themselves as the central focus of the language learning environment, pupils will continue to drop out. We must allow learners to interact, interrelate, negotiate, puzzle, initiate, create and generate.

(Batters, 1988)

FINAL REMARKS

Teachers remarked in these and other interviews (see Clark and Trafford, 1995; 1994) on the disproportion of male and female pupils in top sets, which has encouraged some schools to continue with a mixed-ability policy to the end of Key Stage 3, whereas other schools are experimenting with policies of single-sex setting within the mixed comprehensive school. Further research could usefully evaluate such policies, in order to ascertain the effect they have on pupils' self-image and on the dynamics of the classroom.

Motivation is clearly a vital ingredient in a pupil's success or failure in any subject. The nature of the learning process in a modern language appears to be more burdensome and to require a greater degree of concentration than other areas of the curriculum. In order to promote success, ideally pupils need more frequent contacts with the foreign language (in other words, more than the habitual two periods a week in Key Stage 4, which allow so much time to forget and make it so difficult to build on the work of the previous lesson) and more practical work using a variety of media to reinforce work in a more memorable way. The advances in IT have certainly opened up new possibilities. Pupils have been shown to write more when word processing (Gould, 1980; Atkinson, 1992), and boys in particular seem to find reading from a screen more attractive than from the written page. The development of the Internet has made instant communication with the continent more accessible. Looking to the future, the development of video conferencing should serve as a motivating force. Compared with the traditional penfriend contact, it is much more immediate and has the added attraction of a visual element to make this foreign tongue seem much more real to our pupils. Healthy exchanges and a programme of foreign visits help to raise the profile of language in schools, but for those pupils who for personal or financial reasons are never likely to opt for this sort of experience, the need for contacts with native speakers to give the subject greater relevance is unquestionable (see Chambers, 1994). It is regrettable that at a time when increasing numbers of pupils are studying a modern language to 16, financial constraints have meant that for many schools a foreign language assistant has become a luxury. In such a climate, there is a pressing need for schools to make links with companies in the locality where the use of a foreign language is important, where members of the company can explain to the pupils the contexts in which they require a foreign language and, indeed, where pupils could possibly be placed for work experience to see at first hand a foreign language being used in a work context.

It has, however, long been recognised that the influence the school can bring to bear is insignificant compared with that of parents, peers, the local community and the media and there is therefore a pressing need for

> the promotion of languages. . . outside school as well as inside school. . . . Languages are seen as a significantly low priority by too many people in the UK . . . . We are looking for role models who are UK role models to give examples to pupils of the value of being able to use a foreign language not only in their work environment but in the social and cultural environment.
>
> (Head of Department)

Even more fundamentally perhaps, attitudes towards education generally need to change, so that pupils in general and boys in particular come to value academic achievement more highly. I have focused in this chapter on the particular problems encountered in the modern languages curriculum, but in fact the findings appear to reflect more general trends, (with boys underperforming across the curriculum. Currently, there seems to be an anti-school ethos, notably among working class boys, whereby boys feel under pressure from their peers and possibly their parents to underperform across the curriculum. Girls, on the other hand, may be subjected to social pressure to conform to stereotypes which undervalue their talents and repress their natural abilities (DfEE, 1996). The resistance felt by many boys towards the languages curriculum can only partially be tempered by strategies outlined above; the issues at stake seem to be more entrenched, demanding a radical re-examination of the structure of the whole curriculum and the ways in which both boys and girls are taught and motivated to learn.

REFERENCES

Askew, S. and Ross, C. (1988) *Boys Don't Cry*, Milton Keynes: Open University Press.

Atkinson, T. (1992) 'Creative writing and IT', *Language Learning Journal* (6).

Batters, J.D. (1988) 'Pupil and teacher perceptions of foreign language learning and teaching', Unpublished PhD thesis, University of Bath.

Blackstone, T. (1985) Preface in J. Whyte *et al.* (eds) *Girl Friendly Schooling*, London: Methuen.

Chambers, G. (1994) 'A snapshot in motivation at 10+, 13+ and 16+', *Language Learning Journal* (9).

Clark, A. and Trafford, A.J. (1994) 'A study of the effect of gender on pupil performance and attitudes in modern language learning', University of Sheffield/Department of Employment.

—— (1995) 'Boys into modern languages', *Gender and Education* 7(3).

DES (1983) *Foreign Languages in the School Curriculum* (Consultative Paper).

DfEE (1996) *Highly Able Girls and Boys*, London: DfEE.

Gould, J.D. (1980) 'Composing letters with computer-based text editors', *Human Factors* 23–5.

Harris, S., Nixon, J. and Ruddock, J. (1993) 'School work, homework and gender', *Gender and Education* 5(1).

HMI (1985) *Boys and Modern Languages*, London: HMSO.

Macdonald, M. (1980) 'Schooling and the reproduction of class and gender relations', in L. Barton *et al.* (eds) *Schooling, Ideology and the Curriculum*, Lewes: Falmer.

Mahoney, P. (1985) *Schools for the Boys: Co-education Re-assessed*, London: Hutchinson.

Mickelson, R.A. (1992) 'Why does Jane read and write so well? The anomaly of women's achievement', in J. Wrigley (ed.) *Education and Gender Equality*, London: Falmer.

Ofsted (1993) *Boys and English*, London: HMSO.

Oller, J.W. Jr and Perkins, K. (1978) 'Intelligence and language proficiency as sources of variance in self-reported affective variables', *Language Learning* 28(1).

Powell, B. (1986) *Boys, Girls and Language in School*, London: CILT.

Powell, R.C. and Littlewood, P. (1983) 'Why choose French? Boys' and girls' attitudes at the option stage', *British Journal of Language Teaching* 21(1).

Scott, M. (1980) 'Teach her a lesson: sexist curriculum in patriarchal education', in D. Spender and E. Sarah (eds) *Learning to Lose*, London: The Women's Press.

Stanworth, M. (1983) *Gender and Schooling: a Study of Sexual Divisions in the Classroom*, London: Hutchinson.

Whyte, J. (1986) *Girls into Science and Technology: the Story of a Project*, London: Routledge and Kegan Paul.

3

BALANCING THE BOOKS

Tackling gender differences in reading

Elaine Millard

In the 1990s, it has become evident that boys are not doing as well as girls in many areas of the school curriculum as measured by success in external examinations (see Jesson in this volume) and assessments from Key Stage 1 to Key Stage 3. In this chapter, I intend to suggest that a possible reason for boys' poorer performance in these assessments, which is particularly marked in subjects that require extended written responses, is that they have become insufficiently engaged in the reading process in the first stages of schooling, and have therefore missed out on an essential element of learning from the printed word. I have argued elsewhere, (Millard, 1994: 102; 1997: 19–20) that for a number of cultural and socially structured reasons it is more difficult for many boys to identify with activities which are perceived to be more appropriate for girls than it is for most girls to attempt to emulate boys' achievements. Boys' socialisation encourages them to define themselves as different from girls and to ridicule each other for any signs of interests in activities considered feminine. I have further shown, as I will argue below, that reading fiction in the home is an activity most often enjoyed and shared by girls and women and, as such, becomes less attractive to boys in the middle years of schooling.

My particular interest in the field was prompted by the coincidence of an ongoing research project into reading preferences in the middle years of school with the publication of the OFSTED report *Boys and English* (1993) which drew evidence from the inspections of secondary schools, following the introduction of the National Curriculum (1989–92) Its opening statement was unequivocal:

> Boys do not do as well as girls in English in schools. There are contrasts in performance and in attitudes towards the subject. The majority of pupils who experience difficulty in learning to read and write are boys. Boys' results in public examinations at 16 are not as good as girls', and many more girls than boys continue to study English beyond 16.

It further reported that:

In all year groups girls read more fiction books than boys and tended to have different tastes in reading. Few teachers monitored differences in boys' and girls' reading differences.

Evidence which I collected in the first study, and subsequently reported in *Developing Readers in the Middle Years* (Millard, 1994), had further demonstrated that the practices of reading and writing in school were more in keeping with the self-reported interests of girls. The main reasons for the differences in interest I found then are summarised below.

- *There was a concentration on narrative as the main means of early instruction in reading.* First reading books, whether phonic based schemes or those which are described as 'real' books, mainly tell stories and a linguistic analysis of non-fiction for the primary age range also shows that many information texts for this age are also presented in story form.
- *Teachers discouraged certain kinds of reading material which they considered unsuitable for classroom reading.* Boys said they liked to share and discuss the contents of computer and other hobby-related magazines in their independent reading time but that this was frequently not permitted. They also complained that other books they enjoyed such as *He-man*, *Batman* or *Ninja Turtle* stories or any books in a graphic format were banned in class time.
- *Pupils were given free choice in reading but there was little teacher encouragement for them to develop beyond what they already liked.* Frequently, once children could 'decode print' and had worked through a reading scheme, they were allowed to develop further reading strategies by 'free' reading. The teachers' assumptions were that pupils would progress individually by choosing increasingly more demanding and linguistically complex texts. There was, however, little monitoring of the subsequent progress except for the requirement to keep lists of titles and page numbers in diaries, along with a smiling face, or a 1–5 star-rating system. Poor readers often remained on simple scheme books to the end of the primary phase, reinforcing their sense of failure, and the majority of such readers were boys. Girls on the other hand had more developed networks for sharing and recommending new books to one another.
- *Reading was used as a 'time filler' exercise.* Although all the teachers interviewed claimed that reading was a priority, in the classes observed, other concerns were allowed to eat into the set reading times. Children were sent to tidy up stock cupboards, practise recorders and to finish neat drafts for displays – so reading was seen by the children as something to be done when there was nothing else left to do. Reading almost always occupied a 'dead' slot in the school curriculum such as Friday afternoon or sessions following energetic physical exercise. Children who did not enjoy reading could therefore easily avoid the task.
- *A limited choice of genre was used for shared reading experiences.* In 1990, at the time of this first study, very few KS2 teachers were using whole class or group

readers at KS2, but at KS3 particularly, in Y7, the shared books were dominated by stories dealing with everyday problems which younger teenagers experience, such as bullying, or starting school, relieved by some humour or parody. Boys' preferred texts included more action, horror and adventure.

- *There was a mismatch between pupils' expectations of the importance of reading and its perceived use in school.* When asked if it was important to learn to read, pupils related reading to getting a job and getting on in life but reading in school rarely had a purpose that could easily be related to this. For most pupils reading in school was associated with works of fiction, used primarily, if not exclusively, for leisure. Pupils were often unable to make the necessary imaginative leap to see a connection.
- *Teachers relied heavily on prepared materials such as worksheets and summaries in the National Curriculum subjects.* Where children had a need to read for information it was frequently mediated by teachers' notes or worksheets which prevented non-fiction texts providing an opportunity for reading development.

A careful consideration of these factors suggests that these are conditions which may limit the reading experience of all children. They do, however, discriminate more particularly against boys because boys have also repeatedly been shown by surveys of independent reading habits as less willing to read independently (Whitehead *et al.*,1977; Benton, 1995; Coles *et al.*, 1996) and to have less interest in print-based narrative forms in general. Further, in analysing samples of the narrative writing of the same pupils, I have demonstrated that the reading which girls willingly undertook helped them to shape their written stories more conventionally and more convincingly than the majority of boys who tended to fall back on visual forms of narrative and more speech-based constructions in their narrative compositions (Millard, 1994; 1997).

Differences in the attitude and the experience of the sixteen boys and girls interviewed for the initial survey were so marked that I focused specifically on gender difference in a subsequent study of reading and writing attitudes, drawing on a larger sample of 255 pupils: 121 girls and 134 boys (Millard, 1997). On this occasion, I used an extended questionnaire followed by interviews with both individuals and small groups of pupils. The data collected confirmed that girls were generally more committed and wider readers than boys in the same age group. Of further significance was the finding that it was almost exclusively girls who shared books outside school, both with their peer group and with the other female members of the family. Boys' declared interests lay elsewhere, often in sport or computers. A significant number of boys were identified, whom I labelled 'hypothetical' readers, because the reading they reported remained only a possibility – something they might do if pushed – but which very rarely became a reality. Boys generally knew exactly what they would read if they were asked to do so but did not read voluntarily. The following view is typical of this group:

I don't read much but if I did I would read in bed. I can read a chapter a night. If I found a good book I would recommend it to my friends if they asked. At my primary school we didn't have much time to read you had to finish your work. I don't think I'm a good reader because I dislike reading.

(Boy, age 11; Millard, 1997: 89)

The survey also highlighted significant divergence in narrative taste in boys' and girls' choice of magazines, films and computer programs. Moreover, an experience of different forms of narrative could be readily identified in their own particular writing styles. A focus on a variety of contexts in which reading took place also highlighted significant variations in access to particular literacy experiences. I concluded that both the social practices of the school and those of the wider community worked together to create contexts in which reading contributed to the establishment of a gendered identity for the reader, an identity with which girls more readily identified than boys of a similar age and ability. I further suggested that the differences in boys' and girls' experience was sufficiently marked as to make them 'differently literate' (Millard, 1997).

A decline in the sustained reading of extended works of fiction in leisure time is a marked feature of modern culture, equally as applicable to parents as to their adolescent children. It can no longer be assumed that pupils will encounter sufficient experience of reading continuous prose from their private reading at home. Recent surveys undertaken by researchers in Nottingham (Coles *et al.* 1996) and Roehampton (1994) corroborate the findings of my more individualised research studies in their suggestion that the range of children's private reading has shrunk. Both of the latter national surveys reveal children's preference in the middle years for popular authors such as Roald Dahl and later for series fiction, and periodical reading. Educationalists, particularly teachers of English, continue to value narrative's embodiment of the history of particular cultures and wish pupils to access a wide range of forms in order to become effective readers. It must therefore be acknowledged that most children need more direction to ensure that they encounter increasingly complex and demanding texts. School practices which rely heavily on children's individual preferences ignore large areas of recorded experience, and the disparity between homes where book reading is encouraged and those where it rarely features further works to increase inequality of access to school literacy. Differences in exposure to reading also increase with age, and decline most sharply between the ages of 11 and 14. At every age the larger surveys confirm that boys read fewer books and spend less time on their reading than girls. (Whitehead *et al.* 1977; Coles *et al.*, 1996; Roehampton, 1994). Junior schools, therefore, have a major role to play in ensuring that pupils have been introduced to a wide range of genres and formats as part of the experience of the school curriculum. In particular, it is at KS2 that reading requires the most careful nurturing and monitoring so that secondary teachers may build on a foundation of developed interests and methods of understanding.

Moreover, there is a need to consider what should, or indeed can, be done about the specific gender differences revealed by my own and similar studies of reading habits (Coles *et al.*, 1996; Benton, 1995; Roehampton, 1994). My first suggestions, then, will address ways of adapting the current approach to reading in ways that are more 'boy friendly', using the model of 'girl friendly maths' (Walden and Walkerdine, 1985), without losing hold of practices that have encouraged girls' positive achievements. One way of interpreting boys' alienation from school subjects is to read it as a sign that the curriculum does not properly engage all pupils' interest and that it is boys in general who have been shown to be less willing to tolerate work perceived as having little personal relevance or which lacks clear direction. The following recommendations are therefore initially aimed at promoting a whole classes' range and motivation in reading, on the basis that boys will be prompted to take more interest in a topic that is given a high profile in the curriculum and where success is openly rewarded (West, 1986). There are some specific activities suggested, however, which draw on other kinds of reading identified in the study as of particular interest to large groups of boys. It will be up to the teacher to decide whether these are to be specifically targeted at boys in the class or shared with girls.

AUDITING INDIVIDUAL PUPILS' READING

The first step teachers need to take is to form a clear picture of the reading habits of the individuals who make up their classes. Although a knowledge of national reading trends may be helpful in creating a general picture of reading habits, each child makes a personal construct of what it is to be a good reader from a wide range of cultural contexts. Teachers can only form a complex picture of an individual's reading experience through a personal interview informed by a reading questionnaire, or by means of a reading history, jointly constructed by teacher and pupil. My research employed a questionnaire in narrative form whose basic questions were as follows:

Stories of Reading

Stories can be told about all kinds of happenings, especially if they have developed over a period of time.

Write the story of how you learned to read and the reading you do now. It will help your teacher find out the kinds of books you enjoy reading and the sort of reading you did in your last school. Write as much as you like.

Here are some of the things you might wish to include:

(The introduction is designed to be read out and discussed by the teacher presenting the questionnaires to the class. It acts as an invitation to writing.)

I. Learning to read

Who taught you to read?

Did you find it easy or hard to learn?

Write down the names of any of the first books you can remember reading.

II. Reading at home

What kinds of books do you enjoy most now?

Where and when do you enjoy reading?

Do you like reading to other people? (reading out loud).

Do you share or swap books with anyone else?

Who reads most in your family?

III. Reading at your last school

What books did you read at your last school?

How were your reading times organised?

What kinds of books did your teacher read to the class?

Sections I–III request information about the respondent's previous experience of reading and aims to discover how reading is perceived by the pupil at home and at school.

IV. TV programmes

Make a list of your favourite television programmes.

Is there any kind of programme that you particularly enjoy?

Do you have a television in your own room?

V. Comics and magazines

Which do you buy and which do you read?

What do you like about them?

VI. Computer games

What games do you enjoy and how long do you play on your computer each day?

(Sections IV–VI ask for information about leisure activities which compete with reading.)

VII. Time and place

Where and when do you read most often?

Do you read most at home or school?

This question was to discover whether the respondents read from their own choice and independently of school organisation of private reading time.

VIII. Comments

What have people ever said to you about your reading? (parents, teachers, friends)

To finish off how would you complete the following?

I think my reading is . . . .

The questions may be expanded or narrowed to meet the needs of particular classes and teaching contexts. (See also the developmental Primary Language Record (Barrs *et al.*, 1988: 14–15), which gives clear examples of conferences of older children and teachers.) A wider range of both reading and alternative narrative interests need to be taken into account when constructing such reading histories. Pupils can record, in addition to both fiction and information texts, their interests in film, media and computer simulations and games. These details help to build a more complex picture of the influences on children's literacy development, tastes and the range of texts, both written and visual, that they may use to sustain their own writing.

PROVIDING ACCESS TO BOOKS

In 1977 Whitehead *et al.* reported that the provision of books by the school could be shown to play an extremely important role in determining what children read. The two studies I have completed provide further confirmation that schools make an important difference both to the overall amount of reading undertaken in the middle years and the ways that individuals see themselves as effective readers. Libraries can make a real contribution to enthusiasm for reading, but there is an enormous variation in the role libraries are given in schools. The librarian of one inner city comprehensive school in the survey organised liaison between the English department and its feeder primary schools so that the children arriving in September had a book waiting in the library which they had ordered on a preliminary visit to the school in Y6. This helped to establish an early interest in the school library and its lending system which was developed throughout the children's subsequent time in school. Most departmental and library stocks need to be supplemented with a range of books aimed at capturing boys' narrative attention as well as tapping into all pupils' interest in information about hobbies and out of school literacy. It is important to encourage library-based research to develop habits of critical literacy,[1] while simultaneously making an effort to enthuse all young readers in reading, yet this cannot be done on outdated texts which serve a limited range of interests and represent a limited range of genres. Boys interviewed for this study, in particular, reported that they found many of the books that were provided in school libraries unappealing and outdated. In particular, geography reference books often reflected a world that no longer existed and which took no account of the enormous changes to national boundaries and political identities of the recent past. It is an area where particular attention is required, although out of date covers on popular fiction were seen as most off-putting by the group of pupils I interviewed about library access.

Further, it is not sufficient to address the use of libraries by prescribing one or two sessions of information skills in the first year of secondary school and hope the habit will transfer to the rest of the curriculum. The model of skills-based instruction which is bolted on to the curriculum is one that is equally unproductive in helping pupils gain confidence with information technology (see Opie in this volume). Work in both these areas, that is information processing and access through books and technology, needs to be embedded within meaningful curriculum activities which create authentic reasons for use. Teachers of subjects other than English should consider the opportunities they provide for library research so that encounters with texts become a routine part of every aspect of learning. The Y7 pupils in my studies reported very little time spent in reading primary sources or searching for information in subjects other than English. It is therefore well worth schools setting aside in-service time for the selection of book and electronic resources, where possible using professional advice. Many existing school libraries need to be culled ruthlessly to remove outdated volumes which have no relevance, or are misleading in their content, and those which no one cares to borrow. It is not surprising that many teachers and librarians are reluctant to throw out books when this results in empty shelves. However, the preservation of books with unappealing, dated formats and irrelevant information only serves to discourage many pupils from library use. School libraries also need to adapt to the new technologies by providing access to CD-ROMs and the Internet or World Wide Web. Parents of one secondary school in the survey, with a large library area, not always well used, suggested the setting up of tables for role play games, surrounded by books that would build on this particular interest. Certainly, all schools should have a range of newspapers and special interest magazines for quick reference and an area of the library where talk is positively encouraged. Long periods of silence were reported as least acceptable to the boys in the study who were always the ones to break up the imposed hush of a timetabled private reading or library session.

MATCHING READERS TO BOOKS

Two things are required for establishing good reading policies in schools: a wide provision of well-chosen resources and teachers and librarians who know them well and have time to match pupils to appropriate texts. School librarians can contribute effectively to this matching of child to book in the early stages of secondary school if pupils are given sufficient curriculum time to make choices and discuss their selections with them. One librarian of a Derbyshire secondary school had created a series of small icons for the spine of fiction books which drew pupils' attention to texts of a particular genre – a ghost shape for mysteries, a tank for war stories. Librarians have also discussed creating 'surprises' in the library by a judicious mingling of fact and fiction in displays and categories that were frequently used.

Pupils should hear books of all kinds being well read by a wider variety of people, both on tape and in the flesh. Stories read aloud capture the listeners' imagination, in a way that is often lost in the regular grind of 'getting through' a class novel, chapter by chapter, with an activity tacked on at the end of each block of reading. Subjects other than English could use such readings to engage pupils' interest in particular topics, places or people. Literature is a rich resource, which has always been seen as particularly applicable to the humanities but one that can be equally well exploited in science and technology through accounts of experiments, new discoveries and the lives of important scientists. All teachers in training should be given help in developing the ability to read aloud well.

It may be more productive at times to whet children's appetites with glimpses of a book which they can later follow up for themselves. One Wiltshire school has experimented with paired reading aloud as part of a KS3 Personal Reading Programme. Pupils were encouraged to choose a reading partner with whom they could work over the period of a term on the shared reading of an agreed text. Significantly, the teachers had found that only 14 per cent of the boys compared with 36 per cent of the girls had been asked to read aloud since starting their secondary school. They suggest that reading aloud in a structured activity 'may well result in an improvement in students' involvement and engagement with texts and may influence the amount and variety of personal reading' (Bennett, 1996: 41). Similarly a project I completed for SCAA to encourage weaker boys' reading by pairing the boys with a younger boy for whom they were asked to choose a book was successful in engaging them in reading aloud to their partner. The opportunity to prepare and practise their chosen reading motivated them to work hard on an area that is frequently neglected in the middle years of schooling.

WORKING WITH HOME AND THE WIDER COMMUNITY

Home has been repeatedly shown to exert a powerful influence on the early development of pupils' attitudes to reading (Hannon, 1995; Weinberger, 1996) and the studies I have recently completed suggest this influence continues in the later years (Millard, 1994; 1997). My next point, therefore, is that schools should make efforts to secure the continuing support of parents and carers of both sexes for the promotion of activities associated with reading. Book lists with suggestions for suitable birthday and Christmas presents would help parents to select presents for their children with more confidence, and can be even more effective if pupils are involved in reviewing and recommending new titles. Male members of families need to be involved in school initiatives to promote book buying and promoting an interest in reading. There is growing evidence to show that because mothers are most engaged with helping with reading in the early years the activity seems less relevant to boys. Fathers' opinions need to be solicited and their tastes in reading taken into account when purchasing and recommending books. Schools have used 'Book Weeks' to invite a range of people associated with the school to come into the library and read a favourite story. Local sportsmen, the community policeman, traffic wardens and the owner of the local shop from which children buy sweets are all worth targeting. In one initiative organised for Sheffield's Year of Reading (1996) members of Sheffield United FC were invited to select books to recommend for reading in school. The players made a selection which included poetry and information texts and a range of fictional genre in addition to football stories and these were used to create reading lists to motivate pupils to 'Read a Team'– that is, eleven books from favourite players to be read in a term.

SHARED READING ACTIVITIES

A balance of reading that leads pupils to re-evaluate their emergent view of the world is badly served, however, by a concentration on a personal choice of narrative fiction, which goes unchallenged or developed by interaction with a teacher or an interested adult. More attention therefore needs to be paid to the books chosen for shared reading in class. There is anecdotal evidence from inspections and curriculum audits to suggest that in the middle years of school teachers' choice of books has been overinfluenced by the demands of projects and topics. Similarly, the secondary school curriculum is now heavily dominated by 'the classics' required by the National Curriculum (Benton, 1995: 108). The study of a work of fiction for its own merits needs to be better promoted at an earlier stage in the English curriculum so that reflective reading approaches are well established by the end of KS2. This does not always mean that all children in a particular class should share the same book, ignoring questions of taste as well as ability. Group reading of a selection of interesting texts will serve just as well as a forum for the exchange of views and the organisation of DARTs (Directed Activities Related to Texts) activities such as deducing the opening of a story from its ending, or resequencing a complex narrative that has been cut up to be restructured. It has been the experience of teachers in the survey that such activities, carefully organised, provide a focus for all pupils' reading and are a good stimulus to many boys who appear eager to solve a problem or get an answer quickly.

WORKING WITH POPULAR CULTURE AND OTHER MEDIA

Pupils benefit from discussing the forms of popular culture that are of topical interest to them in order to understand the features that are common to their production – the romance element in the *Point Horror* series, for example. Teachers can draw pupils' attention to the ways in which different narrative structures such as quests, romance, riddle tests and rescue – the common stock of both popular and classic literature – represent different ways of gaining competence and agency in the world. The difference in boys' and girls' narrative preferences need to be openly discussed and compared so that the contrasting positions offered in their messages about gendered identity can be understood.

Well-structured analysis of aspects of cultural representation builds upon pupils' prior knowledge; for example, comics and magazines may be shown to construct a wide range of cultural representations of both old and young characters, which can be categorised and compared. Pupils may have begun to consider such issues for themselves as in the case of one boy in the study who gave a detailed account of changes in the image of the *Beano*'s Dennis the Menace which he thought had affected the age group buying the comic.

Teaching based on cultural analysis model can be fed back into a study of more literary forms. For example, an analysis of advertising media may be used to encourage interest in literary aspects of language through a close, detailed and analytical reading of both magazine and television texts. Television and film adaptations may provide a stimulus for reading complex narratives and provide an alternative way into books as different as Mary Norton's *The Borrowers* and Jonathan Swift's *Gulliver's Travels*. Evidence from current reading surveys shows that there is an upsurge of interest in books whenever they appear as film adaptations. However, evidence of whether children actually read the original classics they include in their lists is quite inconclusive. My own research tends to show that most read abridged and graphic versions of the longer works and may confuse video and film narrative with print in making their lists of books they have 'read'. Therefore, in order to make good use of their awakened interest, pupils' reading of the original text needs to be directed and supported by a suitable task. For example, a class might compare the print and media interpretation of a key episode in a story, to identify what has to be added or omitted in the adaptation.

CATERING MORE DIRECTLY FOR BOYS' TASTES

In order to improve boys' motivation more whole class activities based on the boys' current preoccupations should be considered. A starting point is to change the balance of texts selected for class or group work to include more of the action and humour which are a constant feature of boys' recorded preferences. It is also important to focus on the identification of facts and narrative structure as well as the analysis of feelings and character when working with narrative. Outcomes from reading adapt well to a problem-solving approach and can be presented in a variety of forms using charts, time lines, graphs and other visual forms. For example, a group of Y9 pupils were making a chart to show the prominence of the characters in particular acts of *Romeo and Juliet*. They devised a key using hearts, crossed rapiers and skulls to indicate whether the character fell in love, was involved in a fight or died in the scene studied. The balance of work needs to be handled carefully, however, to avoid slippage into a stereotyped view of what is of interest to boys in general. It would be a retrograde step to destroy opportunities for the discussion of feelings in English lessons, where the study of literature offers a safe arena in which difficult issues and personal responses may be addressed. It is important, nevertheless, to create a balance that allows for a variety of textual encounters, rather than relying on a dominant emphasis on a personal response to issue-based narratives. Many of the boys I have interviewed clearly had a range of interests not included in current school provision and such needs should be of prime importance when new books are being selected.

COMBINING FACT AND FICTION

Another school response has been to develop work in English which combines a range of fiction and non-fiction texts. This allows a focus on questions beyond those of relationship and feelings. One English department introduced work based on a collection of books about wolves, which included natural history texts and anthropological studies as well as myth and fables. The materials to be read were as diverse as the Microsoft CD-ROM, *Dangerous Creatures*, and works of fiction such as Gillian Cross's *Wolf* and humorous retellings of *Little Red Riding Hood* such as *There's a Wolf in My Pudding* by Henry Cecil Wilson. Pupils were asked to consider the representation of wolves in a number of works of fiction, including that of the werewolf, and to discuss whether these had any basis in fact. Working from fiction to fact allowed for an interest in the information content of stories to play a central role in the reading process, something which is repeatedly reported by boys as a motivation for reading. A second group of teachers turned the process about and worked from fact to fiction as in one Y7 group's survey of venomous beasts. Factual information about snakes and poisonous spiders was used in the composition of poems describing the creatures. The first poems were further developed into descriptive images of human beings who aroused the same emotions. Here pupils' thinking developed from understanding facts to an imaginative response, which was then further developed into symbolic and metaphoric representation.

MANAGING READING FOR LEARNING

Although the teaching of fiction is well justified in English lessons as one way of working towards a more critical literacy, it should not be allowed to carry the whole weight of socially significant interaction with texts. More activities which encourage an active reconstruction of meaning from information sources are required. Therefore the second major focus from within which equal access to literacy development is to be planned begins with an audit of the opportunities for this kind of critical reading which are provided within the whole curriculum. Evidence from my own research studies and projects such as that of Webster *et al*. (1996) suggest that too much information is presented to pupils as worksheets or on blackboards, restricting the opportunities for pupils to reconstruct meaning from primary sources for themselves.

For example, Webster *et al*. analysis of the literacy events in the curriculum of both primary and secondary schools provides convincing evidence that children are not required to read by their teachers sufficiently often or trusted to make their own written meanings from the texts presented to them. Too much of the work which the researchers observed had meaning only within a school context and was irrelevant to the world outside. They reported:

> One of our observation categories is specially focused on pupils con-structing their own writing, whilst another category focuses on engage-ment with different text forms, such as personal reading, or reading a . . . text for information. . . . In 76 per cent of cases, generating or redrafting of writing was never observed. In 12.5 per cent of the cases where pupils were generating their own writing, it was for less than a total of ten minutes out of a 55–minute lesson. Reading engagement was never recorded in 78 per cent of the cases, whilst in only 7.5 per cent of cases were periods of reading for more than ten minutes in total recorded.
>
> (p. 113)

This research echoes the earlier work of Lunzer and Gardner (1979) whose studies in the late 1970s found that pupils were required to read in short bursts and frequently had sections of topic books preselected by their teachers for copying into their books.

Sadly the practice of copying out information is even being reintroduced into some English lessons, where teachers anxious for their pupils' SAT performance are encouraging them to copy out plot summaries of Shakespeare plays, because 'they must at least know the plot'. Some primary schools, however, have a better developed practice in helping children make sense of information and engaging their active learning skills at KS2 than do the various subject areas in KS3 of the secondary curriculum (Millard, 1994).

PROVIDING FOR TECHNOLOGICAL CHANGES TO LITERACY

Establishing literacy development as a key learning goal in all subjects, particularly during the middle years (KS2 and KS3), would ensure that curriculum planners gave thought to the wider applications and uses of reading and writing in society. These often require different modes of reading than those appropriate to continuous prose narrative. Computer literacy needs to be carefully defined and better understood for the purposes of curriculum development. It is imperative that all schools rapidly gain full access to information technology to support pupils' learning. In this I include teletext services such as Ceefax as well as interactive media on the Internet and the World Wide Web. There exists a range of areas on the Web dedicated to the needs of children, including school-based communications. However, a very brief surf of individual pages on the Web reinforces the view that boys have greater access than girls and that the families already involved in their own pages have predominantly academic lifestyles. Currently, boys report a greater interest in the new forms of literacy than do the girls (Millard, 1997). On the one hand this means that IT provides a valuable medium for motivating boys, but on the other, that girls may well be falling behind in this newer form of literate behaviour if schools do not ensure their equal participation at a time when their confidence is greatest. A further emphasis for the literacy curriculum is for schools to develop rapidly access to on-line literacies in order to prevent the exclusion of the less advantaged from a new and powerful communication tool.

EQUAL ACCESS FOR ALL?

I intend now to return to my initial analysis of the advantages girls enjoy in the school curriculum as evidenced from SATs and GCSE examination which suggest they are achieving well in the system. However, it is important to be wary of concluding, therefore, that girls are doing well in terms of their future learning or accumulation of what may be defined in terms of Bourdieu's (1990) cultural capital.[2] Girls' interests in school may prove to be too narrowly focused on producing the older established cultural forms which please their teachers, such as, for example, long continuous prose narratives. They may be less practised in developing flexible responses to learning in other subjects.

Boys' attitudes, however, currently claim our immediate attention, not the least because the result of their alienation from school culture (Willis, 1977; Connell, 1989; Mac an Ghaill, 1994) and its literacy practices is being mirrored in a relative lack of progress as measured by the examination system. It is therefore important that teachers of younger boys take steps to draw them more actively into a classroom community of story book readers and narrative writers by making provision in their resources for differences in tastes and by planning classroom activities around them. However, while addressing the problems created by boys' indifference to, and sometimes alienation from, the varieties of reading and writing most often featured in school, it seemed to me that they were symptomatic of a much larger concern. The majority of boys appear to be far less tolerant than most girls of activities which they consider irrelevant to their lives outside school (see also Clark is this volume and Scott (1980), on girls' greater tolerance of boring school work). Girls, on the other hand, largely enjoy the 'literacy curriculum', whatever its function, often importing their interest in reading and writing to more practical subjects, as when producing carefully documented projects in technology, for example. There is some ground then to consider boys' gradual alienation from school as an important statement about the relevance of the current curriculum to all pupils' needs.

If we also take into account the range of boys' literacy interests outside school, and their greater show of interest in the new technologies (an aspect discussed in greater detail by Opie in Chapter 5), it becomes clearer that girls also have an interest in a critical reappraisal of school literacy practices. Although girls currently appear to be doing better than boys in terms of school work we need to question further whether their expressed literacy preferences are the best preparation for a changing world literacy. (White, 1986, 1990; Teese *et al.*, 1995, Millard, 1997). Looked at more critically, current differences in boys' and girls' performance may well signify that groups of advantaged boys are already staking a claim to more powerful means of communication while actively avoiding school book learning. It may therefore follow that, as men, they will continue to gain more powerful access to the most influential discourses embodied in the interrelated media of film, computer and CD-ROMs. Without carefully planned provision the newer forms of literacy may be restricted to those in advantaged positions thereby widening the gap between the information rich and those with no, or very limited, technological resources. The issues which I have raised in the final section should motivate schools to identify ways in which all the members of the school community can be encouraged to exercise a more authentic and critical literacy. By that I wish to indicate learning embodied in a range of practices which encourage pupils to become increasingly critically aware of their world through an equal access to, and familiarity with, both the printed and the electronic page.

NOTES

1 I define this as the ability to question texts and their role in structuring meaning in addition to accessing and using their contents. *Critical literacy* is also the title of Lankshear and McLaren's (1993) collection of essays which interrogate the interrelationship of literacy, politics and praxis in modern schooling. The essays refer frequently to the literacy projects of Freire and Giroux who advocate the importance of developing a critical consciousness, in their education of peasant populations. In this chapter I use critical literacy therefore to relate to both the direct experience of the learner and the ability to critique power relations in constructing knowledge. Critical literacy can be best understood as a way of making meaning from texts and in writing which seeks consistently to question the underpinning

of the ideas that are generated in the process.

The utopian aim of a critically literate population is discussed at greater length in the concluding chapter of this collection.

2 Cultural capital is used by Bourdieu in his structuralist analysis of the ways in which schools reproduce, indeed reinforce, cultural and economic inequalities. He shows how the language, discourses and cultural preferences of dominant groups are adopted and rewarded by schooling to the exclusion of other classes. Closely related is Bernstein's earlier identification of a 'restricted' code which disenfranchises working class pupils. See Bernstein, B. (1997) *Class, codes and control*, Vol. 3, London: Routledge and Kegan Paul. Both theorists have been much criticised for 'labelling' or even 'blaming the victim'; however, the concept of such 'capital' helps me to theorise about the advantages enjoyed by children who have books which are closest to school texts provided for them in the home, these children being predominantly middle class. Bernstein has recently (1996) re-examined his 'code' theory in *Pedagogy, symbolic control and identity*, London: Taylor & Francis).

REFERENCES

Barrs, M., Ellis, S., Hester, H. and Thomas, A. (1988) *The Primary Language Record: Handbook for Teachers*, London: Centre for Language in Primary Education.

Bennett, C. (1996) 'Making allowances – developing reading aloud with a Year 7 Class', in A. Howe (ed.) *Boys and English: Discussion Documents, Inset Materials and an Account of Development Work in Three Wiltshire Schools*, Trowbridge: West Publications.

Benton, P. (1995) 'Recipe fictions: literary fast food? Reading interests in Y8', *Oxford Review of Education* 21: 108–11.

Bourdieu, P. (1990) *The Logic of Practice* Trans. R. Nice, Cambridge: Polity Press. (Original work published 1980.)

Clark, M. (1976) *Young Fluent Readers*, Oxford: Heinemann Educational.

Coles, M., Fraser, V. and Hall, C. (1996) *The Children's Reading Choices Project*, Interim Report (sponsored by W. H. Smith), Nottingham University.

Connell, R.W. (1989) 'Cool guys, swots and wimps: the interplay of masculinity and education', *Oxford Review of Education* 15(2): 291–303.

Hannon, P. (1995) *Literacy, Home and School Research and Practice in Teaching Literacy with Parents*, London: Falmer.

Lankshear, C. and Lawler, M. (1987) *Literacy, Schooling and Revolution*, Lewes: Falmer.

Lankshear, C. and McLaren, P.L. (1993) *Critical Literacy, Policy, Praxis and the Postmodern*, Albany, NY: State University of New York Press.

Lunzer, A. and Gardner, K. (1979) *The Effective Use of Reading*, London: Heinemann Educational.

Mac an Ghaill, M. (1994) *The Making of Men: Masculinities, Sexualities and Schooling*, Buckingham: Open University Press.

Millard, E. (1994) *Developing Readers in the Middle Years*, Buckingham: Open University Press.

—— (1997) *Differently Literate: Boys, Girls and the Schooling of Literacy*, London: Falmer.

Roehampton Children's Literature Research Centre (1994) *Contemporary Juvenile Reading Habits*, Roehampton Institute (British National Bibliography Research Fund, Report 69).

Scott, M. (1980) 'Teach her a lesson: sexist curriculum in patriarchal education', in D. Spender and E. Sarah, *Learning to Lose*, London: The Women's Press.

Teese, R., Davies, M., Charlton, M. and Polesel, J. (1995) *Who Wins at School?: Boys and Girls* in *Australian Secondary Education*, Department of Education Policy and Management, The University of Melbourne, Australia.

Walden, R. and Walkerdine, V. (1985) *Girls and Mathematics: the Early Years*, Bedford Way Papers, London University Institute of Education.

Webster, A., Beveridge, M. and Reed, M. (1996) *Managing the Literacy Curriculum*, London: Routledge.

Weinberger, J. (1996) *Literacy Goes to School: the Parents' Role in Young Children's Literacy Learning*, London: Paul Chapman.

West, A. (1986) 'The production of readers', *The English Magazine: Literature* (17), Autumn: 4–22.

White, J. (1986) 'The writing on the wall: beginning or end of a girl's career?', *Women's Studies International Forum* 9: 561–74.

—— (1990) 'On literacy and gender', in R. Carter (ed.) *Knowledge about Language and the Curriculum*, London: Hodder & Stoughton.

Whitehead, F., Capey, A., Maddren, W. and Wellings, A. (1977) *Children and their Books*, Final Report of the Schools Council Project on children's reading habits 10–16, Basingstoke: Evans/Methuen Educational.

Willis, P. (1977) *Learning to Labour*, London: Saxon House.

4

SCIENCE EDUCATION FOR ALL?

Towards more equitable science education

Jon Scaife

SEX, GENDER AND ATTAINMENT DIFFERENCES IN SCHOOL SCIENCE

Assessing learning

'Girls getting ahead'
'Boys buck the trend and come out on top'
'Schools urged to focus on low achieving boys'

These national newspaper headlines are an indication of the recent political weight given to children's attainment in school. Data on children's curriculum perfor-mance is not in short supply in education but it is by no means straightforward to interpret. Indeed, it sometimes appears that the emerging message has so much 'spin' on it that the original data is no longer relevant. Consensus, though rare, is occasionally reached. One broadly supported view to emerge in the 1990s, for instance, was that schools have increasingly come to be seen as a waste of time by one particular group of students. Her Majesty's Chief Inspector of Schools admitted in March 1996 that white working class boys are failing in schools and, in a rare moment of humility, he declared that he did not know why (Woodhead, 1996). His view was supported by Rowe, a researcher from Melbourne, Australia: 'Increasingly girls prefer being at school significantly more than boys. We're almost in danger of developing an educational underclass – consisting of boys' (Rowe, quoted in Pyke, 1996). A survey of secondary-aged students conducted by the University of Keele revealed that school work is more 'uncool' for boys than girls, boys are 'out' four nights a week compared with girls' once, boys rush their homework compared with girls, and boys' motivation falls from Year 8 onwards (Evans, 1996). School inspection data collected by the Office for Standards in Education (OFSTED) has shown that the overall performance gap between girls and boys increases with the overall performance of the school. The implication is that if standards rise, the gap will widen!

The current view that girls have overtaken boys in examination performance at 16 in England and Wales masks a social class effect, according to research by Bentley (reported in Hofkins, 1996). In independent and grammar schools, girls are outperforming boys in physics and are on a par with boys in chemistry, while boys are scoring higher in biology. In comprehensive schools, however, girls, and especially girls from working class backgrounds, are opting out of science as far as they are allowed by taking it as a single curriculum subject, while boys tend to take science as a double subject. It could be possible to read into the fact that girls have caught up in science that science must now be 'girl friendly'. Bentley's data reveals what an incomplete picture this would be.

International surveys of achievement

Despite their undoubted interest, international surveys need to be treated with some caution. This is because achievement is not universally defined. An extraordinary achievement in one cultural and historical context may, somewhere else, hardly rate at all. Although this makes direct comparison hazardous, Gipps and Murphy (1994) consider that there are measured differences in performance in science tests between the sexes, with boys scoring higher. The difference between boys and girls in Britain has reduced over the years 1970 to 1990. It is not clear to what extent the tests reflect 'actual differences in achievement', however. This is because the authors of the surveys do not generally question the construct as they define it for assessment, or the type of test item used (the 'construct' is the bundle of knowledge supposed to be operating in response to the task or test item). This has frequently resulted in the conclusions (i) that girls have underachieved and (ii) that 'there is something lacking in girls, who are then encouraged to behave more like boys' (p. 113). This explanation, that girls underachieve because they are deficient in some way, is sometimes referred to as the 'deficit model'.

The Third International Maths and Science Study (TIMSS) produced data on the science performance of 9 and 13 year olds in Europe, the Americas, Africa, the Middle East, the Far East and Australasia. The results, reported in November 1996, revealed an improvement in English children's performance in science compared with other countries since the previous survey in 1991. (*The Times Educational Supplement* declared that our 13 year olds are now: 'At the top of division two in science – or at least, the kind of science measured by tests'.) About 80 per cent of the test questions in TIMSS were multiple choice format. In three-quarters of the participating countries boys outscored girls. Year 9 boys in England scored an average overall mark in science of 562 compared with 542 for girls, despite the tests being conducted at precisely the time when boys' school performance was raising great alarm. Boys outscored girls in each of the science categories of physics, chemistry, earth, life and environment, with the biggest difference being in chemistry.

Data such as this supports the conclusion that boys usually do better in science than girls *within the same country.* However, girls from some countries perform much better in science than boys from other countries. This led Gipps and Murphy (1994) to draw the following conclusion on the traditional nature–nurture issue: 'there is no genetic determinant of performance: if girls in one country can score higher in maths or physics than boys in another, the cause of differential performance must be environmental rather than biological' (p. 113).

Evidence from the UK

Research teams for science were established in 1978 and national surveys of children's knowledge, understanding and skills in science took place from 1980 to 1984. This was followed by analysis and further research.

From an overall view of the APU data, three key factors emerge as significant in influencing science performance, particularly for girls. The first is the perceived *purpose* of the task: 'The purpose defines what knowledge students consider appropriate to draw on . . . . The APU results indicate that girls' purposes are more often at odds with those of science assessors than boys and their performance more frequently misinterpreted as a consequence' (Murphy, quoted in Gipps and Murphy, 1994: 149). The second factor is the nature of the task *content*:

> The differential effect of task content on pupils was noted across the surveys, yet assessors assume that the content of a task is largely irrelevant. These content performance effects arise from the combination of avoidance by some students, and the heightened confidence of others.
>
> (p. 149).

By way of illustration, suppose that a pupil's ability to take readings from the scale of a measuring device is to be assessed. From the assessor's point of view, the task could be set using kitchen scales or, equally well, a voltmeter. From the pupil's perspective, however, the choice of content may strongly influence the perceived difficulty of the task. The third factor is *context*:

> Typically girls tend to value the circumstances that activities are presented in and consider that they give meaning to the task. They do not abstract issues from their context. Boys as a group conversely do consider the issues in isolation and judge the content and context to be irrelevant. This latter approach is generally assumed in assessment practice.
>
> (Murphy, in Gipps and Murphy, 1994: 150)

Murphy relates this context effect to the tendency of boys to outperform girls on multiple choice tests. In the APU science tests with 15 year olds, for instance, boys were less comfortable than girls with assessment requiring a free response, but the positions were reversed with multiple choice tests.

Language is fundamental to students' interpretations of purpose, content and context. Gipps and Murphy report that:

> One of the overwhelming findings of the APU science surveys was that students failed to achieve on items not because of errors but because of answering alternative tasks. It is possible to alter the content of a test to advantage or disadvantage certain groups while maintaining the construct that the test is said to be assessing.
>
> (p. 183)

Content (and also context and purpose) is thus a design feature of the task and as such it is within the teacher's influence.

Of the many detailed findings, here is one that seems to illustrate the content effect and perhaps, also, the context effect on performance:

> The *extreme* discrepancy in the performance of girls and boys on questions featuring electricity appears to be a particularly firmly established phenomenon. Girls' weakness in this area was evident across the framework and was not confined to questions demanding conceptual understanding. Whenever a circuit diagram or an actual circuit was featured in a question, girls performed at significantly lower levels than boys.
>
> (p. 135)

Teachers who are aware of this potential aversion will be better placed to plan lessons to counteract it.

Gipps and Murphy conclude that there is 'little support' in the APU findings for biological explanations for differences in performance: 'differences across subjects are reduced when curriculum background is controlled or when out-of-school experience is taken into account, indicating that differences in achievement are related to differences in opportunity to learn to a large extent' (p. 146).

Evidence from the USA

National Assessment of Educational Progress (NAEP) surveys have been conducted since 1969. Differences in performance between the sexes emerged in the physical sciences: (i) 'The performance gap in physics between 11th grade girls and boys was found to be extremely large, and it could not be explained by differential course-taking patterns'; and (ii) the 'proficiency gap' between boys and girls increased, in some cases, with course taking. Chemistry course taking particularly improved boys' scores.

The NAEP surveys included data on children's informal science-related experiences. These are illustrated in Tables 4.1 and 4.2. APU data has been added to the second table for comparison.

Noting the similarity between the British and American findings, Gipps and

Table 4.1 Differences among 9 year old boys and girls in terms of the percentages claiming to have worked or experimented with particular named topics

Topic	% pupils		Discrepancy in favour of	
	Boys	Girls	Girls	Boys
Batteries and bulbs	61	47		
Magnets	68	57		
Floating and sinking	58	48		
Dissolving	55	54		
Living animals	65	63		
Mirror	41	43		
Seeds	61	64		
Living plants	63	68		
Shadows	43	48		
Sound	55	67		

Source: 1982 USA national survey data; Johnson and Murphy (1986)

Murphy infer that there is a 'cross-cultural phenomenon of gendered societal expectations in support of the environmental hypothesis concerning differential learning opportunities' (p. 177).

Research following on from the NAEP surveys cited several factors considered likely to be influential in bringing about performance differences in science. These were teacher expectation, typically higher for boys than girls; teacher–student interaction, typically more challenging with boys during questioning; textbook content; parental attitude; peer attitude.

Lockheed *et al.* (cited in Gipps and Murphy, 1994) reviewed sex and ethnic

Table 4.2 Differences in the percentage of young boys and girls reporting use of particular measuring instruments at home or otherwise out-of school*

Measuring instruments	% 9 year olds		% 11 year olds		Discrepancies in favour of	
	Boys	Girls	Boys	Girls	Girls	Boys
Compass	65	52	69	48		
Microscope	54	40	49	34		
Stopwatch/clock	57	45	66	52		
Spring balance	35	25	28	20		
Hand lens	86	81	70	59		
Metre stick	67	62	22	16		
Thermometer	81	83	53	49		
Weighing scales	84	87	75	81		

Source: 1982 NAEP and 1984 APU national survey data; Johnson and Murphy (1986)
*   ■ indicates American 9 year olds, and ■ British 11 year olds

differences in American middle school maths and science, including NAEP data in a wider context. They commented that performance differences tended to be thought of as arising from supposed 'deficits in cognitive ability' rather than from the assessment process itself, despite the latter 'relying upon task and apparati associated with upper-middle class white males' (p. 181).

End-of-course examination performance

Harding's research in the late 1970s indicated that in examinations at 16+ in science:

- boys from mixed schools outperformed girls from mixed schools;
- girls from girls' schools outperformed girls from mixed schools;
- boys from comprehensive schools outperformed girls from comprehensive schools.

Harding suggested that the achieved performances may be context related and that this may contribute to sex-based performance differences (Gipps and Murphy, 1994: 211–12).

The ratio of boys to girls entering the three traditional science 'A' levels from 1988 to 1992 inclusive were as follows: physics 3 (boys per girl), chemistry 3:2 and biology 2:3. In the A–C grade band in 'A' level physics girls outperformed boys. Gipps and Murphy, and others, account for this by suggesting that the subject tends to 'select' girls who are more highly motivated on average than the boys who take physics.

Newbold's analysis in 1980 of boys' and girls' performance in 'A' level sciences led him to suggest that the major factor contributing to boys outperforming girls is the skill demanded by the test item. 'This would suggest that it is the constructs used to define achievement and how mode of assessment mediates these that need to be explored in a search for "fairness" in examinations' (Gipps and Murphy, p. 214). In other words, (i) some skills are more readily demonstrated by certain pupil groups than others, for example boys in Newbold's study; and (ii) assessment tasks are generally not neutral with respect to all pupil groups and may turn out to emphasise some skills rather than others, for example those shown more often by boys, as above.

EQUITABLE ASSESSMENT IN SCIENCE

Can science learning be assessed in ways that do not disadvantage either sex?

Evidence like that summarised in the previous section is informative about the comparative performance of particular groups of pupils but it also sheds light on processes of assessment and on what is being assessed.

Gipps and Murphy (1994: 256–77) point out how fragile the rock of assessment is, on which so much faith is placed. They declare that 'there is no such thing as a fair test, nor could there be'. Any interpretation of data is shaped by the nature of the test. In particular, the validity of conclusions about student performance rests on the nature and quality of the assessment process.

> It is widely accepted that affective factors mediate students' performance in assessments . . . a task with a particular mode of response, rather than measuring the construct assumed, may, for some students, only measure their level of confidence in themselves with regard to the domain being assessed . . . there is a need to explore *characteristic* responses to assessment tasks.

This would involve exploring student's preferred modes of expression of knowledge on identified constructs.

Equipped with this knowledge, teachers would then be able to plan the inclusion of an appropriate range of tasks, requiring a variety of modes of response, at least some of which would match each student's strengths. In particular, if the assessment process aims to recognise students' best performance, then it would seem appropriate to use different modes with different students. One way of approaching this would be to offer choices to the student. The open-book, time-unlimited exam is an example which may be suitable for older learners.

The APU science surveys also highlighted an instance where student choice enhanced performance: 'when girls were able to establish tasks for themselves, rather than working with established tasks which were to them less relevant, their performance was better than that of boys' (p. 269). There is an interesting corollary to this: although pupil assessment normally operates with individuals, if some pupils work better in groups, should their work be assessed in groups?

Another example of flexibility in approach to assessment which has improved girls' performance in physics is reported from South Australia (p. 275). Contexts were only included if they were integral to the particular physics problem; the language of questions was simplified (note that this does not imply that the corresponding constructs are simpler); equal status was accorded to different ways of answering questions; and a list of key words was provided. It may also be more equitable to identify students' end-of-course examination work by number, or other code, than by name. This is because, as Goddard-Spear (1983) found, a science assignment was marked lower by teachers when it was said to be by a girl than when it was said to be by a boy! (Gipps and Murphy, p. 150).

Teacher expectation

It has been asserted (e.g. Roychoudhury *et al.*, 1995; Volman *et al.*, 1995; Guzzetti and Williams, 1996; Staberg, 1994; Weinburg, 1995) that the subject of science is essentially masculine and tends to repel girls by tacitly forcing masculine values on them. Could it then be said that teachers, through being successful in science teaching, contribute to the continuation of an inequitable domain in education, albeit unwittingly?

We tend to rate more highly those behaviours that are closer to our own cultural norms. If a teacher is a well-assimilated member of a professional community successfully practising western, masculine science, he or she is likely to respond more positively towards those students who adopt the same view of science. When that view of science is compatible with students' broader social norms, the students are more likely to succeed, and the dominant view of science will be reinforced. If, however, western, masculine science is perceived as an alien culture by some students, they are seen as misfits.

It is well known that teacher expectation has a powerful influence on children's progress in school. If teachers are (unknowingly) drawn to hold relatively low expectations of some groups of pupils then there is a distinct possibility that the performance of these groups will be depressed as a result. I have seen this catch student science teachers unawares. Despite their familiar (and welcome) tendency to enter the classroom full of idealism and liberal values, some have responded with ingrained intolerance of 'alternative' pupil approaches to doing science. These alternatives have generally been associated with pupils who are not middle class, or not white, or not boys. The first two categories, non-middle-class and non-white, can evoke a sense of threat – Gillborn calls it the 'myth of the Afro-Caribbean challenge' (Gillborn, 1990). Teacher expectation of girls is different. Gipps and Murphy report that teachers tend to consider more girls than boys to be average. Boys are more likely than girls to be regarded as high achievers or low achievers. The result of this, especially for student teachers, is predictable. Boys stand out, either for 'good' or 'bad' behaviour, and demand teacher attention. It may come as a relief to the teacher when girls are content to be 'average'!

Underachievement

No biological characteristic has been identified that distinguishes groups of people on the basis of aptitude at assessment tasks. (For example, boys may well tend to outscore girls on multiple choice tests, but I am aware of no biological reason why.) It could be assumed, therefore, that any large group of pupils, however constituted, is broadly the equal of any other large group in terms of such aptitude. If such a

Table 4.3 The physics gap between boys and girls*

Subcategory	Age	England	Wales	Northern Ireland
Applying biology concepts	11			
	13			
	15			
Applying chemistry concepts	13			
	15			
Applying physics concepts	11			
	13			
	15			
		10 20 30 40	10 20 30 40	10 20 30 40

Source: Girls physics weakness (1980–4 APU national survey data); Johnson and Murphy (1986)
* Differences in mean scores shown as a percentage of common standard deviations, averaged over the period 1980–4. Bars to right indicate performance gap in favour of boys, those to left in favour of girls

group then scores lower than other groups in assessment tasks it could be said to be an 'underachieving' group. An example is given in Table 4.3.

The notion of 'underachievement' has been criticised because it locates the problem within the pupils. The example in Table 4.3 was said to be evidence of a *problem with girls*. However, according to Levidow (1987: 249):

> The APU's obsession with such statistical comparisons presupposed that the assessment methods had the same meaning for all children, regardless of cultural difference. It precluded any wider discussion of what causes 'underachievement', much less of how to measure what counts as achievement.

Remaining with the above example, a complete rejection of the idea that the problem is with girls could lead to the view that the problem is entirely with physics. An alternative perspective would be to view girls and physics as interacting in a social system, in which the 'problem' is then to do with the interaction. For a development of these views see Roychoudhury et al. (1995).

GIRLS' EXPERIENCES OF SCIENCE CLASSES

In Riley's work with girls in three London schools, black girls were found to be especially keen to have access to science and technology subjects, with woodwork particularly popular. When asked what subjects the pupils would add into the curriculum, these were the replies:

I'd bring things like physics . . . there was SCIZ, which is a combination of all three sciences, but not enough of us chose it, so they crossed it off. . . . And I would offer things like technical drawing, 'cos some girls are interested in that. I want to do computers.

(Kay, a black girl)

The world's changing. Engineering, woodwork and things like that. Just for fun, to see what it is like . . . . More to do with business, science and engineering, and woodwork – that sort of thing.

(Wendy, a black girl)

The girls' views were illuminating, on both their own and their black male peers' experiences in school:

Girls are more determined . . . 'cos my mum encourages me more than my brother.

(Marion, a black girl)

Boys of our age are kind of Casanovas. They've got their mind on other things. In my class, girls work harder.

(Yvonne, a black girl)

I think parents bring up the girls stricter . . . . Boys tend to muck about, try to be big . . . . They can behave.

(Marcia, a black girl)

This last rider, the boys *can* behave, connects with some sharp observations that some of the girls made about interactions between teachers and black boys. The girls reported a tendency for teachers to hold negative views about the black boys and to be unaware of appropriate ways of responding to their 'non-conforming' behaviour. For instance:

The teacher should sort of understand . . . what they are really like and then they would get on good . . . like if a coloured boy came in . . . and messes about, the teacher gets angry, which I agree [with] but if they sort of just ignore the boy . . . he'll go and sit down and be quiet and behave himself.

(Yvette, a black girl, in Riley, 1994: 70)

The black girls generally felt that their experiences in school tended to be better than those of black boys.

Riley's view of the girls in her study was that black girls tended to resist gender stereotyping more strongly than white girls. A particular positive influence on black girls' experiences in one school was the support for the aspirations, academic and extracurricular, that they received from the staff.

In a meta-analysis of a number of studies conducted between 1970 and 1991 Weinburg (1995) drew the following conclusions:

1 Positive attitude towards science tends to result in higher achievement. This applies generally to all children.
2 In order to achieve high scores, a positive attitude towards science is particularly necessary for girls. It is particularly the case with girls that low performance accompanies a negative attitude towards science.
3 Over the period in question, boys' attitude towards science has been consistently more positive than girls'. This has applied to all of the science subjects and has not appeared to vary with time.

The evidence above suggests that teachers would be well advised to explore strategies that lead to students, and particularly girls, having more positive views of science study. It is commonly said that boys attempt to dominate the social environment in science classes. They do this through monopolising teacher time and attention, dominating discussion and question–answer sessions and taking the lead in practical activities.

Guzzetti and Williams (1996) report some classroom strategies adopted by the science teacher (Williams) to reduce sex-based inequity in his lessons. Observation of laboratory work and small mixed-sex group work had revealed that in Williams' lessons:

1 The males tended to restrict opportunities for the females to speak.
2 Females' contributions to discussions were not on a par with males'.
3 Females had fewer conversational rights.

In 'refutational discussion' boys tended to assert propositions and counter-propositions (e.g. 'That's wrong because . . .') while girls spoke rarely and then tended to comment by questioning (e.g. 'Shouldn't that be . . .?). Guzzetti and Williams considered that the girls' actions were 'consistent with socially learned norms of gender-appropriate language behaviour' (p. 11).

The students, especially the girls, were well aware of gender inequity in the frequency and style of speaking in class. Questionnaire responses showed the girls experiencing self-doubt and lack of self-confidence, while the boys were willing to assert themselves. Students were asked to rate each other's physics knowledge. A girl who was toprated by 50 per cent of the boys and 28 per cent of the girls was incredulous to learn of this. She commented: 'I don't think of myself like that at all! Physics is my hardest class. I don't like to talk in class. I'm not sure of myself' (p. 14).

The teacher attempted to reduce sex-based inequity by setting up some single-sex group work and by taking care to call on equal numbers of boys and girls in class discussion. Despite these actions, discussion still favoured the boys. The researchers found that 'female students were restrained by their fear of the male students (not of the teacher) and of challenging the social norms that permeated classroom interactions'. Guzzetti and Williams drew an interesting conclusion from this study: that students should be encouraged to become explicitly involved in reflecting on what goes on in their classes. Teacher intervention, they argue, is insufficient on its own.

In a study of Swedish children aged 13 to 15 in chemistry, physics and technology classes, Staberg (1994) found that girls adopt and are given the role of 'keeping the lesson together'. Like Guzzetti and Williams, Staberg found girls doubtful of their understanding in science. Anna, for instance, was regarded as a 'bright' girl but she admitted that during her physics lessons she feels as is if: 'I don't know any physics, I don't understand anything. But when I come home I understand somehow . . . but I always think that I don't understand anything.'

In Staberg's view, girls and boys learn in different ways: 'Girls prefer knowledge connected with their own and others' lives, while boys are interested in apparatus, things and making things'. According to one pupil, Klara, 'You do experiments but you have no idea of what use they have in real life'. Boys tended to play in science, both with apparatus and with each other. They interacted competitively whereas girls preferred collaboration, using books, reading and writing. Girls were also critical of the fast tempo and the rapid flow of information in science lessons. This is understandable if it is the case that girls tend to look for connections within new knowledge and between old and new knowledge. Boys, it seems, are more comfortable with a linear flow of knowledge.

On the issue of social roles in class, Staberg commented on how diligent boys tend to be mocked by their peers, with the implication that being studious is a feminine trait. Girls, on the other hand, were criticised both for being successful in science and for failing! Staberg states that in science 'boys have always been the norm for "pupils"'.

AN INTRODUCTION TO FEMINIST PERSPECTIVES ON SCIENCE AND SCIENCE EDUCATION

For a few years I have included a card-sorting activity designed to elicit graduate pre-qualified teachers' views about the nature of science. One of the cards mentions feminist science. There always seem to be reactions to this card: 'What *is* feminist science?' 'Is there such a thing?' 'This one's a load of rubbish, isn't it?' I would classify the majority of expressed views as lying somewhere between bemusement and rejection. I think this is more than just a student reaction; many practising science teachers would, I suspect, also express bemusement towards, or rejection of, the idea of 'feminist science'. But, as Roychoudhury *et al.* (1995) point out, a feminist pedagogy is not male antagonistic: the aim is not

> to shift the loyalty from a male perspective to a female one, but to achieve a more holistic approach towards understanding the world . . . to add

another viewpoint instead of using the dominant one . . . to enthuse girls
. . . not to thwart boys' interest in science.

(p. 900)

{Haggerty (1995) argues that in spite of much recent work on gender and science, little has changed, either in the nature of girls' and women's experiences in science education or in the conceptualisation of what science might be. Her view is that science must become responsive to the needs and views of girls and women.} Teachers are often unaware of the difference between encouragement and gender harassment and this lack of awareness is not addressed in most professional development programmes, where the issue 'will be avoided by those most in need of change'. Haggerty is in no doubt that science is a gendered activity. She quotes Sjoberg and Imsen to illustrate the learner's perspective:

> Gender is a fundamental attribute in most cultures. To be a genderless person or to have a genderless identity, is inconceivable . . . . The under-representation of girls in natural science has to be interpreted in terms of culture. Science in most cultures is socially defined as a masculine domain. Boys engage in science and technology to reinforce their mascu-linarity – while this is not a way for girls to become feminine. For a girl, a choice of science may lead to sanctions from her feminine peer group – and from boys!
>
> (Sjoberg and Imsen, 1988, in Haggerty, 1995: 2)

Haggerty also draws attention to the perspective of the woman teacher, a figure sometimes overlooked in the research literature compared with the female learner. Time is seen by many teachers as so limited that any aspirations for serious professional development or reflection are abandoned, or even hostilely rejected. Drawing on Apple and Jungck (1992), Haggerty observes that the time trap is deeper for women, given that 'the gender cultures of our patriarchal society dictate that women are the primary home-makers and child care-givers' (p. 5).

What of women who have been academically or professionally successful in science? Haggerty's view is that they may regard themselves as exceptional and believe that their success reflects their dedication, effort or aptitude, rather than seeing the lack of other successful women as a systemic problem. Such people, she suggests, 'are likely to feel like outsiders, rather than feeling empowered or part of the science culture' (p. 7).

How, then, would feminist science differ from contemporary science? Draw-ing on the writings of Sandra Harding, Evelyn Fox Keller and Barbara McClin-tock, Haggerty suggests that feminist science would have the following characteristics:

- a more *holistic* and *personal* approach, making science more generally accessible and valid;
- an approach that seeks to *know* and *understand* phenomena, rather than to dominate and control nature.

Drawing from Sandra Harding, Roychoudhury *et al.* show how 'feminist standpoint theory' (FST), allied to a constructivist approach (in which the learner's role as an active constructor of knowledge is acknowledged by the teacher), can contribute to the construction of a more equitable context for learning in science. (Though the authors describe a feminist–constructivist approach to science education for adults, much that they describe is informative and relevant to the education of children.) FST contains the premise that the different social experiences of males and females result in them having different views on life events, different ways of interpreting and making meaning, and thus different 'standpoints'. If science is dominated by a male, western culture then it is to be expected that it will be perceived differently from male and female standpoints. Roychoudhury *et al.* state that 'many women are *strangers* to science because the logic of science dominated and developed by men can never be totally compatible with women's standpoints'. If women are to engage with science, they have to alienate themselves from their non-science life experiences and attempt to adopt a male standpoint, something that may be impossible for many women. Roychoudhury *et al.* argue that the development of feminist science is not an attempt to run two threads – feminist and masculinist – in parallel but to broaden the culture of science by including female views and ways of knowing and learning.

Suggestions for feminist-informed science teaching include:

- providing opportunities for students to connect what is being encountered in the science class with other life experiences;
- valuing individual and collaborative working;
- building in longer project work to allow students to become personally involved in this aspect of their science learning;
- accommodating the interests of students in deciding the focus of project work and how and where to do the work;
- providing choice of various modes of assignment work.

Roychoudhury *et al.* report the evaluation of a science course constructed along the above lines. The students were men and women who were not science specialists; they were taking a science course as part of a qualification in junior school teaching. Particular points were these:

- 'The most exciting feature of science for the female students . . . was the connection with life' (p. 916).

73

- 'Freedom of choice was appreciated by the majority of students' (female and male).
- The students benefited significantly from a caring and supportive learning environment.

The authors consider that the course embraced the students' interests and thereby incorporated both male and female viewpoints, enriching it for all participants. They argue that current science and science education are incomplete and inherently weakened through non-inclusion of a feminist perspective. They believe that it is essential for students to do science work in situations of interest to them and that for women, this is: 'an absolute necessity to legitimise their views and their work'.

PRACTICAL ACTION: SCHOOL AND CLASSROOM INITIATIVES

It is over a decade since the GIST (Girls into Science and Technology) project (Whyte, 1986) alerted the science education community to the gendered nature of school science. In the light of evidence of continuing bias in science education, limiting the performance of girls and other groups of students, it is important to examine some of the practical approaches that have been taken with the aim of making science education more equitable. Some of these are research based and some are teaching based. Many of these initiatives are experimental. Conclusions can only be drawn tentatively. I will not argue, for instance, that it has been shown that sex-segregated teaching produces *this* result or *that* outcome. The situation is generally too complex for one-to-one causal relations to emerge. In this respect there is something in common between equitable teaching and 'good teaching'; in each case it is hard – perhaps impossible – to specify what the constituents are, yet this does not prevent it happening!

Science textbooks

Walford's analysis of science textbooks is quite well known. He found that of the illustrations in physics textbooks in use in schools, 80 per cent showed males only. When females did feature, typically they were either partly clothed or nursing or cleaning (Walford, 1980). In twenty-three 'O' level chemistry books Walford (1981) found 258 illustrations of only males and 26 of only females. Again, men were typically in science-active roles and women were typically not. The conclusion is inescapable: either such images make no impact, in which case they could have been gender balanced in the first place; or they do make an impact, in which case they should have been gender balanced!

Single-sex classes?

Girls opt out of science, and physical science especially, as soon as they can. There is evidence, however, that girls in all-girl schools are less likely to follow this trend than are girls in mixed schools. So why not experiment in mixed schools by setting single-sex classes?

> A drastic decline in girls' performance in state schools at the highest level has occurred since co-education was introduced. In the early 1970s girls gained the best A level results in England and Wales; now they trail behind state-school boys and independent pupils of both sexes.
>
> (McCrum, 1995)

This initiative has been taken in several English schools (Nash, 1995). In one, a girls-only GCSE physics class was set up. The following results were reported by Gillibrand and Braun (1994):

- 'by far the most important factor to emerge was the girls' increased confidence in their ability to learn and use physics';
- the girls rated highly the greater pupil co-operation in the girls-only class; this occurred in the sharing of ideas, equipment and information;
- on the teaching of other subjects, most of the girls preferred mixed-sex groups, with the possible exception of mathematics.

Dore (1995) reports further experiments in two schools in Essex, England, with all subjects being sex segregated in one case. From the perspective of being a head-teacher in a mixed comprehensive school, Marland (1983) regards the establishment of some single-sex classes as both feasible and potentially attractive: 'I can certainly see occasions when there would be argument for introducing some single-sex work into a mixed school. It may be very helpful for getting over a particular hurdle at a particular time.' Gender stereotyping and peer pressure constraining subject choices is one such 'hurdle'. But Marland lists several drawbacks of setting up single-sex classes: they may reinforce some stereotypes; they are based on the questionable assumption that the boys all have similar needs and the girls all have similar needs; and they may act to conceal deeper issues that are contributing to gender-based differences in schools.

Teacher attention

It is often reported that teachers' attention in class is drawn more to boys than to girls. One teacher, quoted in Harris and Rudduck (1991) said that, 'Girls are overwhelmingly used in mixed-sex schools as a means of socialising boys and making it more comfortable for teachers'. Her experience as a science teacher convinced her that when boys entered the school at age 11 they were more enthusiastic and more confident about the subject than were 11 year old girls. She believed that rather than narrowing this gender gap, secondary school experience resulted in girls becoming progressively *less* confident in science, relative to boys. She reports a micro-scale experiment that she tried in one of her classes.

> I have taken a deep breath and done something really quite dramatic with a particular group. I laid the law down for one lesson in science, a practical science lesson, and I said that no boy was to approach me for any assistance whatsoever. I said I would choose who I would work with. Nobody must track a path to me. I made this clear to the boys and I explained why. And I made a profound discovery: when you have the nerve actually to do it and you believe in it enough, it works. The boys, including the really dominant boys in the group, sorted themselves out, got on and were not disruptive . . . . I challenged the boys to accept that this lesson they would be in charge of their own learning and it wasn't that I went around sorting out the girls because they were less good. What I did was to take time to admire the girls' work, to move among them in a positive way and to enjoy being with them because I thought, in the context of the way science lessons go, that was important.
>
> (Harris and Rudduck, 1991)

Teaching to motivate girls in physics

In an illustration of research-informed curriculum development, Ramsden (1990) reports the setting up, carrying out and evaluation of a project that was aimed at increasing the interest of 13 and 14 year old girls in physics. A pupil questionnaire elicited views about physics topics. Light was consistently popular and electricity was consistently unpopular (cf. the APU findings reported earlier, concerning girls' negative responses to questions involving electricity). Ramsden constructed two teaching schemes, on energy and on electricity. Evaluation of the pupils' reactions to the new schemes was conducted by questionnaire and by pupils' subsequent subject choices. The schemes, taught by the author and by her colleagues, appear successfully to have met the aim of raising the girls' interest.

SOME CONCLUSIONS

Whyte (1986), drawing out implications for teaching from the GIST project, commented on the unwillingness of the profession to accept the issue of equity:

> there seem to be five elements, which in combination constitute a virtually impenetrable barrier to girls in science and technology . . .

1. a belief in biological determinism
2. a belief in 'cultural' determinism
3. denial that a problem exists
4. traditional views about sex roles
5. apprehension that boys will suffer from positive discrimination for girls

Plus ça change! Despite the recent furore about underperforming boys, girls in the UK and in most other countries continue to do less well in science on average than boys. Research in the last decade has reinforced and extended the arguments of Whyte, Kelly and others in the GIST project that school science is a gendered practice and a gendered domain of knowledge. As has been pointed out in this chapter, many aspects of school science may contribute to the maintenance of the gender gradient: teacher expectations; the meta-messages in science books, videos, IT and other resources; a curriculum which is clinical and detached rather than referred to human experiences; the contexts and applications in which science concepts are situated; the norms of behaviour in science classrooms; the forms and styles of assessment; and the epistemology of school science, in which knowledge is frequently seen as a way of controlling nature.

It is not the case, of course, that school science is the 'cause' of gender bias in science. The role of the school is strongly bound up with broad social construc-tions of science, masculinity and femininity, in which, for example, scientific and technological toys are marketed and bought as boys' toys and children arrive at school with well-established notions of gender. Teachers do, however, occupy positions of considerable influence and autonomy within their own classrooms. There are ways forward, through measures such as the following:

- establishment of the view that girls can do science just as successfully as boys, reinforced through acknowledgement of the value of girls' contributions in science lessons;
- resistance to the expectation that 'boys are the norm for pupils' in science;
- critical evaluation of teaching resources and materials;
- broadening of the contexts in which science is applied, to include human and 'everyday' situations;
- adoption of a broader range of pedagogic styles, accommodating more than an expert-led, closed and analytic epistemology;
- employment of a wider variety of assessment media and formats, including untimed, open-book and collaborative assignments.

It seems plausible – even reasonable – that school science, as an evolving practice, must inevitably pass through a stage where gender bias is an issue, if only on account of the interlinked histories of state education and science. Continuing tolerance of bias is, however, increasingly hard to justify. It is for contemporary teachers and educators to ensure that in the next millennium, writers referring to GIST are not moved to exclaim: *plus ça change, plus c'est la même chose!*

REFERENCES

Apple, M.W. and Jungck, S. (1992) 'You don't have to be a teacher to teach this unit: teaching, technology and control in the classroom', in A. Hargreaves and M.G. Fullan (eds) *Understanding Teacher Development* (pp. 20–4), New York: Teachers' College Press.

Dore, A. (1995) 'Heard the one about the Essex girls?', *The Times Educational Supplement* 31 March: 3.

Evans, A. (1996) 'Perils of ignoring our lost boys', *The Times Educational Supplement* 28 June: 20.

Gillborn, D. (1990) *'Race', Ethnicity and Education*, London: Unwin Hyman.

Gillibrand, E. and Braun, R. (1994) 'Physical challenge', *The Times Educational Supplement* 11 March.

Gipps, C. and Murphy, P. (1994) *A Fair Test? Assessment, Achievement and Equity*, Buckingham: Open University Press.

Guzzetti, B.J. and Williams, W.O. (1996) 'Gender, text and discussion: examining intellectual safety in the science classroom', *Journal of Research in Science Teaching* 33(1): 5–20.

Haggerty, S.M. (1995) 'Gender and teacher development: issues of power and culture', *International Journal of Science Education* 17(1): 1–15.

Harris, S. and Rudduck, J. (1991) *Keeping Gender on the Agenda*, QQSE Portfolio, Division of Education, University of Sheffield.

Hofkins, D. (1996) 'Class is factor for girls', *The Times Education Supplement* 12 January: 10.

Johnson, S. and Murphy, P. (1986) *Girls and Physics*, APU Occasional Paper No 4, London: DES.

Levidow, L. (1987) '"Ability", labelling as racism', in D. Gill and L. Levidow (eds) *Antiracist Science Teaching*, London: Free Association Books.

Marland, M. (1983) 'Should the sexes be separated?' in M. Marland (ed.) *Sex Differentiation and Schooling*, London: Heinemann.

McCrum, G. (1995) 'Return to the days of single-sex classes', *The Guardian* 14 March.

Nash, I. (1995) 'Single-sex science to break up stereotype', *The Times Education Supplement* 31 March: 2.

Pyke, N. (1996) 'Male brain rattled by curriculum "oestrogen"', *The Times Education Supplement* 15 March: 8.

Ramsden, J.M. (1990) 'All quiet on the gender front?', *School Science Review* 72(259): 49–55.

Riley, K.A. (1994) *Quality and Equality*, London: Cassell.

Roychoudhury, A., Tippins, D.J. and Nichols, S.E. (1995) 'Gender-inclusive science teaching: a feminist-constructivist approach', *Journal of Research in Science Teaching* 32(9): 897–924.

Staberg, E. (1994) 'Gender and science in the Swedish compulsory school', *Gender and Education* 6(1): 35–45.

The Times Educational Supplement (1996) Editorial, 22 November: 18.

Volman, M., van Eck, E. and Dam, G. Ten (1995) 'Girls in science and technology: the development of a discourse', *Gender and Education* 7(3): 283–92.

Walford, G. (1980) 'Sex bias in physics textbooks', *School Science Review* 62: 219.

—— (1981) 'Do chemistry textbooks present a sex-biased image?', *Education in Chemistry* 18: 1.

Weinburg, M. (1995) 'Gender differences in student attitudes toward science: a meta-analysis of the literature from 1970 to 1991', *Journal of Research in Science Teaching* 32(4): 387–98.

Whyte, J. (1986) *Girls into Science and Technology: the Story of a Project*, London: Routledge and Kegan Paul.

Woodhead, C. (1996) 'Boys who learn to be losers', *The Times* 6 March: 18.

5

WHOSE TURN NEXT?

Gender issues in information technology

Clive Opie

Uses of IT are found everywhere in the world beyond the classroom and will play a major role in the extension of opportunities for employment. They are already so integral to the everyday practices of both teachers and pupils that it is imperative that the school curriculum focuses on offering equal access to boys and girls. The explosion of innovation since IT's inclusion as a core subject of the National Curriculum ten years ago, coupled to the marked acceleration of learning potential through new educational networks, make it essential that all schools begin to rationalise their learning environment. New communication networks facilitate a cost-effective and rapid connection to many sources of information including remote libraries, museums and developed databases.

However, as in other areas of the curriculum, the historical roots of the subject and its beginnings in the technology department have already left a mark on the implementation of IT policies in school. This fact, coupled with prevailing cultural and social factors which make home computing available only to those with a comfortable income, and even then less accessible to girls, has created a picture that is very far short of a democratic ideal.

In British secondary schools, the first school-based computing courses in the form of computer studies, computer science and information technology (IT) were for the most part set up by male teachers, as offshoots of maths, physics or technology courses, and were attractive mainly to young, technologically minded, male pupils, often disparagingly referred to by their peers as 'nerds'. Such courses were frequently restricted to examination groups in the upper half of school and option choices ensured girls were invariable in a minority. However, with the 1988 Educational Reform Act (ERA) and the inclusion of IT in all statutory subjects' orders within the National Curriculum (NC) as well as the requirement for all pupils to study IT as a subject in its own right, a mechanism was provided whereby equality of access, usage and experience could be addressed. This chapter provides a review of the literature which examines the relationship of gender issues to IT, both prior to 1988 and following the ERA reforms, looking also wider afield for relevant studies. It considers whether educationalists' efforts to counterbalance gender inequalities in IT within schools and to secure equality of access have been successful. There are four areas of concern. The first examines pupils' attitudes towards aspects of technology in school. Here the weight of both recent evidence and past research suggests that boys have been encouraged to build more positive attitudes to computers than girls. As Turkle suggests, most women came to computing later than men. She writes:

> Women look at computers and see more than machines. They see a culture that has grown up around them and they ask themselves if they belong . . . . It is a world predominantly male, that takes the machine as a partner in an intimate relationship.

(1988: 42)

The second section, which considers teachers' attitudes to IT, reveals a more contradictory picture. For although teachers seem to be becoming increasingly more positive towards the use of computers across the curriculum, thereby helping to redress the gender imbalance, most 'IT teachers' are still predominantly male, and only a third of other subject teachers as yet actively involve themselves in working with IT. This raises the question of teaching styles and subject content, and the identification of IT with masculinity.

The third section looks at the issue of access to IT in schools and in the home, where its presence has rapidly increased in the last few years. The picture which emerges, however, creates much cause for concern, for generally home provision favours boys, as parents often choose to buy computers for their sons rather than for their daughters. Therefore in addition to there being quite limited access in schools, which impacts on the learning opportunities provided for both sexes, home access limits the experience of girls. Further, the existing provision of specialist courses tends to be dominated by males, perpetuating the gender imbalance.

The final section considers how far government policy has succeeded in redressing the past gender inequalities in IT, suggesting that practice in schools often works against the interests of those who are less confident users of machines despite the fact that NC orders aim to promote equal opportunity. It is suggested that unless teachers adopt a change in styles from promoting individual, competitive use, to a more holistic, co-operative small group approach such orders will have little effect.

The chapter concludes with a series of recommendations for schools aimed at helping teachers to address gender bias in the current IT curriculum. It recognises, however, that teachers are working under enormous pressure, with relatively limited resources, and so this section also argues that schools cannot redress the issue of gender and IT without significant external support in terms of providing hardware and opportunities for staff development in order to increase teachers' confidence in the use of IT in the classroom.

81

PUPIL ATTITUDES TO IT

It has been argued that pupils' own attitudes to IT, particularly the disinterest of many girls, provide the key factors in blocking schools' attempts to provide equal access to the new forms of learning. In an ideal teaching environment IT would be integrated seamlessly into everyday classroom practice. As argued in previous chapters, pupils bring with them views on which activities are appropriate to which groups of pupils and gendered views are more intractable among young men. Commentators such as Seymour Papert have suggested that computer teachers, in particular, have reinforced 'scientific' attitudes through what he describes as a 'supervaluation of the abstract' and an emphasis on 'abstract-formal knowledge' (Papert, 1993: 148).

He argues that work with computers does not have to be abstract but can be firmly based in concrete experience. A more positive curriculum where IT is presented in a way that is more concrete and therefore 'ordinary', personally interesting and appropriate to both sexes and their everyday work patterns would ensure a more balanced application of technology and, more importantly, a social reconstruction of its general value to both sexes. The indicators are that IT becomes less threatening when it is properly integrated into the everyday practice of each subject. Sadly, current research indicates that this is far from the present state in secondary schools, where an increase in the common requirements for IT, coupled to pressure from examination classes, has often made access to computers even more technologically biased and male dominated through a skills-based approach located within existing computer studies departments. English teachers currently report having a struggle to gain a fraction of the time they would like to spend with their classes on working with word processing and the editing of texts, while few schools offer direct access to information and retrieval systems in a way that is easily accessible to their pupils. This issue will be discussed further in the final section of the chapter alongside the question of 'delivering capability in IT'.

Although the computer has been hailed by educationalists as 'the children's machine' (Papert, 1993) there is a weight of evidence which shows such marked differences in boys' and girls' orientation to the new technology that would lead us to conclude that computers are more often seen by parents and children as 'toys for the boys'. In *Girls and Computers*, for example, Hoyles (1988) cites the work of Wilder *et al.* (1985) who in a survey of attitudes of 1,600 4 to 16 year old pupils found that boys and girls alike perceived computers to be more appropriate for boys than for girls. In addition, although both sexes were reported as being positive to computer use, at all ages more boys than girls actually liked computers. Other studies (Drambrot *et al.*, 1985; Harvey and Wilson, 1985; Collis and Williams, 1987; Levin and Gordon, 1989; Martin, 1991) relate similar findings as does the more recent work of Kirkman (1993) which showed that compared with females, males were more enthusiastic towards computers, more confident with them and rated themselves better at using them. The most recent publication which echoes the same view is a cross-cultural study involving Japanese and Swedish 16 year olds by Makrakis and Sawada (1996), which showed that regardless of the country, males reported higher scores of usefulness, aptitude and liking for computers. They suggest that in these countries the persistence of gender differences in attitudes to computers, despite a general rise in computer awareness, indicated a failure in the way gender issues were being addressed and tackled in schools. One difficulty may be explained by the very different levels of access to computer technology available in pupils' home environments. A current, but as yet unreported, survey of the home access of Y7 and Y9 pupils conducted at Sheffield University revealed marked patterns of difference in computer ownership between boys and girls which will be discussed in more detail below.

The evidence would then seem to suggest that, despite positive intervention to reduce the gender imbalance, there is still need for more positive action and that although this state of affairs should give us real cause for concern, we should not be at all surprised by it. Firstly, pupils' responses in school reflect the well-documented differences in their early socialisation, including factors such as parental attitude, gender role identity and the prevalent images of computer users given by the media. An example of the extent of parents' different responses to boys' and girls' early achievements was recorded in Solomou's recent study of (1996) nursery children's use of IT. As part of her home/school observations she recorded the number and nature of parents' questions to teachers about their children's work in school. She found that the fathers who visited the nursery were more likely to ask about their child's computers and both parents raised questions about computers in relation to sons much more frequently than in relation to their daughters' achievements.

Earlier research studies confirm these differences. Levin and Gordon (1989) and Loyd et al. (1987) found that males are more likely to own a computer and that the increased access in the home is directly related to a positive attitude towards computers. Harvey and Wilson (1985) also found that difference in positive attitudes towards computers was closely linked to 'owners' and 'non-owners' rather than gender differences. We can surmise that as the move to home-based personal computers continues to increase, the number of girls who come to school familiar with machines will increase accordingly and girls will develop a more positive attitude as a matter of course. Similarly, although Durndell (1991) reported that boys created many of the problems for girls in the IT classroom by endorsing sex-stereotyped views; interestingly they also showed that older girls were significantly less likely to endorse sex-stereotyped views than their male peers. The indications are, then, that as the use of computers and IT becomes more accepted, sex-stereotyped views will diminish.

There is a temptation, therefore, to think it is less essential to address existing gender imbalance in IT because as technology becomes more widely used, pupils will achieve this transition in a more natural and sustainable way. Unfortunately, the speed of advances in technology means this is not an option we can take for our current pupils. Currently, the National Council for Education Technology (NCET) is conducting a major development project to examine the present low levels of girls presently entering IT careers and identifying the criteria which exist where girls do succeed. The project *Attracting Girls to IT* cites the following factors as contributing to low expectations:

> girls are likely to take on more passive roles when working alongside boys. Lack of access to role models, lack of awareness on the part of careers advisers and teachers, inflexible employers, poor recruitment practices, lack of parental and social encouragement . . . aggressive computer games and many more factors have been blamed.
>
> (NCET, 1996)

As will be argued in the following sections there are other central issues which need to be addressed if a gender imbalance is not to be perpetuated in delivering IT capability in schools.

TEACHERS' ATTITUDES TO IT

Research evidence suggests that there has been a significant narrowing of the gender difference in teachers' attitudes to IT and in their willingness to use technology for their own purposes. Although this is encouraging, unfortunately this gender neutrality is not reflected in most school practice. Male teachers still dominate computer science courses, which ensures that men are usually in control of both the teaching of skills and in organising classroom access to the hardware and networks. This, of course, sends a particularly gendered message to pupils. Similarly, access to new forms of communication such as e-mail and the Internet are more often directed through computer science departments than other departments within the school. More significant, however, are the images of appropriate gender behaviours and attitudes which teachers carry around with them and which directly reinforce a view of IT as a male-dominated sphere of activity.

Research by Spear (1985) found that 49 per cent of teachers (sampled across all subjects) viewed technical subjects as of key importance to a boy's general education while only 24 per cent rated them as very important to that of girls. Work published a few years later by Durndell *et al.* (1990) showed that the major reason for lack of girls' interest in computing courses in higher education was a result of predominance of males in these subjects which created the male-orientated atmosphere described earlier by Turkle. Even more recently, Groundwater-Smith and Crawford (1992) found, in their survey of New South Wales secondary schools, that 80 per cent of those responsible for the management of school computing resources were male and that across the curriculum the proportion of confident staff users of computers ran at 2:1 in favour of male teachers. Indeed this picture is much more widespread inasmuch as an international study by Reinen and Plomp (1993) showed that in many countries computer use in schools is dominated by men. Perhaps more worrying from this work was that less than half the schools, from the twenty-one countries from which data was collected, had a special policy for the promotion of equal opportunities for boys' and girls' use of IT. The impression which most pupils gain is that work with computers is particularly male. This does not create a particularly constructive picture if the aim is to convey to pupils that it should be a gender-neutral activity.

However, an interesting study by Elkjær (1992) provides an alternative view of the issue surrounding teachers' attitudes, arguing that whereas some writers maintain that girls have a 'problem' with IT, in fact it is boys – or some of them – who create the major difficulty for girls in defining what is appropriate in their relationship to the subject. It is because, she argues, 'their (boys and men) relationship is defined (more or less implicitly) as an ideal which girls and women ought to emulate'. Elkjær has identified two spheres of learning, both of which are differentiated by gender. The first is the 'private sphere' around computers where the learner needs to master the social relations required for close teamwork. This is more closely associated with girls' and women's ways of working. The second is the 'public sphere' which revolves around discussion about applications and capability and which is more often controlled by boys and men. The difference, she says, 'has become a matter of habit to the extent that we hardly think about it'. In relation to the subject content itself she presents 'two spheres of content', one related to a comprehension of computer applications – the science of computers, stereotypically connected with men and masculinity – and the other to discussion of the humanistic and social scientific nature of the applications and consequences of computers – the IT of computers – connected with women and femininity.

She goes on to show that although there is little difference in girls' and boys' motivation for choosing IT as a subject and that the girls know that the boys are not necessarily better than they are, they do know that the classroom is the boys' domain. She then contrasts the spheres of learning to show that in the private sphere, girls develop computer expertise without any anxiety and this provides them with a certain 'latitude' to their specific formation of identity. Boys, on the other hand, can be highly problematic in this sphere of learning in that those not competent in computer skills are busy denying their incompetence, causing classroom difficulties and ultimately restricting both their own and others' development. In the public sphere of learning the situation is more problematic for girls. It is not that girls do not have the ability or knowledge to participate but that they are prevented from expanding in this arena by the dominating behaviour of some boys who believe, again stereotypically, that this sphere of learning is connected with aspects of masculinity. In her words, ' the presence of, and oppression by, boys and men, prevent girls and women from developing fully'. In short, Elkjær argues, it is the boys who create the problem in the IT classroom and not the girls, so teachers' beliefs, that girls and women were less effective computer users, which is expressed through their teaching styles, should be seen as a social invention.

Further interesting case study material (albeit from a very small sample of pupils in an Australian primary school), which supports this view, is provided by Singh (1993). He argues that boys gain a position of power because they are able to employ a socially constructed view of technocratic masculinity to their advantage in the classroom. The position is heightened by the response of the classroom teacher who confirms the boys' claim to computer expertise by engaging them in setting up work in the classroom. Singh further claims that through this dual action a fiction about computer knowledge and competency is socially constructed within the classroom. Boys are interpreted as 'risk taking', 'experimental' and 'technologically competent' while girls are positioned as 'inactive', 'passive' and 'rule followers'. Girls then have to mediate between conflicting social relations:

> They must struggle to negotiate a positioning for themselves as 'nice and good', 'carriers of messages', the 'domestic', the 'subservient' while at the same time, these daughters of professional career mothers, must struggle to be, 'not nice', to be 'powerful', 'active' and to gain credit for their computing skills.

We see then from this and earlier work by Adams (1985) that teachers believe gender bias is a condition which is external to schooling. However, good teaching styles and positive role models can counter gender inequality and have a dramatic effect on girls' perception of their ability in IT. Where there is more student self-directed work, girls tend to be mutually supportive, which encourages increased confidence and as a consequence greater achievement. There are therefore sound arguments for single-sex classes when computer skills are being introduced to a year group or at least single-sex groupings. This prevents the 'hands over shoulders' syndrome found where boys take over a keyboard to 'help' girls with a computer-based task.

There is also a general acceptance (Madsen and Sebastini, 1987) that the greater the computer proficiency of teachers, the more likely they are to use them and to

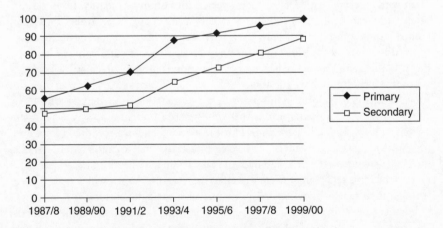

Figure 5.1 Teachers reported as 'confident' in use of IT

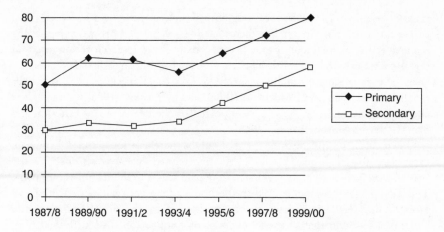

Figure 5.2 Teachers reported as regularly using IT

exhibit less anxiety towards them. There is further evidence that teachers' positive attitudes also rub off on students, leading to improved performance (Moore, 1988) and this position seems to be supported by more recent studies (Downes, 1993) of teachers who provide a positive role model. However, although teachers' confidence in the use of IT has increased as indicated by DfEE statistics presented in Figure 5.1, the number of those who actual use it in their teaching is much lower (Figure 5.2).

As was noted earlier, non-specialist teachers are more anxious than their pupils when it comes to using IT. Robertson *et al.* (1995) suggest three possible reasons for this: a greater conservatism amongst teachers than pupils; teachers' anxiety at having to introduce yet more innovation; and differences in perception in that pupils see them just as machines to be used whereas teachers may be perceiving them as 'potential pedagogical tools that they are as yet adequately prepared to use'.

The most important lesson to take from this section is that it is important for teachers not to be overinfluenced by stereotypical attitudes. A more sensible way forward would be to redress any gender bias experienced in their teaching by providing positive role models of learning and by monitoring the abilities of all pupils to ensure that boys do not dominate the groups set up in the classroom.

ACCESS TO IT IN SCHOOLS AND THE HOME

There is a continuing underprovision of resources for the development of IT in all but the most privileged schools, which prevents full access for all pupils, and this despite the NC's recognition of IT's increasing significance. Kirkman (1993) found that 22 per cent of students had never used a computer during the final year of their middle school education and, overall, 85 per cent of those who had been given access had used a computer less than ten times. What is more worrying, in the context of the major focus of this book, is that all the research reviewed so far seems to indicate that it is girls who are always given the least 'hands-on' experience. This is evident from the research related to IT use for 10–12 year olds highlighted by Siann and MacLeod (1986) and by Deakin (1985) for secondary and higher education levels, and is supported by the later work of Harrison and Hay (1991) and Durndell *et al.* (1990).

One must therefore conclude that not only is there a serious lack of 'hands-on' experience for all pupils in school, but this limited access is seriously gender biased, with boys constantly seeking to dominate access to the school's computers. This pessimistic view is mirrored in the home where yet again access privileges boys. Culley (1986) in a research project funded by the Equal Opportunities Commission found that of the 39 per cent of a cohort of 974 fourth- and fifth-year pupils (491 boys and 483 girls) who reported having access to a computer in their home, 27 per cent of them were boys and only 12 per cent girls. The fact that this was the case even amongst pupils taking computer studies courses highlighted that at this time girls were inevitably at a disadvantage in terms of computer access.

It appears the picture has not significantly changed in the intervening years. Kirkman (1993) showed that from a study of 199 Y8 students (102 girls, 97 boys), although 55 per cent of students used a computer at home there was a gender imbalance with significantly more boys (70 per cent) than girls (38 per cent) using them. His findings are also supported by a study undertaken by Levin and Gordon (1989). More recent studies have further confirmed boys' greater access.

Millard, investigating leisure time competition with reading in nine groups of Y7 pupils (134 boys, 121 girls), found that far more boys reported playing on computers as a favoured home activity. Over half of the boys surveyed played on a computer for longer than one hour each day and only 15 per cent reported having no computer access. In contrast, over half the girls either did not use a computer at all or described themselves as very infrequent users (Millard, 1997: 69–70).

In a more recent, and as yet unpublished, study of Y7 and Y9 pupils' use of computers in the home to support their school learning, Millard and Opie have found similar differences in the patterns of usage and access for boys and girls (Figure 5.3).

Boys were far more likely to have a computer in their own room than were girls and to describe themselves as using it a lot and of using it to help when doing homework. There were, however, also significant class differences with children from schools in more affluent areas reporting more computer use than those from poorer socio-economic areas. Where girls had been given home access to personal computers and supported in their use of it, they were equally enthusiastic about its use to support their school work. Two boys and two girls in one school were identified as often choosing to produce work on the computer for their English teacher without being asked to do so. Interviews revealed that these pupils had supportive professional parents who themselves used PCs at home for work.

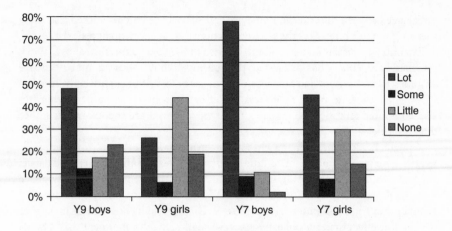

Figure 5.3 Home computer access (unpublished results)

Significantly, however, the majority of the younger girls rarely described themselves as very good with computers, and though the Y9 girls had become a little more confident in judging their abilities, only 10 per cent of them claimed to be very good at computing, compared with over a third of the boys (34 per cent) who rated their own abilities highly. Although the numbers involved in this survey are too small to provide conclusive evidence, we suggest that each of the schools involved did make a difference to pupils' attitude, but that access at home played a more significant role in orienting pupils to learning in this field. This small study confirms the findings of earlier work and suggests that it is essential to ensure more access to computers in areas where home ownership is limited or where the patterns of inequality found in access to early literacy will be replicated in relation to the new information and communication technologies.

Further, Kirkman's (1993) survey provides evidence to corroborate the notion that an average students' IT experience comes significantly from home use. More importantly, when home and non-home computer users were compared, the former were shown to be both more enthusiastic and confident in using computers. Home computer users also perceived computers as more useful. However, what gives rise to greatest concern is that Kirkman also found that these same home users were also successful in commandeering significantly more time on computers in school.

Girls therefore are at a double disadvantage. Not only are they given less access to computers in the home with all the associated disadvantages noted by Kirkman, but boy home users' increased confidence results in them gaining more time on computers in schools which has already been shown to be quite limited. It follows that non-home-user girls lose out in every conceivable way, and along with the less computer-literate boys do not receive their fair share of 'hands-on' experience (Martin, 1991). Groundwater-Smith and Crawford (1992) recorded a similar imbalance between the sexes in home use and school use, but also noted that there was a lack of awareness on the part of teachers that such inequalities exist.

By contrast, there is some counter-evidence to the views expressed above. Work by Shashaani (1993) has suggested that although boys showed more positive attitudes to computers and this was related, perhaps not unsurprisingly, to computer experience, no relationship was found between home computer ownership and computer attitudes. Shashaani's findings, however, are the exception rather than the rule.

It might be concluded from what has been recorded hitherto that computer-related courses in schools have little effect in redressing the gender imbalance. Martin's work (1991), however, suggests otherwise in that he found strong evidence that pupils' affective reactions to working with computers were determined by whether they took computer-related courses. Gender and having a home computer had a lesser effect than school experience, strengthening the argument that schools need to be active in encouraging all pupils to learn computer skills.

In conclusion, the picture that emerges of access to new forms of literacy is disturbing in its disregard for most girls' continuing lack of 'hands-on experience'. There are also important social issues related to access in schools serving communities in the lower socio-economic bands. Added to this financial limitations make opportunities for increasing IT resources in schools very limited and in some schools the computers available for pupils' individual work bear little resemblance to the windows environments encountered outside the classroom. There is therefore an urgent need to evaluate how computers are used in the curriculum to provide for increased individual access. In particular girls, and less computer-literate students, need to be monitored to ensure they are given their fair share of computer time. This means that computers need to be integrated into the whole curriculum and not restricted to a particular named area or subject specialism.

GOVERNMENT POLICY, THE NATIONAL CURRICULUM AND IT

The introduction to this chapter described how many existing IT departments developed initially from technologically based areas of the curriculum which were generally male. These subjects, located in specialist suites within school, often regulate access to all the school population's computer facilities including e-mail and the Internet. This continues to be the case in many schools, despite the 1995 revised orders for the NC which have designated the use of IT in all subject areas.

The position of IT in schools has become increasingly uncomfortable therefore for many IT co-ordinators. On the one hand, IT remains an NC subject in its own right with distinct programmes of study. On the other hand, IT is prescribed as a resource for teaching and learning in every other subject of the NC with the exception of physical education.

In order to give a picture of current provision in schools the National Council for Educational Technology (NCET) has described four basic responses, collated from schools' responses to these NC requirements, which range along a continuum from courses totally delivered through IT departments to those which are fully integrated into all subject areas. These are described as:

- a centralised approach
- a skills core approach
- a kick start approach
- a cross-curricular approach.

Each approach is described by NCET as bringing both advantages and accompanying problems in terms of organisation and the deployment of IT resources within a school. A centralised approach is based on a clearly defined, taught programme often delivered as a single period a week throughout KS3 and KS4. The intention is to ensure quality in the delivery by keeping teaching within an existing IT department. However, the danger, as we can see from the research studies described above, is that IT may then be presented as the prerogative of a particular kind of teacher and restricted to that person's teaching style and the sessions provided may be limited to practice sessions rather than to developing confidence in IT's independent use. Teachers in other subjects may lack motivation to develop its use in a particular area and aspects of IT may be taken out of context and seem irrelevant. Once more pupils who have no home access and therefore see no real purpose for their work are penalised more.

A skills core approach is cross-curricular in delivery. Each department integrates IT in work which is already taking place and the IT co-ordinator's role is to monitor its use throughout the school. Although there may be a danger of not covering all aspects of IT, this approach ensures that pupils meet IT skills in a meaningful context and with a wider range of staff than in the previous model.

Some schools described giving their pupils a 'kick start' at the beginning of their secondary schooling, providing Y7 and Y8 with dedicated IT lessons each week and encouraging subject areas to take over responsibility later. Here problems may occur because of the difference in understanding and attitude of different members of staff so that IT may not be an integral part of all subject teaching. In some schools the key strands of IT have been 'up for grabs' and different departments have agreed to deliver a particular aspect. In this situation the introduction of databases may well be limited to use in a particular subject such as science, and pupils lose the opportunity to develop their expertise related to another area that interests them more. A completely cross-curricular approach is at present less widespread in schools as it depends on a wide range of staff having proficient IT skills. In the last two models, pupils who already have good IT skills may well be used by individual subject teachers to support work in the classroom, perpetuating the kind of inequality in 'hands-on' experience described above. It is, however, more likely than the first two models to encourage all pupils to see work with IT as an essential aspect of all teaching and learning.

A key to the effective implementation of a whole school policy is the necessity for all teachers to have access to support and training. Currently NCET suggests that only 34 per cent of secondary teachers report using IT regularly in their work and this statistic has remained constant for the past seven years. NCET refers to teachers still uninvolved in IT as the 'missing two thirds' and these teachers will need significant support and training opportunities in order for technology to be integrated as a normal and integral part of all children's learning.

RECOMMENDATIONS

The last section of this chapter will identify some areas for schools to develop their practice in the interests of all pupils.

From the earliest years those responsible for small children need to be encouraged to give girls as well as their brothers opportunities on computers at home and in the nursery, recommending software tools for them to use in order for the gender gap to close. Schools have a role to play here by helping parents to acquire the computer skills alongside their children. We also need to gain a greater understanding of pupils' individual experiences which create a positive attitude to technology both in and out of school.

Every school needs a whole school policy which not only develops a clear anti-sexist pedagogy but also plans for effective teaching in IT. This should involve a detailed audit of who uses the technology and where it is located in the school to avoid the confinement of the hardware to a realm of technology and hard science. There needs to be a flexible and adaptable use of resources in order that meaningful learning experiences can be provided across the curriculum. All pupils and teachers need to see computers as a learning tool in use across the curriculum. The development of a more reflective curriculum which aims to relate pupils' experiences to issues of gender divisions in society would also help.

On the issue of resources there is much of Levi Straus's bricoleur in many teachers, which creates a willingness to make do and mend in the face of limited resources and insufficient technical support. However, if much of the work that pupils are asked to do in school draws on outdated and slower technology than that generally available to them outside, then the subject will not seem relevant, however strong the rhetoric about greater access to job opportunities.

Teachers' attitudes and teaching styles are very important when IT capability is being developed. Where sexism occurs in the educational process it needs to be tackled in a systematic and educational way. It is important to build upon the personal experiences of pupils and enable them to test out their own ideas within a supportive framework. This may require a decreasing emphasis on competitive individual learning and an increase in co-operative group work activities. Such an approach has been shown to help girls acquire skills more easily.

As Unwin argues in Chapter 10, subject choice and career guidance need to be constructed particularly carefully to discourage gender-biased selection by pupils. Guidance should make clear that IT as a subject in its own right is appropriate for both boys and girls. This will be more convincing if all pupils have powerful models of different patterns of computer literacy to draw on, having experienced its effective use in English, modern languages and the humanities as well as a support for learning in science and maths.

As pupils increase their understanding of the nature of the new forms of communication they need to be drawn into an evaluation of the role of computers and IT in society. They also need to be helped to reflect on the 'knowledge and understanding' of the courses they are being offered in a context that promotes discussion of social and personal responsibility.

CONCLUDING COMMENTS

While it is tempting for IT teachers to suggest that the way their subject was initially set up in schools has made it too difficult to implement all of these recommendations, it would be socially irresponsible and inequitable not to make serious attempts at change. The findings enumerated above indicate that intervention strategies which concentrate solely on equality issues surrounding take-up and access will not necessarily translate into effective personal action for many pupils, particularly the girls. Attention must also be paid to addressing the social influences affecting attitudes and access to computers at home and in the workplace and the ways in which the use of the new forms of technology has already significantly changed everybody's lives.

REFERENCES

Adams, C. (1985) 'Teacher attitudes towards issues of sex equality', in J. Whyte et al. (eds) Girl Friendly Schooling, London: Routledge and Kegan Paul.

Collis, B.A. and Williams, R.L. (1987) 'Cross-cultural comparison of gender differences in adolescents' attitudes towards computers and selected school subjects', Journal of Educational Research 81: 17–27.

Culley, L. (1986) 'Gender differences and computing in secondary schools', Loughborough Department of Education, Loughborough University of Technology.

Deakin, R. (1985) Women and Computing, London: Macmillan.

Downes, T. (1993) 'Student-teachers' experiences in using computers during teaching practice', Journal of Computer Assisted Learning 9: 17–33.

Drambrot, F.H. et al. (1985) 'Correlates of sex differences in attitudes and involvement with computers', Journal of Vocational Behaviour 27: 71–86.

Durndell, A. (1991) 'The persistence of the gender gap in computing', Computers in Education 16: 283–7.

Durndell, A. *et al.* (1990) 'Gender differences and computing in course choice at entry into higher education', *British Educational Research Journal* 16: 149–62.

Elkjær, B. (1992) 'Girls and information technology in Denmark – an account of a socially constructed problem', *Gender and Education* 4(1): 25–40.

Groundwater-Smith, S. and Crawford, K. (1992) 'Computer literacy and matters of equality', *Journal of Information Technology for Teacher Education* 1(2): 215–29.

Harrison, C. and Hay, D. (1991) 'High-technique of manual skills', *Education Guardian*, 7 February.

Harvey, T.J. and Wilson, B. (1985) 'Gender differences in attitudes towards microcomputers shown by primary and secondary school pupils', *British Journal of Educational Psychology* 57: 114–21.

Hoyles, C. (1988) *Girls and Computers*, Bedford Papers/34, Institute of Education, University of London.

Kirkman, C. (1993) 'Computer experience and attitudes of 12-year-old students: implications for the UK National Curriculum', *Journal of Computer Assisted Learning* 9: 51–62.

Levin, T. and Gordon, C. (1989) 'Effect of gender and computer experience on attitudes towards computers', *Journal of Educational Computing Research* 5(1): 69–88.

Loyd, B.H. *et al.* (1987) 'Gender and computer experience as factors in the computer attitudes of middle school students. Special Issue: Sex differences in early adolescents', *Journal of Early Adolescents* 7: 13–19.

Madsen, J.M. and Sebastini, L.A. (1987) 'The effect of computer literacy instruction on teachers' knowledge of and attitudes towards microcomputers', *Journal of Computer Based Instruction* 14: 68–72.

Makrakis, V. and Sawada, T. (1996) 'Gender, computers and other subjects among Japanese and Swedish students', *Computers in Education* 26: 225–31.

Martin, R. (1991) 'School children's attitudes towards computers as a function of gender, course subjects and availability of home computers', *Journal of Computer Assisted Learning* 7: 187–94.

Millard, E. (1997) *Differently Literate: Boys, Girls and the Schooling of Literacy*, London: Falmer.

Moore, B.M. (1988) 'Achievement in basic math skills for low performing students: a study of teachers' affect and CAI'. *Journal of Experimental Education* 67: 38–44.

NCET (1996) 'Attracting girls to IT', http: //www.ncet.org.uk/info-sheet/girls.html (August).

Papert, S. (1993) *The Children's Machine: Rethinking School in the Age of the Computer*, New York: Harvester Wheatsheaf.

Reinen, I.J. and Plump, T. (1993) 'Some gender issues in educational computing use – results of an International Comparative Study, *Computers and Education* 20(4): 353–65.

Robertson, S.I. *et al.* (1995) 'Computer attitudes in an English secondary school', *Computers in Education* 24(2): 73–81.

Shashaani, L. (1993) 'Gender-based differences in attitudes towards computers', *Computers in Education* 20: 169–81.

Siann, G. and MacLeod, H. (1986) 'Computers and children of primary school age: issues and questions', *British Journal of Educational Technology* 17(2): 133–44.

Singh, P. (1993) 'Institutional discourse and practice. A case study of the social construction of technological competence in the primary classroom', *British Journal of Sociology of Education* 14(1): 39–58.

Solomou, K. (1996) 'Nursery school children and computers: gender-related differences', Unpublished MEd dissertation, University of Sheffield.

Spear, M.G. (1985) 'Teachers' attitudes towards girls and technology', in J. Whyte *et al.* (eds) *Girl Friendly Schooling*, London: Routledge and Kegan Paul.

Turkle, S. (1988) 'Computational reticence: why women fear the intimate machine', in C. Kramarae (ed.) *Technology and Women's Voices: Keeping in Touch*, New York: Routledge and Kegan Paul.

Wilder, G. *et al.* (1985) 'Gender and computers: two surveys of computer related attitudes', *Sex Roles*, 13: 3.

6

ECLIPSED BY ETON FIELDS?

Physical education and equal opportunities

Alan Skelton

> The Battle of Waterloo was supposedly won on the playing fields of Eton. In the future, the same may be said of one or two Olympic medals.
>
> (*The Times*, 1996d: 37)

> The best days of my life at school were spent when we had some form of cricket, or soccer, or rugger.
>
> (John Major, reported in *The Times*, 1996b: 6)

INTRODUCTION: A 'NATIONAL SPORTS CRISIS'

The summer of 1996 witnessed two major sporting events in which 'our' national teams were involved: the European Soccer Championships and the Olympic Games. In the former the English team reached the semi-finals resurrecting – with the aid of the media – the type of football fervour not seen since the World Cup of 1966. Eventual defeat against Germany appeared to put large sections of the nation into mourning and some supporters expressed their disappointment by going on the rampage through London streets (see *The Times*, 1996a). In the Olympics the national team also did less well than was hoped. Two of our best contenders in the athletic events – Linford Christie and Sally Gunnell – not only failed to get medals but, more significantly, failed really to compete: Christie because he was disqualified in the 100 metre final for two false starts (which some reporters claimed was his way of avoiding likely defeat and humiliation) and Gunnell because of an injury in the semi-finals. Apart from a small number of successes, there was a general feeling that as a nation we were under-performing across a wide range of sports and as the Games came to an end, the papers were full of inquests, ultimatums and doom and gloom reports (e.g. 'Who do we blame for a national failure?' *Independent*; 'Olympic shame over Britain's medal tally' *The Times*, both 5 August 1996).

The government responded swiftly to this 'national sports crisis'. John Major unveiled a further stage in his 'Raising the game' initiative, which was introduced in

1995 to 'revolutionise' British sports performance. The second wave of the initiative involved pumping £100 million into national sports facilities to enable all leading sports to have their own national academies. The government also used the initiative to link the crisis in national sports performance to school physical education (PE). It did this by outlining plans for 'sportsmark' awards to be given to those schools doing most to develop and improve sporting achievement. It also outlined plans for the creation of specialist sports secondary schools/colleges. These schools would be allowed to select half of their intake on the basis of pupils' sporting abilities and if they were able to raise £100,000 of private money, they would receive an extra £100 per pupil from the Department of Education and Employment for the encouragement of 'sporting excellence' (see TES 1996a: 4). Together these initiatives gave the impression that little sport was taking place in schools and that urgent remedial action was necessary if the country's fortunes on the international sports stage were to be improved.

SCHOOL PE AND THE GOVERNMENT'S RESTORATIONIST EDUCATIONAL POLICY

The government's response to the events of summer 1996 needs to be understood in the context of a much longer attack on school PE which it has waged, with some conviction, over the last ten years. This attack has sought to discredit what might be loosely termed as an emerging 'New PE' (see Evans, 1990) and to restore competitive team sports as the central defining element of the subject. The government has used both discursive strategies and direct structural intervention (e.g. National Curriculum changes to PE) in its struggle to control the 'official discourse' of the subject (Evans and Penny, 1996). For example, in the latter half of the 1980s, the government, together with large sections of both the popular and more 'respectable' press and other media, strongly criticised PE teachers for undermining the place and importance of competitive team sports in UK schools. The public were led to believe that PE was being taught by a new breed of left wing radicals who, 'driven' by progressive educational ideals, were intent on subjecting children to an impoverished diet of co-operative, non-competitive and non-sporting activities (Today, 1986). Despite research reports which demonstrated that competitive team games still dominated PE in the UK (Murdoch, 1987), prime-time 'serious' programmes like Panorama (March 1987) subjected its viewers to images of deserted playing fields contrasted with shots of sporting heroes from the past. The message being presented was clear: PE in schools was to blame for poor sports performances on the international stage and young, inexperienced, left wing PE teachers were undermining the country's strong sporting tradition through a set of practices underpinned by outdated notions of egalitarianism.

Several years later following the Educational Reform Act of 1988, National Curriculum Working Groups were set up by the Secretaries of State for England and Wales to advise on attainment targets and programmes of study for individual subjects. In July 1990 the Working Group for PE was established and in December of the same year it produced a progressive Interim Report. In specifying three attainment targets (planning/composing; participating/performing; and appreciating/evaluating), the Report implicitly recognised the value of *conceptualising* and *reflecting* on the nature of PE activities, in addition to the more obvious *performative* aspect of the subject. In identifying six key activities (games, dance, gymnastics, athletics, swimming and outdoor activities) for programmes of study for *all* students up to the end of Key Stage 3 (it was recommended that at Key Stage 4 those pupils not taking a GCSE in PE should experience three of the six activities), the Report was also implicitly contesting dominant traditions in PE, notably competitive team games for boys and dance/gymnastics for girls (Flintoff, 1993). The Report devoted a whole section to equal opportunity issues which included the following statement:

> working towards equality of opportunity in physical education involves not only widening and ensuring access. It involves the understanding and appreciation of the range of pupils' responses to femininity, masculinity and sexuality, to the whole range of ability and disability, to ethnic and cultural diversity, and the ways these relate to physical education.
>
> (DES, 1991: 18)

It is instructive to note how these progressive elements were gradually filtered out of National Curriculum PE (NCPE) between 1991 and 1994 in the final making of the original National Curriculum and in its remaking post-Dearing (SCAA, 1993). Through discursive strategies, direct intervention, and structural control over the membership, remit and timings of NCPE Working Parties, the government was able to change the final content and ethos of NCPE considerably, or in other words, 'what is now thinkable in the practices of PE' (Evans and Penny, 1995: 194). For example, in a letter dated 19 February 1991, Kenneth Clarke, as Secretary of State for England, refused to accept the three attainment target proposals of the Interim Report, protesting that PE was an 'essentially active subject' which was characterised by 'performance' as its 'single most important element'. In commenting on the six areas of activity identified in the Report, Clarke doubted the justification for including all of them during Key Stages 1–3 (he doubted, in particular, whether outdoor education should be a compulsory part of a statutory PE curriculum). The Final Report of the 'original' NCPE Group (June 1991) sought to effect a compromise between its original intentions and the Secretary of State's response. It agreed to specify one attainment target which, whilst recognising the central place of activity/performance in PE, would also include planning and evaluation elements. Whilst it retained its commitment to all of the original six activities for Key Stages 1–2, it recommended greater flexibility for Key Stage 3. It stated that although pupils should at some point experience all the six activities (apart from swimming due to resource implications) between ages 11 and 14, in any one school year pupils would only need to experience four activities, one of which should be games and one either dance or gymnastics. With information on equal opportunities, gender issues and cultural diversity moving from chapter two of the Interim Report to figure merely in the appendices of the Final Report, there are clear indications here of significant changes – in terms of content and emphasis – being made to the PE that was initially conceived by the National Curriculum Working Group. These changes, however, were reflected in NCPE as defined by the final statutory orders (DES/Welsh Office, 1992).

Further changes to NCPE were introduced following Sir Ron Dearing's recommendations (SCAA, 1993) that the content of all National Curriculum subjects should be reduced. A PE Advisory Group was set up in January 1994 to review NCPE. As this group began to meet, there was considerable coverage about the issue of school sport, or rather, the lack of it, in the popular press (*Daily Express*, 1994). In April, Ian Sproat, the Minister for Sport, submitted a detailed report to the Prime Minister entitled 'Blueprint for the revitalising of School Sport' which set out an outline for a return to five core games – cricket, football, rugby, netball and hockey (see *The Times*, 1994). As Evans and Penny (1995: 189) suggest, it is unlikely that it was merely accidental that this discourse on sport suddenly 'appeared' in the public arena. Together with the tight regulation of the review process through its quango SCAA (which decided the terms of reference, membership, deadlines and what evidence was submitted to the Advisory Group) and through the setting of a dominant discursive field (PE = sport) within which the Advisory Group had to deliberate and reach its conclusions, the government was able to exert considerable influence on the NCPE which emerged from the process. It was finally recommended that games along with dance and gymnastics should be compulsory activities for pupils between the ages of 5 and 14 (Key Stages 1–3). At Key Stage 3, it was decided that a reduction in the PE curriculum could be achieved by splitting areas of activity (apart from games) into 'half units' and by recommending that pupils take three full units of activity each year. Games was to be taken by all pupils as a *compulsory* full unit and one further full unit plus two half units were to be taken from dance, outdoor and adventurous activities, athletics or gymnastics. At Key Stage 4 (14–16 years), it was recommended that pupils take two activities. Although initially these were not specified, later intervention by SCAA and the Secretary of State ensured that games (read competitive team games) were to be compulsory at Key Stages 1–4 in the post-Dearing 'New NCPE' which emerged in November 1994.

The government's attempt to implicate schools in the 'national sporting crisis' of summer 1996 therefore needs to be understood and located within an ongoing political strategy. As part of a general restorationist policy which has set out to revive 'traditional' educational practices over the last ten years or so (through populist appeals to 'common sense', 'standards', 'efficiency' and 'discipline'), it has sought to reduce PE to sport even though the majority of those involved in the PE profession see competitive team games as only one small part of the subject. Through discursive strategies (PE = sport), direct intervention and structural control over the process and mechanisms of 'curriculum development', it has managed to define NCPE as an essentially practical subject, stripped of any academic content, pedagogical intent and cultural significance. In the following section I consider what implications this has for equal opportunity issues in PE.

PE AS SPORT: IMPLICATIONS FOR EQUAL OPPORTUNITIES

> Sport is so important because it affects the whole character of a generation, let alone its health. And when I say sport I do not mean aerobics, stepping up and down bars or countryside rambles . . . . What I mean is properly organised team games . . . particularly of the traditional games of this country: soccer, cricket, hockey, rugger, netball.
>
> (Iain Sproat, January 1994, cited in *TES*, 1996b: 4)

As PE becomes eclipsed by sport, there is a very real danger that it will gradually become more and more acceptable for there to be unequal opportunities in PE. PE as sport implicitly reflects and reproduces a *particular* view of PE and therefore promotes the interests of those people who hold this view. If PE as sport becomes normalised over time through the circulation of sport discourses and practices then it is likely that the interests of those who see sport as just one small part of PE may well become marginalised and/or perceived as inappropriate.

PE as sport reflects and reproduces an inherently male view of the subject. NCPE privileges traditional games which originated in the English public schools of the nineteenth century (see Parker, 1996a). These games were used to develop physical and emotional toughness in boys and to encourage the broader values deemed essential for the maintenance and continuation of British imperial supremacy (Mangan, 1981; Holt, 1989). PE as sport marginalises those activities which are associated with the dominant female PE tradition – namely, gymnastics, movement and dance (Flintoff, 1993) – and blatantly ignores the fact that many girls in school actively dislike competitive games (Wright, 1996). It also disregards those alternative PE movements such as the 'New PE' which, in the light of feminist thought, contained elements which sought to challenge the competitive individualistic ethos of traditional male PE. Put simply, therefore, PE as sport fails to offer equality of opportunity for boys and girls since it draws unequally on male and female PE traditions.

Looked at in a different way, however, it could be argued that girls and women can reappropriate PE as sport and use it for their own emancipatory purposes. For example, McCrone (1988) suggests that participation in sport enables women to challenge traditional feminine stereotypes (e.g. frail, passive, dependent) and thereby to become more self-determined. From this perspective, PE as sport would be viewed as a good thing for women since female PE traditions developed out of restrictive Victorian notions of femininity (e.g. exercise was viewed as a means to produce attractive feminine wives and healthy potential mothers – see Atkinson,

1978). As Pedersen (1990) notes, however, women are rarely allowed to participate in sport on equal terms with men owing to the enforcement of dress codes and rule changes which make the game less taxing (and therefore more 'appropriate') for them. In this way, women's sport is typically interpreted in a way that sustains the identification of strenuous physical exertion with masculinity. It is also important to point out that access to a male-defined PE curriculum does little to challenge that curriculum itself, and the power relations that constitute it. Equal opportunities for women through PE as sport can only be achieved, therefore, by seeking to become a member of the 'male club' (Salisbury and Jackson, 1996) which for some women would clearly be a contradiction in terms (see Weiner, 1985).

In the light of recent work on the heterogeneity of masculinity (e.g. Connell, 1995; Mac an Ghaill, 1996) we also need to consider *which* men are served by a PE defined as sport. We need to look through the myth of a 'monolithic masculinity' (Siedler, 1991) to see how different groups of boys and men are likely to engage and be positioned by the subject as currently defined. Does PE as sport provide equality of opportunity for *all* boys? Recent studies of PE in secondary schools suggest that not all boys enjoy the tough masculine culture which surrounds competitive games-playing (Parker, 1996b). Boys (and male PE teachers too – see Skelton, 1993) bring a wide range of culturally divergent masculinities into school, yet PE as sport forces a particular version of masculinity (a 'culturally restricted' one – DES, 1991: 17) on them. It is up against this imposed masculinity that boys struggle in order to develop their own gender identity. This involves at the very least trying to resolve personal ideals with dominant cultural expectations and practices. What emerges is a range of possible responses. For example, some boys become victims of the macho PE culture and are effectively excluded from PE activities. Others strategically comply to the informal demands of this culture yet retain private reservations about it. And finally hard boys actively take up, 'for their own', the thrusting masculinity which constitutes PE as sport (see Parker, 1996b). Through the imposition of a particular view of masculinity, therefore, PE as sport excludes some boys from the PE curriculum. It also actively constructs dominant ('hegemonic') and subordinate physical masculinities in boys; that is, a masculinity premised on physical power and strength.

So although all boys may technically have equal access to the PE curriculum, the culturally specific nature of that curriculum (and the particular version of masculinity which underpins it) serves to limit the opportunities of boys who do not share its assumptions and values. But even for those pupils who do, can we really talk in terms of PE offering 'opportunities'? Can a PE curriculum which brutalises boys by encouraging them to distance themselves from feeling be considered an 'opportunity'? The relationship that working class boys have with the PE curriculum is a further case in point. Whilst many working class boys may vigorously take up PE as sport, is this an opportunity or a cultural restriction? For example, some anti-school working class boys (e.g. 'The Macho Lads' – Mac an Ghaill, 1994) may be attracted to PE as sport owing to its essentially active, practical nature and its culture of abrasive masculinity. PE offers the boys a context within which they can claim a source of power given that the social power available in and through the academic curriculum is not available to them (see Connell, 1989). But in taking up the power available through the physical culture of PE as sport, working class boys make themselves amenable to the implicit values of that culture and the covert messages carried by its practices. In competitive games, some of the key messages carried relate to the notion of meritocracy. The games suggest that anyone, irre-spective of their social position, can achieve sporting excellence if they have ability and are prepared to work hard. This sentiment is reflected in the gushing *Times* report of Redgrave and Pinsent's victory in the coxless pairs rowing final at the Olympic Games:

> We in Britain should celebrate not merely a memorable gold medal, but two men's contribution to the symbolism that Olympic sport holds for ordinary life: an achievement through hard work for no gain other than personal satisfaction.
>
> (*The Times*, 1996c: 26)

Here then is the rub for working class boys. 'Opportunities' in PE as sport carry with them the subtle suggestion that success – on the sports field and in life in general – is an entirely personal affair which has nothing to do with material and/or cultural advantage/disadvantage. Some working class boys who are embracing a project of social mobility through schooling may be particularly amenable to this message. And for anti-school working class boys PE as sport may help 'explain' *their* academic failure.

For boys of the middle class, 'opportunity' in and through PE as sport may also be a misnomer. As already stated, the separation from self that PE as sport assumes and requires may have long term emotional consequences (Rowan, 1997). Further-more, for some middle class boys, achievement both on and off the sports field may serve to mask their cultural advantage in the classroom, making material rewards accrued through their ascendancy up the meritocratic ladder seem 'justly' earned. Others who become the 'wimpish', 'academic' victims of PE as sport or those who hold private reservations about its vulgar aggressiveness may channel their energies into the academic curriculum. Success here may lead to power and status and access, therefore, to a form of masculinity which is built on hyper-rationality, 'credentialism' and position in the social hierarchy. Men who claim such power may feel, however, that they lack the physical masculinity that was offered to them during their schooldays. The need to regain a *real* masculinity through an abrasive physicality can represent one of a set of interrelated factors which can sometimes lead men to express violence with women and other 'lesser' men (Miles, 1992).

PE as sport furthermore assumes and reinforces compulsory heterosexuality (Rich, 1986). In and through sport, boys are encouraged to reject their own femininity and to see women, gay men and effeminate men as 'other'. Any behaviour deemed feminine is subject to constant surveillance and ridicule and much of boys' 'identity work' (Brittan, 1989) in sporting activities is devoted to demonstrating and continuously 'proving' the boys' masculinity. Of course PE as sport also offers girls greater opportunities to participate in sport but, as noted earlier, they are seldom allowed to participate on equal terms and their performances are interpreted in ways that maintain the identification of strenuous physical activity with masculinity. It may also be the case that many girls take up sport to work on *their* femininity; here identity work may involve using sport to produce a slim, 'attractive' body (Bartky, 1988) reproducing the 'tyranny of slenderness' (Wright, 1996) in the west. In these ways, PE as sport vigorously polarises the gender identities which are deemed appropriate for young women and young men. It shifts the balance away from co-educational PE which offered an opportunity to blur the boundaries of separate male and female PE activities and processes. Whilst evidence suggests that girls lose out in co-educational PE owing to boys' control over activities, space and the teacher's attention (Scraton, 1985; Flintoff, 1993), its potential cultural significance should not be underestimated. PE as sport hardens up the boundaries between what PE is considered appropriate for girls and boys. It thus creates a clear male/female dualism which is necessary for and constitutive of compulsory heterosexuality. Working to improve the opportunities of girls in PE must ultimately depend, therefore, on linking issues of gender to issues of sexuality. As Townley (1993) suggests:

> Equal opportunities initiatives in education will never result in lasting change until working to dismantle heterosexism and homophobia is seen as an integral part of working for gender equality.
>
> (p. 323)

CONCLUSION

In these rapidly changing times of 'high modernity' (Giddens, 1990) or *postmodernity* (Usher and Edwards, 1994), leisure and sporting opportunities in the western world are becoming ever more diverse and wide ranging. Simultaneously people are beginning to question the role of the physical in their lives and demanding different things from the available resources. There are hyper-technology gyms where people receive seemingly 'personalised' programmes which they then use to submit their bodies to greater and more total self-regulation and surveillance. A privileged few are trying out the first wave of virtual reality machines which allow one to 'sense' bodily movement whilst standing still. And there are people who, influenced by some of the new social movements (see Connell, 1995: 125), refuse to engage in many taken for granted bodily practices owing to their broader impact on the environment.

At a time then when we should be seriously engaging with the question of what a genuinely *inclusive* PE curriculum should look like as we move towards the twenty-first century, a culturally specific and *exclusionary* curriculum – PE as sport – has

LIVERPOOL
JOHN MOORES UNIVERSITY
AVRIL ROBARTS LRC
TEL. 0151 231 4022

been imposed on schooling. This curriculum seeks to restore a bygone age where competitive games were used to train the cultural elite and sublimate the real interests of those 'less suited' for leadership. PE as sport therefore appeals to neo-conservative factions in the British political Right through its 'old' 'cultural supremacy' line. Yet it also manages to resonate with the seemingly more contemporary concerns of neo-liberal factions by offering to produce those values – competitive individualism – which are believed to be essential for 'our' economic interests in global markets (see Ball (1990) for a discussion of the different internal factions of the British political Right).

There is a real need to move to social democratic alternatives for PE. A useful basis for dialogue has been provided by the original National Curriculum Working Group which produced a progressive Interim Report. It included sport as one part of PE rather than its defining characteristic. It recognised the need for a 'critical review of prevailing practice . . . and often the willingness to face up to long held beliefs and prejudices' (DES, 1991: 18). As we approach the millennium it is important that pupils experience a wide range of activities in PE, so that they can use these experiences to help them make decisions about their present and future lifestyles. There needs to be real opportunities for girls and boys in co-educational classes which will require PE teachers to develop greater sensitivity to context. Pupils can benefit from a greater depth of experience in PE which may be offered by providing opportunities for them to reflect on their activities. Critical frameworks may be particularly useful here to bring into question the taken for granted assumption that 'working on your body' is inherently good and worthwhile. But it is precisely these frameworks that are silenced when PE is reduced to an 'essentially active subject' (Clarke, 1991). Characterising PE as a practical poor relation to 'academic' subjects closes down its transformatory possibilities and reproduces the mind–body dualism that a restorationist curriculum assumes and requires.

REFERENCES

Atkinson, P. (1978) 'Fitness, feminism and schooling', in S. Delamont and L. Duffin (eds) *The Nineteenth Century Woman*, London: Croom Helm.

Ball, S. (1990) *Politics and Policy Making in Education*, London: Routledge.

Bartky, S. (1988) 'Foucault, femininity and the modernization of patriarchal power', in I. Diamond and L. Quinby (eds) *Feminism and Foucault: Reflections on Resistance*, Boston: North Eastern University Press.

Brittan, A. (1989) *Masculinity and Power*, Oxford: Blackwell.

Clarke, K. (1991) Letter to Ian Beer, Chair of National Curriculum Physical Education Working Group, 19 February.

Connell, R.W. (1989) 'Cool guys, swots and wimps: the interplay of masculinity and education', *Oxford Review of Education* 15(3): 291–303.

—— (1995) *Masculinities*, Cambridge: Polity Press.

Daily Express (1994) 'Hour a day to make pupils good sports', *Daily Express* 22 January: 1.

Department of Education and Science (1991) *National Curriculum Physical Education Working Group: Interim Report*, Cardiff: DES Welsh Office.

Department of Education and Science/Welsh Office (1992) *Physical Education in the National Curriculum*, London: DES.

Evans, J. (1990) 'Defining a subject: the rise and rise of the new PE?', *British Journal of Sociology of Education* 11(2): 155–69.

Evans, J. and Penny, D. (1995) 'Physical education, restoration and the politics of sport', *Curriculum Studies* 3(2): 183–96.

Flintoff, A. (1993) 'Gender, physical education and initial teacher education', in J. Evans (ed.) *Equality, Education and Physical Education*, London: Falmer.

Giddens, A. (1990) *The Consequences of Modernity*, Cambridge: Polity Press.

Holt, R. (1989) *Sport and the British*, London: Clarendon.

Independent (1996) 'Who do we blame for a national failure?', *Independent* 5 August: S10–11.

Mac an Ghaill, M. (1994) *The Making of Men: Masculinities, Sexualities and Schooling*, Buckingham: Open University Press.

—— (ed.) (1996) *Understanding Masculinities*, Buckingham: Open University Press.

Mangan, A.J. (1981) *Athleticism in the Victorian and Edwardian Public Schools*, Cambridge: Cambridge University Press.

McCrone, K.E. (1988) *Sport and the Physical Emancipation of English Women 1870–1914*, London: Routledge.

Miles, R. (1992) *The Rites of Man*, London: Paladin.

Murdoch, E. (1987) *Sport in School*, London: Sports Council.

Parker, A. (1996a) 'Sporting masculinities: gender relations and the body', in M. Mac an Ghaill (ed.) *Understanding Masculinities*, Buckingham: Open University Press.

—— (1996b) 'The construction of masculinity within boys' physical education', *Gender and Education* 8(2): 141–57.

Pedersen, J. (1990) 'Sport and the physical emancipation of English women 1870–1914 (K.E. McCrone)', reviewed by J. Pedersen, *Gender and Education* 2(1): 107–9.

Rich, A. (1986) 'Compulsory heterosexuality and lesbian experience', in A. Rich (ed.) *Blood, Bread and Poetry*, London: Virago Press.

Rowan, J. (1997) *Healing the Male Psyche*, London: Routledge.

Salisbury, J. and Jackson, D. (1996) *Challenging Macho Values: Practical Ways of Working with Adolescent Boys*, London: Falmer.

SCAA (1993) *The National Curriculum and its Assessment*, London: School Curriculum and Assessment Authority.

Scraton, S. (1985) 'Losing ground: the implications for girls of mixed physical education', Paper presented at the British Educational Research Association, Sheffield.

Siedler, V. (1991) *Recreating Sexual Politics*, London: Routledge.

Skelton, A. (1993) 'On becoming a male physical education teacher: the informal culture of students and the construction of hegemonic masculinity', *Gender and Education* 5(3): 289–303.

The Times (1994) 'Blueprint for revival of school sport', *The Times* 8 April: 1.

—— (1996a) 'England fans riot after defeat', *The Times* 27 June: 1.

—— (1996b) 'Major starts £100m race to give Britain a sporting chance', *The Times* 25 July: 6.

—— (1996c) 'Redgrave stands supreme among the Olympian elite', *The Times* 29 July: 26.

—— (1996d) 'Talent blooming on Eton's fields', *The Times* 29 July: 37.

—— (1996e) 'Olympic shame over Britain's medal tally', *The Times* 5 August: 7.

The Times Educational Supplement (1996a) 'Selection to be based on sports ability says premier', *TES* 26 July: 4.

—— (1996b) 'Man with a teeming vision', *TES* 26 July: 4.

Today (1986) 'Barmy Britain', *Today* 11 July: 1.

Townley, C. (1993) 'Lesbians play football too: widening the gender debate', *Gender and Education* 5(3): 321–4.

Usher, R. and Edwards, R. (1994) *Postmodernism and Education*, London: Routledge.

Weiner, G. (1985) 'Equal opportunities, feminism and girls' education: introduction', in G. Weiner (ed.) *Just a Bunch of Girls*, Milton Keynes: Open University Press.

Wright, J. (1996) 'The construction of complementarity in physical education', *Gender and Education* 8(1): 61–79.

7

SHIFTING THE GOALPOSTS

Girls, women and soccer

Jerry Wellington

INTRODUCTION

Because the game of soccer permeates so deeply into much of our national life, it provides the perfect case to illustrate general points related to the gendered curriculum. In its practice and organisation can be found the effect of attitudes, comments and media coverage, as well as the structures and institutions (or lack of them) in place which inhibit the participation and development of girls, not least in our schools. The male dominance of the sport is also protected by the pseudo-biological arguments which have been used for decades to restrict access and participation.

Hence the rationale for, and value of, considering soccer as part of a book on unequal opportunities. This chapter does not advocate that girls and women should play soccer. No one should attempt to force that upon them, or on boys and men (especially on cold, wet, windy days). The chapter starts from the simple premise that girls *should have the opportunity* to play soccer if they so wish. This simple premise, as argued later, has many implications. For example, it implies that girls should have the freedom to play without jibes or harassment, the encouragement to play if they want to, and opportunities and structures enabling them to play both in and out of school. It also has implications for the way soccer is organised and run, and for the way it is 'covered' by the media.

The chapter begins with a brief sketch of the history of soccer for women and its current position in this and other countries. I then turn to the backbone of the chapter. On a positive note, I review the events and policies which have facilitated girls' participation in the game. But more importantly, I then focus on the factors which have acted against girls' participation in soccer. This section includes a review of past research into constraints (both real and imaginary) and also reports interview data with a range of respondents. Towards the end of the chapter some ways forward are suggested which could provide girls and women with the opportunities and structures to play soccer in the future.[1,2]

HISTORICAL ASPECTS

Women's football has a fascinating history which can only be dealt with briefly here (see Williamson (1991) for some excellent accounts, despite the rather questionable title of his book). Its early history seems to stretch back to the start of the eighteenth century when an annual ritual near Inverness involved women kicking a stuffed animal bladder around, using trees as goalposts. The best documented era seems to stretch from the late nineteenth century to the early 1920s. This era includes a decade or so when women's football reached its peak, despite an FA ruling in 1902 banning any of its teams from playing matches against 'lady teams'.

The real catalyst, sadly, was undoubtedly the advent of the First World War when women's football began to grow largely around northern factories which increasingly employed women as part of the 'war effort'. Many games were played for charities and war funds, often at the large grounds of the time such as Stamford Bridge (Chelsea), White Hart Lane (Tottenham) and Goodison Park (Everton). Teams in the south began to grow and clubs such as Lyon's Cafe in London, Bath Ladies (a 'non-factory' team, of course) and Plymouth Ladies grew up to match their northern rivals. But the most famous team of the era was Dick, Kerr's Ladies founded at a munitions factory in Preston. On Boxing Day 1920 they attracted a record crowd of 53,000 at Goodison Park (far more than are allowed to view Everton men now). The gate receipts were a record at over £3,000, while nigh on 10,000 would-be paying customers were locked outside the Goodison gates. That Boxing Day appears to have been the zenith for women's soccer. In the early 1920s, ladies charity matches had been attracting average crowds of 12,000 (Williamson, 1991) but problems were about to arise. Critics were beginning to question the 'suitability' of football for women at the same time as rumours were being spread about the destinations of the funds raised at the popular charity games. The first major reversal came when an FA resolution in 1921 deemed football to be 'unsuitable for females' and banned FA clubs from staging women's matches. As is the case today, few women's clubs had their own pitches and facilities and so games could only be staged by the minority such as Bath Ladies who had their own ground. The women fought back by forming their own FA in 1921 which, despite the efforts of the male FA, was able to gather 150 clubs in England.

However, the women's game would never again rise to the heights of the 1920s. Subsequent history of women's football is more hazy and largely unresearched (Williams and Woodhouse, 1991) but the above sketch of its golden era serves amply to provide lessons for today. A summary of some of the main events is given in Table 7.1.

A history of constraints

The history of women's football is fascinating (Lopez, 1997) not least because it illustrates the perennial constraints and barriers to its development, which closely

Figure 7.1 A 1990s team

Figure 7.2 Two 1930s footballers
Source: Getty Images

parallel other aspects of the gendered curriculum. The lack of structures and the imposition of decrees, largely from the FA in 1902 and 1921, virtually killed it as a mass spectator sport. The FA has much ground to make up before it can compensate for its past neglect. The formation of a women's association in 1921 proved to be too late to preserve women's football as a mass attraction. The lack of their

Table 7.1 A brief chronology of girls'/women's football

Early 18th century	Scotland – annual ritual near Inverness (trees as goalposts, stuffed animal bladder)
1894	Brighton High School for Girls forms a football club
1895	Northern versus Southern Ladies at Crouch End (North 7 South 1)
1895	Ladies match in Newcastle attracts 8,000 people
1902	FA instructs its member teams not to play matches against 'lady teams'
1914–18	Women's football grows during the First World War, especially around northern factory teams, e.g. Dick, Kerr's of Preston
	Many games played for charities
1918–21	Games increasingly played at large grounds, e.g. Stamford Bridge (Chelsea), White Hart Lane (Tottenham) and Goodison Park (Everton) to accommodate the large crowds (approved by the FA)
1920	Teams form in the south, e.g. Lyons (Cafe) Ladies in London
1920	Bath Ladies formed (a 'non-factory' team)
1920	Dick, Kerr's Ladies tour France
1920 [Zenith]	Boxing Day: Dick, Kerr's v. St Helens Ladies attracts a crowd of 53,000 at Goodison Park (10,000–14,000 locked out) Gate receipts of £3,115
1921	Ladies' charity matches attracting an average of 12,000 spectators
1916–21	Dick, Kerr's alone raises £50,000 for charity
1920–1	Critics question suitability of football for women
1921	Rumours abound concerning destination of funds raised by women's football for charity
1921	5 December: FA resolution deems football 'unsuitable for females' and bans FA clubs from staging women's matches
post-1921	Women's football staged only where clubs have own facilities, e.g. Huddersfield Atlanta, Dick, Kerr's, Bath Ladies
1921	English Ladies FA formed (150 clubs in England)
1922	Hey's Ladies, based around a Bradford brewery, become England's prominent team (the 'new guard')
1922–60s	Hazy history, largely unresearched
1939	England v. Belgium women's international
1965	Kerr's Ladies finally disbanded (played 800 games, raised over £70,000 for charity)
1969	Women's FA of England formed
1984	WFA finally invited to affiliate to the FA
1984	England women's team reach the first UEFA Cup Final
1985	Football League clubs encouraged to support formation of affiliated women's teams
1988	First women's international at Wembley
	England women beat Italy 2–1 to win the 'Little World Cup'
1990	Football Trust allocates £150,000 to women's game
1991	334 women's clubs registered with the WFA (about 9,000 players)
1991–2	National Women's League founded
1993	Women's FA subsumed by FA

own facilities, i.e. grounds, pitches and social and indoor facilities, proved to be a major factor in the demise of women's football – just as the same vacuum hampers the growth of the game now.

Pseudo-biological arguments about women's minds and bodies have been used repeatedly to prevent their active participation in soccer and other sports. Teeter (1985), for example, cites the use of ideas in the Victorian era from the embryologist Von Baer on adolescent psychology – their effect was to promote sports for boys and young men but deny them to girls and young women. A similar story is told by Mills (1994) of the Second World War era when 'common beliefs' were held that participation in sport could make women infertile, coarse, unfeminine and possibly immoral. A full account of these historical barriers can be found in Vertinsky's (1994) account of late nineteenth century beliefs about female exercise and McCrone's (1988) book on women in English sport from 1870 to 1914.

These beliefs and attitudes restricted the active part of women in sport and often maintained their role as spectators (even in baseball, despite the formation of a national league for 'Girls' in 1943). This dubious role of girls and women admiring and cheering on athletic men seems to have originated in the USA where female cheerleaders provide a common media focus in televised sports. It is also a role not uncommon in other countries – witness the 'kickabouts in the park' where the men play and the women watch on. As Berger (1972) expressed it: 'Men act, women appear.'

WHO'S PLAYING NOW – HERE AND ELSEWHERE?

We are repeatedly told that we live in an 'information society', but it is never pointed out that the information available to us depends totally on who is collecting it, why, and what categories they use. Thus, if we look in *Social Trends* for example (which provides a wealth of information on the society we live in) we can see at a glance, in the section on lifestyles and leisure pursuits, the number of men playing football – but no data are provided on women in soccer (Table 7.2). We see instantly how many do yoga, aerobics or tennis, but lo and behold there is no entry for football.

Newspaper reports vary in terms of the figures they publish. The 1993 *Independent on Sunday* reported Graham Kelly (the FA's chief executive) as saying: 'There are just under 10,000 players today – that could be increased tenfold in five years' time.' (*Independent on Sunday* 26 April 1996). The same paper in 1992 reported that FA predictions spoke of 5,000 women's teams by the turn of the century and 100,000 players. It is difficult to determine to whom we should turn to provide the 'hard data'.

The FA have been extremely helpful in supplying me with *some* facts and figures. Data from their sheet ('An overview of women's football since 1993', which extends over two sides of A4) indicate that the number of women and girls playing football in England has trebled in the last seven years to 21,500 registered players.

Table 7.2 In the so-called information age, the data we have depends on who collects it and what they are looking for

United Kingdom	Percentages[1]							
	16–19	20–24	25–29	30–44	45–59	60–69	70 and over	All aged 16 and over
Males								
Walking	45	46	48	48	47	45	33	45
Snooker/pool/billiards	56	47	34	23	14	8	3	21
Swimming	23	19	19	21	12	8	3	15
Cycling	37	19	21	16	11	6	5	14
Soccer	44	27	19	9	2	0	0	9
Golf	15	13	12	11	9	7	3	9
Females								
Walking	40	41	41	41	42	36	20	37
Keep fit/yoga	29	28	26	22	14	8	6	17
Swimming	26	25	22	24	14	8	3	16
Cycling	14	12	8	9	7	4	2	7
Snooker/pool/billiards	26	17	6	4	2	1	0	5
Tenpin bowls/skittles	9	9	5	4	2	1	0	3

Source: General Household Survey, Office of Population Censuses and Surveys: Continuous Household Survey, Department of Finance and Personnel, Northern Ireland
1 Percentage in each age group participating in each activity in the four weeks before interview.

Making comparisons

Figures in tens of thousands sound impressive, but in comparison with the number of males (estimated at over 1.5 million), given the opportunities and the structures to play soccer in the UK, they are minimal. Similarly, it is informative to compare our situation with that in other countries. For example, the history of soccer in the USA is very different from our own and very illuminating. The first women's soccer there, in 1907, was college based and a 1930 survey of 120 American colleges showed that women's soccer was occurring in 58 per cent of them: 'In the United States before mid-century soccer was almost exclusively a women's game' (Lee, 1983: 240). This history may account for the huge popularity of the American female game now and its strength relative to that of the men.

The women's game is also far stronger than here in many other European countries, especially the Netherlands (39,659 girls and women), Denmark (39,000), Norway (60,000) and Germany, with an amazing total of 706,336 registered girl and women players. This may show that Germany is highly efficient at registering players – but even if we add the FA estimate of 100,000 girls who have played some football through school and community initiatives, the UK figures fall far short of participation per head of population in all the other European countries, except Portugal which only has an estimated 690 registered women players.

FACILITATORS AND CONSTRAINTS

Any account of factors encouraging and promoting girls' football through history will be a short one. Few structures, rulings, policies or attitudes have existed to lend any real encouragement. Attitudes of both men *and* women, policies and rulings such as the FA ban of 1921, myths about women's physique and mentality, and coverage by the media of both men's and women's football have all pulled against it and continue to do so. In history there have been events which almost by accident have promoted the women's game. Thus the First World War, by creating a shortage of men alongside a jingoistic drive to raise money for charity, gave the women's game a chance to flourish. But this was only at the top level with teams like Dick, Kerr's and Plymouth Ladies. There is little evidence to suggest that the game at grass roots level received a boost. Thus, although the game grew as a spectator sport, participation was for the few, rather than providing an outlet or a source of health and pleasure for the many at park or school level. Similarly, the extensive media coverage of the time, with its treatment of the big charity matches as some sort of freak show, did nothing to promote soccer as a sport for all girls/ women. Reports tended to focus more on what the women were wearing than how they were playing, as the following excerpt from the *Manchester Guardian*, telling of the famous 1895 North v. South match, shows:

> The ladies of the North wore red blouses with white yolks, and full black knickerbockers fastened below the knee, black stockings, red beretta caps, brown leather boots, and leg-pads. The South wore blouses of light and dark blue in large squares, and blue caps, the rest of their dress being the same as the other team. A few wore white gloves and some discarded caps altogether. One or two added a short skirt above the knickerbockers.
>
> (Quoted in Williamson, 1991: 4)

The *Manchester Guardian* went on to say that 'when the novelty has worn off I do not think that ladies football matches will attract crowds'. How wrong the newspaper was – as the events of Boxing Day at Goodison Park twenty-six years later were to prove.

The modern game does admittedly have more facilitating factors in its favour. There are now ten regional girls'/women's leagues in the UK, an active Women's FA 'within' the FA, and occasional media coverage which promotes rather than ridicules. The existence of strong structures and high participation rates in other countries such as the USA, Italy and Scandinavia has also acted as a spur, if not a facilitator. In many cases the encouragement and influence of parents, family, friends and sometimes teachers provides the necessary conditions for growth. A study by Brown *et al.* (1989) showed that the influence of 'significant others' is a major factor in maintaining the involvement of 'female adolescents' in physical activity. But girls first need to be attracted into participating and often the deterrents outweigh the attractions. The interview data reported later in this chapter shows that family members are significant, often fathers and brothers who already play the game. In my view, we are still at the stage where the best way forward is to look at the constraints in the hope of removing some of them, rather than to concentrate solely on improving the positive factors – hence my concentration below on the barriers and constraints before turning to ideas for positive action.

'It's just not natural': Myths about females and football

We just don't like males and females playing together. I like feminine girls. Anyway, it's not natural.

(Ted Croker, Chair of the FA in 1988, *The Times* 26 August 1988)

The argument about certain habits and activities being 'natural' has a long history, not only in sport but also significantly in the history of science. As Willis points out, it is often used as an argument for a certain ideology because of its apparent autonomy from biased interpretation (discussed in Williams and Woodhouse, 1991: 88). But what does it mean to say that something is not natural? It is often no more than an expression of disapproval. The accusation of being 'unnatural' could equally be made of flying in an aeroplane, drinking purified water, using contraceptives, reading by artificial light, or cleaning our teeth with a toothbrush. The 'un-natural' argument is clearly vacuous yet it is still commonly used and is certainly present in the minds of girl soccer players:

People are a bit negative about girls football – they don't think it's natural kind of thing.

(Girl soccer player, age 14)

One woman player whom I interviewed recalled that she was told at school that she could not play football because girls' knee joints were 'not up to it'. The implication of this is that hockey and tennis are fine for knee joints but not soccer. Similar assertions about the female physique and the dangers of de-feminising as a result of sports have been extensively used, as Williams and Woodhouse discuss (1991: 88 and 92). None of these 'physiological' explanations have any support from scientific or medical evidence. As Birke and Vines (1987) point out, there are many parallels between women's exclusion from sport and from science. They critically examine the 'biological arguments' used to 'show' that women are 'inferior' in science and also to limit women's participation in sport. They point out that biology itself is subject to change.

Perhaps the classic case of this argument in practice occurred in 1984 when the Inner London Education Authority (ILEA) argued against girls' football with the assertion that:

Women have many other qualities superior to those of men but they have not got the strength and stamina to run, kick, to tackle and so forth.

(Quoted in Hargreaves, 1994: 177)

In practice, this led to a ban on young girls playing in mixed football teams until 1990, which effectively stopped them from playing at all. In fact, the FA capitulated in that year and allowed girls to play in mixed football until the age of 11. In reality, as I argue later, this did nothing to help promote the game for girls, and (in my view) attempts at 'mixed football' have inhibited the participation of girls in soccer.

Girls won't go out once it's cold. If they do they just stand around and complain.

(PE teacher, quoted in Scraton, 1992: 71)

A similar argument to the unnatural and unfeminine allegation has been reported by Scraton (1992) in discussing responses to the weather. She reports some remarkable views from a range of school PE teachers related to girls and soccer. Wet, muddy, cold playing fields were seen as unsuitable for 'the girls':

Once the fields are muddy it just isn't worth taking the girls out. They complain and nobody achieves anything.

I think it's a bit different for most boys. They seem to not mind going out in the cold. Probably boys are so much more active that they don't feel it the same.

(Scraton, 1992: 49)

These and other similar quotes which Scraton reports are remarkable for the assumptions that the teachers quoted (presumably teachers with PE qualifications) are making. For example, we should question whether any children have to be sent out onto muddy fields to get cold and whether boys enjoy getting cold. Are boys immune to the cold? Why can they not all wear warm, suitable clothing such as waterproofs, track suits, gloves and woolly hats as most professional footballers do in training? Does 'the cold' stop women from going on the ski slopes? Are boys really more active than the girls – do they have a different metabolism? The in-built assumptions and prejudices underlying the above quotations are endless and relate closely to the 'it's just not natural' assertion.

There's no future in it

I used to play hockey as well as football so the teachers used to try and make me play hockey instead. They said that I should choose to play hockey because with football I wouldn't get anywhere . . . they just said women had nowhere to go in football.

(Joanne Broadhurst, woman international soccer player, quoted in Williams and Woodhouse, 1991: 98)

This is an argument which often surfaces in discussions of girls soccer, including in my own interviews:

My dad told me to stick to netball because if I do I might get to play for the county.

(Girl player, age 14, on giving up soccer)

This constraint, unlike the first two, has some evidence to support it. Structures which would allow girls and subsequently women to pursue a future in soccer are few and far between. Playing football for the county is possible in some parts of the UK but not in all, and structures that do exist are not widely known or publicised in the media or by schools. In these circumstances it is difficult to argue with the opinion expressed by the girl's father in the quotation above.

But in my view the future argument should not be overemphasised. It is important for girls to get enjoyment and other benefits from their present activities. Frankly, very few boys have a future in football as professionals. But what they do have is a clear view of where they can enjoy the sport as older boys, men and even veterans, whether in parks, sports clubs or just the local rec. Girls do not have this 'view', simply because the opportunities and structures do not yet exist.

Role models and the media

It is well known that girls have few, if any, role models in soccer (or in other sports; Creedon, 1994) to look up to. Even the comic character 'Bess of Blacktown' who in 1933 was the female equivalent of Roy of the Rovers (reported by Williamson, 1991: 94) has no contemporary counterpart. Football magazines and fanzines for women are virtually non-existent, and 'mainstream' magazines such as SHOOT contain virtually no coverage of female soccer. Hargreaves (1994: 149) talks of the power of the hidden ideology in comics and magazines. Comics for young boys give football a high profile:

Football is treated as an adventure, a way of being macho and 'one of the boys' in a separate world of masculinity. Girls are never portrayed playing football, and are only occasionally seen looking on.

Television rarely screens the women's game, even during the Olympics and the World Cup. As Williams and Woodhouse (1991: 32) report, when England reached the final of the UEFA Cup in 1984 the game was hardly mentioned in the British press, whereas their opponents, Sweden, arrived with a 'TV crew and 36 press personnel'. In the UK, television commentators and 'experts' are entirely male. In fairness, radio stations such as BBC's Five Live now have two female reporters, but they are heard and rarely seen.

Even the more intelligent male commentators, such as Alan Hansen, keep reminding us that 'it's a man's game' (usually meaning that soccer is a contact sport, so why not just say that?). When television coverage of women's soccer does occur it is at best tongue-in-cheek and at worst demeaning:

> The language of the male commentators is regularly and often quite explicitly riddled with observations about the appearance of female per-formers and with sexual innuendo.
>
> (Hargreaves, 1994: 165)

The 1995 documentary on the 'Doncaster Belles' portrayed them as coarse, uncouth, foul mouthed and 'hard', simply by its choice of which scenes to show and which comments to include. My own experience of our club playing against their junior teams is that the Belles set excellent standards, with an excellent organisation on limited funds – none of which were portrayed in this documentary. Quite rightly, Graham Kelly of the men's FA was disturbed by the documentary and reportedly (*Independent* 11 March 1996) sent the club a 'sharp letter' about the tone of the programme (although the real target for the complaint should have been the BBC). The club itself became extremely wary of any future media coverage despite the need to raise funds – an impossible dilemma to resolve.

An American study of television coverage of women's sport (Weiller and Higgs, 1992) found that, in the late 1980s and early 1990s, it received far less air time, fewer cameras at each event and often condescending, trivialised comments. The stereo-typical image of the female athlete was reinforced rather than challenged. More-over, newspapers virtually ignore girls' and women's soccer.

Negative attitudes and the 'culture'

The culture argument is similar to the natural or biological arguments in that it acts almost as a sentence or argument 'stopper'. How many times has the assertion 'It's just part of the culture' been used to justify or excuse an attitude or practice that is, quite simply, wrong? To use a fictitious example, cutting off someone's hands if they steal may be part of a culture, but it does not make that practice right. The 'culture argument' carries no moral weight.

There is some past research on culture and attitude in women's sport, though little specifically on soccer.[3] A 1987 study (Fasting, 1987) focused on the fact that men and women belong to two different cultures and this influences the way they are socialised into sport. As a result, sport has played little part in women's lives. Similarly, a study in the same year by Varpalotai (1987) showed how girls at a summer camp experience the contradictory roles of woman and athlete, and the effect that socio-cultural attitudes to this tension have on practices. Varpalotai

118

discusses the 'hidden curriculum' in formal education (see next section) and the socialisation processes in informal experiences which inhibit girls' participation in sport.

Earlier in the decade, a New Zealand study (Shallcrass et al., 1980: 65–7) suggested that 'contemporary attitudes' were a major constraint to women's involvement in sport and showed that their 'recreational opportunities' did not receive the same financial, political, educational or media support as the men's game. They argued for increased representation of women at policy-making level in sport. It seems, though, that little changed through the 1980s and into the 1990s.

My own interview data shows that both spoken comments and the body language of spectators can act as a deterrent:

> It annoys me a bit when people gawp at us playing football and think it's weird.
>
> (Girl, age 14)

The girls talked of 'sexist, patronising comments', such as 'girls can't play football'; 'as if you can play football'; 'mind your make up'; or 'Wow . . . she can actually play', as being commonplace. However, some of the girls whom I interviewed felt that it was as much the attitudes and past experiences of girls themselves which acted as a barrier:

> A lot of girls are afraid to try . . . a lot of people think 'I'm a girl, I can't play football', but basically they've never tried. They don't want boys making fun of them and things.
>
> (Girl, 14)

> If they see someone else who's maybe good or has some experience they get a bit embarrassed if they can't play themselves.
>
> (Girl, 15)

> Girls are more interested in non-physical things, like netball.
>
> (Girl, 15)

One girl linked it to the lack of media coverage and role models, so that:

> People think it's not normal to play . . . they don't dare to be different.
>
> (Girl, 14)

Peer group pressure obviously plays a major part, as do attitudes and comments at school. The idea of what counts as 'normal' is a powerful one.

It also seems to be part of the culture that it is not 'normal' for girls and women even to talk about soccer. Mac an Ghaill (1994: 123) illustrates how girls are excluded from everyday conversations about football, even if they are spectators themselves:

ANN MARIE: . . . the men teachers say that they treat boys harder and they do in a way, but there's still a togetherness about the way they behave.

DAWN: That's especially in things like PE. Some of us go to the matches [football] but the teachers, the men teachers would never talk to us like that.

MM: Like what?

DAWN: It's like they're in a club and girls can't join. The men teachers are the same sometimes even with Miss Eagleton [PE teacher]. Sometimes I feel really sorry for her.

NIAMH: One minute they're telling the boys off and the next they're talking together in a close way about telly programmes and football.

Schools as institutions and the people in them

Schools are complex places and a lot goes on inside them that we neither understand nor are fully aware of. It is very tempting to point a finger at schools, teachers and teacher education – so I will briefly succumb to that temptation. Several authors have looked at the training of PE teachers (see Skelton (1993) and in this volume). One study offering a feminist critique of the way that masculinity and femininity are 'culturally produced' in British PE was made by Sherlock (1987). She argued that a segregated curriculum has resulted from the separate training of PE teachers. In society, the values of masculinity, capitalism and sport have developed in close association and the same values have permeated deeply into the culture of PE.

An earlier, empirical study was made by Lopez (1979) who found that only twelve out of twenty-nine female soccer players surveyed had received encouragement from their PE teachers. My own observations and interview data indicate that this number in 1979 (nearly 40 per cent) was not a bad percentage. Scraton (1992: 49) suggests that women PE teachers may have stronger negative attitudes to soccer than men, as her quotes from female teachers illustrate:

> I have yet to see an elegant woman footballer. I just don't like seeing women playing football. If they did I would definitely want to modify it. The pitch is far too big and the ball too hard.

> Football – I have a personal thing about this. I've been to a woman's football match and there's nothing sorer to my feminine eyes than a big bust and a big behind and the attracted crowd and spectators. . . . I won't let the girls play because it is very, very unfeminine. . . . I feel strongly that I will never let the girls play soccer.

These feelings, related to perceived biological constraints and definitions of femininity mean that football is not included as even a small part of the girls' curriculum:

If girls want to go off and play football then they can go and play in a park or club. It is definitely not our place to encourage those activities in school times.

(Scraton, 1992: 49)

Later in Scraton's book (p. 65) she quotes the way a male Head of Department showed his disapproval as the girls' soccer group left the changing room:

Football, you must be mad – you should have been born a lad.

Hargreaves (1994) gives a similar account of the values underlying PE teacher training when she argues that it continues to 'adhere to the disciplined, fitness and competitive games tradition . . . cementing the images and divisions between "feminine appropriate" and "masculine appropriate" activities' (p. 153).

My own interview data on schools and teachers confirm the presence of these images and divisions:

At school we really had to push to get a girls' team . . . people are all for equality and stuff, but we really had to go out of our way to get a team.

(Girl, 14)

Teachers don't encourage it [soccer].

(Girl, 15)

As for soccer training for girls:

It's when they can fit us in really.

(Girl player, age 14)

If a choice at secondary school was offered, then netball and hockey are included but football is not:

In secondary school they reckon you're not allowed to play physical sports with the boys.

(Girl, 14)

A summary of barriers and constraints

Thus the history of girls' football, more and less recent, is a history of continuing obstacles: institutional, social, structural, scientific (or rather pseudo-scientific) and even semi-legal. Such barriers apply to other sports of course, and indeed other areas of the curriculum. A survey of women in the East Midlands (Glyptis, 1985) identified barriers to their participation in sport and divided them into three types:

1   practical barriers, e.g. time, money, transport;
2   social barriers, e.g. family and gender roles, ethnic variation;
3   personal barriers, e.g. shyness.

This classification ties in with my own discussion and data above. Similarly, a paper by Lumpkin (1984) giving a more historical perspective from the USA identified three major factors in 'girls not having been provided with equal opportunities in sport':

1   physiological differences between the sexes;
2   societal norms and attitudes;
3   organisational rules and support.

In summary then, there is a clear pattern of barriers and constraints to female participation which applies not only to soccer but also to sport in general and arguably to many other areas of the school curriculum and life outside it.

WAYS FORWARD

I would like to turn my attention now to ways in which girls may be offered the freedom to play without comment and constraint in the future. I have divided this section into several arbitrary and overlapping headings: schools, structures, the media, attitudes, investment, in order to analyse future action and policies.

The media and new attitudes – spreading the word

People, especially girls and women themselves, need to publicise their game and tell others of the enjoyment and benefits it can bring. This is where the media can help. Girls themselves can tell their own story but it requires the media to make it public. Women's magazines and newspapers can play a part by devoting space to girls' soccer. Interestingly, women football enthusiasts have 'leapfrogged' the traditional media by going straight to the Internet to report and broadcast. Figure 7.3 shows a few examples of World Wide Web sites on women's football.

The media (and some of the other agents I discuss below) can also help to shape and determine the future of women's soccer so that it may share the positive features of the male game, namely skill, excitement, effort, creativity, intelligence, but none of the negative features. We do not want to create a mirror image of the male game. It is important to exclude the petulance, dissent, aggression (as opposed to effort), vindictiveness, dangerous tackling, gloating in victory and sour grapes in defeat which are the features of the professional sport. If these are elements of masculinity, 'the man's game', let us avoid transferring them to women. As a woman player wrote of the female game (*Independent* 17 May 1992):

We bitch less, we spit less, and we kiss less

The media can play a major role in keeping it that way.

Schools

Opportunity needs to be offered at the primary phase:

> They should have done something early on to get people out of their shell and try it. Then, when you reach secondary school, you're not afraid to try it.
>
> (Girl, 14)

The message from all the girl players I spoke to is that they 'need their own team'. I agree – in my view mixed football at any stage is not the way forward at present (just as mixed science lessons may not have been). Girls need to develop at their own pace; they need special encouragement and coaching. Few girls are taught

The newsletter for the occasional footballer

Girls just want to have fun

AFTER YEARS in the footballing widows wilderness, the girlfriends/wives/female associates/complete-strangers-of-the-opposite-sex-to-the-players-of-Athol-Athletic-who-are-all-men-inc have banded together and have already played two stirring games at the Athol Athletic training complex in Chorlton, Manchester.

Using Mr Stitchface - the old Athol indoor football - the women have managed to attract more people to their training sessions than the Athols have managed recently. On Sunday February 11, nearly 20 people were either watching or playing.

Watch this space for more info...!

[**Next News Story** | **Previous News Story**]

[**Home Page** | **Latest News** | **Fixture List** | **League Table** | **Meet the Squad**]

[**Contact Us** | **Mailbag** | **Photo Album** | **Old News** | **Other stuff**]

Women's Soccer Foundation

Volume Five Number Two

June - July - August 1994

Soccer in Scotland!

by Sheila Begbie, Team Sport Scotland, Girls/Women's Football Coordinator

The first recorded women's soccer match in Scotland was played in Inverness in 1888. The married women in the village lined up to play the single women I'm not sure who aspired to be on which team! This first game, played with an inflated pig bladder, became an annual event. There are recorded matches of Scottish teams in the late 1800's and early 1900's.

However, in the 1920's, the Football Association (FA) in England banned women from playing soccer, thus the demise of the game in England consequently saw the demise of the game in Scotland. The Scottish Women's Football Association was formed in 1972, with one senior national league boasting 10 teams.

Women's soccer stagnated for nearly 20 years with no real development or support from the men's governing body, the Scottish Football Association (SFA). A government initiative to increase the opportunities for players and coaches in Scotland, called Team Sport Scotland, was introduced in 1991. With this and the growing public awareness, women's soccer in Scotland is now a rapidly developing sport.

The Team Sport Scotland initiative, with support from the Scottish Women's FA and the SFA, has seen an increase in the number of girls and women participating in the sport.

Football festivals and player development days are organized regularly on a regional basis. The senior women's league has 28 teams playing weekly, there are now U16 and U13 leagues, with a plan to introduce development squads from le vel U 13 to U 20.

All the major Universities and colleges in Scotland now have women's teams, so girls/women's soccer bears well for the future. With the support from the SFA, the Scottish Women's FA is now based at the SFA's headquarters in Glasgow, giving the Women's FA in Scotland access to the many departments at the SFA, and adding a much more professional outlook to developing the sport in Scotland.

In 1992, Team Sport Scotland in conjunction with the Scottish Women's Football Association organized a conference called Heading for the Future to study models of good practice in Norway and the USA, and to consider adapting their mod els to develop women's football in Scotland. Shortly after the conference, the Scottish Sports Council appointed a full time administrator for women's football. The appointment of Maureen McGonigle has raised the profile of women's football in Scot land.

We have a firm commitment to developing our players and coaches. We have been proactive in offering women only coaching courses, and we have increased the number of qualified coaches from 24 in 1991 to 115 in 1994. Our aim is to inc rease the bank of coaches to help development at the grassroots level. In addition, we have asked Michelle Akers-Stahl and her husband Roby Stahl to come to Scotland to undertake a programme of player and coach developments. Their visit is being an ticipated with excitement, and they will travel to the main centres of women's football to work at the local level and to advance and enhance the development of our players and coaches.

We are aware that we cannot run before we can walk, but it is expected that within the next decade Scotland will develop the many structures required for our players to participate at the level they wish, for our coaches to be continu ally assisted with their own personal development and to build a national team who will be able to compete on a world stage.....we look forward to that journey.

For more information contact:

```
Maureen McGonigle
Scottish Women's Football Association
5 Park Gardens
GLASGOW, SCOTLAND
G3 7YE
Tel: 041 353 1162
Fax: 041 353 1823

        or

Shiela Begbie
Team Sport Scotland
Scottish Football Association
6 Park Gardens
GLASGOW, SCOTLAND
G3 7YE
```

U.S. Women's National Soccer Team Falls to Norway 1-0 in Championship of First Algarve Cup

U.S. Soccer, Contact: Paula Martin

FARO, Portugal (Sunday, March 20, 1994) - The defending world champion U.S. Women's National Team was defeated by Norway 1-0 in the championship match of the first Algarve Cup.

After a scoreless first half, Norway scored the game-winning goal in the 83rd minute when Ann Kristin Aarones hit the back of the net from 15 yards out. Linda Medalen served a cross from the right side of the penalty area to an ungua rded Aarones, who blasted a right-footed shot to the upper left of U.S. goalkeeper Briana Scurry.

Roger LeGrove Rogers, Editor

The material and information in this magazine is copyrighted property of WSW and must be properly credited. Contact us for permission if you wish to use any part(s) of it's contents.
© copyright 1996

EMAIL WOMENSOC@aol.com
English, German, French or Italian Accepted

1996 OLYMPICS

OLYMPICS NEWS AND VIEWS

Link to the Official 1996 Olympics Site

Complete Results

What The Media Said About Women's Soccer in the 1996 Olympics

During the next weeks we will be bringing you some excerpts from media reports about the women's Olympic soccer, and would welcome reports from your home town newspapers particularly if it is also the hometown of a member of the Olympic Team of your country.

You may send by fax, e-mail (if you have a scanner) or normal mail. Please include some information about yourself.

Today I am starting with an excerpt from an article written by George Vecsey in the New York Times, Monday August 5, 1996. In my opinion he is the best sportswriter in the United States today, comparable to the top reporters in Great Britain and Europe.

Figure 7.3 Web sites on women's football

from the toddler stage by their dads, in contrast to the boys. As one girl player with a younger brother put it:

> People think of it as a boy's game . . . the Dads see it as a kind of duty to teach the boys. Boys at school who aren't very good at football are not very highly regarded.
>
> (Girl, 15)

With this special treatment for boys how can girls compete in a mixed setting at primary age? It is analogous to an imaginary situation in which boys are taught to read before coming to school (but not girls) and yet the girls are expected to have the same reading age. No – girls need their own team, their own coaching, special encouragement and their own structures, just as boys' needs in reading require special attention (see Millard in this volume).

LIVERPOOL JOHN MOORES UNIVERSITY AVRIL ROBARTS LRC TEL. 0151 231 4022

Structures for opportunities

There are girls' and women's leagues as we saw above. But they are almost exclusively based round large clubs (often men's clubs) in leagues with a wide geographical spread. Women footballers are travelling hundreds of miles for a game. Is this fair? It does nothing to promote football for women, who clearly (Traill, 1993; Remorini, 1994; Daggett, 1976; Clough et al. 1996; Tappe et al., 1989; Colley, 1986) suffer more from constraints of time, home responsibilities, lack of family support, transport and money than men. Leagues, therefore, which encourage girls' and women's clubs to draw on a wide geographical range to create elite female teams are stifling rather than promoting the game as a participant sport. We need local leagues, local teams with their own independent set-up and their own structure. From my experience, local teams are forced to enter a large regional league, simply to 'get a game', because there are no local leagues. This means that they are forced to compete with teams based round a large club which can attract and select from a range of players and which has at least some resources, such as a kit and transport. This results in a kind of inequality that produces the 'cricket scores' I have witnessed and seen reported: 12–0, 18–1, 15–3.

We need local girls' teams and local leagues – similar to those already available to the boys, but without the unpleasant features.

> I think it would be better to have more local leagues with more local teams. There's plenty of people around and a lot would like to get into it but there's just not a team near them. If more people were encouraged it [girls soccer] would become much more widespread and people would show an interest and recognise it.
>
> (Girl, 14)

Encouragement does not include putting a local team against a large club team and making commiserating noises when it loses 16–0.

Investment

Local leagues, special coaching, single-sex teams in schools, etc., all imply a pattern and scale of investment which is not there at present. Money and sponsorship is going into girls' football but a large part of it is going into the promotion of large leagues such as the Yorkshire Electricity Ladies League, covering a huge geographical area in the north of England (teams are travelling seventy-five miles for some away games). This is an active, well-organised league with good intentions, but it cannot succeed in the creation and maintenance of local teams – indeed, as I have argued, giving small clubs no choice but to enter it can kill them at birth. Money needs to go into setting up new teams, giving them coaching and resources (balls, kits, training facilities) and allowing them time to grow and become established.

Where can this money come from? The National Lottery fund, which was kind enough to pay the Churchill family over £13 million for a collection of wartime papers which only a few hundred people will ever see, could provide the answer. Half that sum would nurture enough local girls' clubs to enable the game really to become supported and recognised. That in turn would lead to a change in attitude, new structures, new policies and new media coverage – the wheel, as Edmund in *King Lear* put it, will then have really turned full circle.

I leave one of my interviewees to sum up:

> Football is a main part of people's lives – we want girls to be part of it too, not just men.
>
> (Girl, 14)

ACKNOWLEDGEMENTS

Many thanks are due to the girls of Millhouses FC (especially Kate Burlaga, Tilly Ross and Hannah Wellington) and others, for their observations and statements. Further information on the club can be found on its Web site, address: http://www.million.co.uk/mgfc.

APPENDIX: QUESTIONS DISCUSSED WITH THE GIRL PLAYERS IN INTERVIEW

- How did you first find out you could play football? Who (or what) encouraged you to play? How did you get started? What opportunities do you have/have you had for playing football?

- What (if anything) put you off? What do you think might put other girls off?
- What do you enjoy about playing football? What do you get from it? What do you dislike about it?
- Should more girls be encouraged to play football? How? What opportunities (structures) could be developed?
- What future do you see for yourself in playing football?

NOTES

1 I use girls/women interchangeably in this chapter. Usually I am referring to girls as females under 18.
2 I sometimes use the term soccer (which is in line with American parlance), although most people in the UK would call it football.
3 For this chapter extensive literature searches were carried out with the help of four Master's students in information studies whom I would like to thank (Angeline Hamilton, Liz Smith, Jayne Potter and Mary Hirst). All the major on-line sources (ERIC, BIDS, SSCI, OPAC, BEI, ASSIA, World Wide Web) were consulted and we also carried out a manual search.

REFERENCES

Berger, J. (1972) *Ways of Seeing*, London, Harmondsworth: BBC, Penguin.

Birke, L.I.A. and Vines, G. (1987) 'A sporting chance: the anatomy of destiny?', *Women's Studies International Forum* 10(4): 337–47.

Brown, B.A., Frankel, B.G. and Fennell, M.P. (1989) 'Hugs or shrugs: parental and peer influence on continuity of involvement in sport by female adolescents', *Sex Roles: a Journal of Research* 20 (April): 397–412.

Central Statistical Office (1996) *Social Trends*, London: HMSO.

Clough, J., McCormack, C. and Traill, R. (1996) 'Girls playing soccer: a case study', *ACHPER Healthy Lifestyles Journal* 43(1): 19–23.

Colley, A. (1986) 'Sex roles in leisure and sport', in D.J. Hargreaves and A.M. Colley (eds) *The Psychology of Sex Roles* (pp. 233–49), London: Harper & Row.

Creedon, P. (ed.) (1994) *Women, Media and Sport*, Beverly Hills, CA: Sage.

Daggett, A. (1976) 'Women in sport', *Sport and Recreation* 17(1): 17–22.

Fasting, K. (1987) 'Sports and women's culture', *Women's Studies International Forum* 10(4): 361–8.

Glyptis, S. (1985) 'Women as a target group: the views of the staff of Action Sport – West Midlands', *Leisure Studies* 4(3): 347–62.

Hargreaves, J. (1994) *Sporting Females*, London: Routledge.

Jones, D. (1980) 'A woman's place?', in J. Shallcrass *et al.* (eds) *Recreation Reconsidered into the Eighties* (pp. 65–7), Auckland, Auckland Regional Authority: NZ Council for Recreation and Sport.

Lee, M. (1983) *A History of Physical Education and Sports in the USA*, New York: John Wiley.

Lopez, S. (1979) 'Investigation of reasons for participation in women's football', *Bulletin of Physical Education* 15(1): 39–46.

Lopez, S. (1997) *Women on the Ball: a Guide to Women's Football*, London, Scarlet Press.

Lumpkin, A. (1984) 'Historical perspectives of female participation in youth sport', Paper presented at the Annual Convention of the American Alliance for Health, Physical Education, Recreation and Dance, Anaheim, CA, 29 March–2 April 1984.

Mac an Ghaill, M. (1994) *The Making of Men: Masculinities, Sexualities and Schooling*, Buckingham: Open University Press.

McCrone, K. (1988) *Sport and the Physical Emancipation of English Women 1870–1914*, London: Routledge.

Mills, B.D. (1994) 'Women's baseball in colleges and clubs prior to 1940', North Carolina, USA.

Remorini, W. (1994) 'An investigation into the constraints affecting women's football in England', M.Sc. thesis in Sports and Recreation Management, University of Sheffield.

Scraton, S. (1992) *Shaping up to Womanhood: Gender and Girls' Physical Education*, Buckingham: Open University Press.

Shallcross, J., Larkin, B. and Stothart, B. (eds) (1980) *Recreation Reconsidered into the Eighties*, Auckland: Auckland Regional Health Authority, New Zealand, Council for Recreation and Sport.

Sherlock, J. (1987) 'Issues of masculinity and femininity in British physical education', *Women's Studies International Forum* 10(4): 443–51.

Skelton, A. (1993) 'On becoming a male physical education teacher: the informal culture of students and the construction of hegemonic masculinity', *Gender and Education* 5(3): 289–303.

Tappe, M.K., Duda, J.I. and Ehrnwald, P.M. (1989) 'Perceived barriers to exercise among adolescents', *Journal of School Health* 59(4): 153–5.

Teeter, Ruskin (1985) 'Educational attitudes and science as impediments to female sport and socialization during the Victorian period', Paper presented at the Annual Meeting of the British Society for Sport History, Glasgow, Scotland, 3 July 1985.

Traill, R.D. (1993) 'Girls playing soccer: resistance or submission? A case study of women's soccer in the ACT', *A Report to the National Sports Research Centre, Australian Sports Commission*, Canberra University (Australia), October.

Varpalotai, A. (1987) 'The hidden curriculum in leisure: an analysis of a girls' sport subculture', *Women's Studies International Forum* 10(4): 411–22.

Vertinsky, P. (1994) 'The social construction of the gendered body: exercise and the exercise of power', *The International Journal of the History of Sport* 11(2): 147–71.

Weiller, K.H. and Higgs, C.T. (1992) 'Images of illusion, images of reality. Gender differentials in televised sport – the 1980's and beyond', Paper presented at the Annual Meeting of the American Alliance for Health, Physical Education, Recreation and Dance, Indianapolis, IN, April 1992.

Williams, J. and Woodhouse, J. (1991) 'Can play, will play? Women and football in Britain', in J. Williams. and S. Wagg (eds) *British Football and Social Change* (pp. 85–108), London: Routledge.

Williamson, D. (1991) *Belles of the Ball*, Devon: R & D Associates.

8

'THAT SPARK FROM HEAVEN' OR 'OF THE EARTH'

Girls and boys and knowing mathematics

Hilary Povey

I rose early, played on the piano, and painted during the time I could spare in the daylight hours, but I sat up very late reading Euclid. The servants, however, told my mother, "It was no wonder the stock of candles was soon exhausted, for Miss Mary sat up reading till a very late hour"; whereupon an order was given to take away my candle as soon as I was in bed. I had, however, already gone through the first six books of Euclid, and now I was thrown on my memory, which I exercised by beginning at the first book, and demonstrating in my mind a certain number of problems every night, till I could nearly go through the whole. My father came home for a short time, and, somehow or other, finding out what I was about, said to my mother, "Peg, we must put a stop to this, or we shall have Mary in a strait jacket one of these days".

(Somerville, 1874: 54)

Had our friend Mrs Somerville been married to La Place, or some other mathematician, we should never have heard of her work. She would have merged it with her husband's, and passed it off as his.

(Letter of Charles Lyell, 23 August 1831,
published in Lyell, 1881: 322)

I have perseverance and intelligence but no genius, that spark from heaven is not granted to the sex, we are of the earth.

(Mary Somerville, notes for an autobiography,
published in Patterson, 1983: 87)

It is clear how Mary Somerville was constructed as having no 'spark': her early enthusiasm and expertise in mathematics were deemed to be incompatible with womanhood. In this chapter I try to uncover how girls and boys are currently being constructed as mathematicians or as 'of the earth' and to question whose interests this (unwanted) dualism serves.

131

In contrast, perhaps, to some other areas of the secondary school curriculum, gender and the teaching and learning of mathematics has been the focus of enquiry and action for some considerable time. I begin with the evidence about the under-participation of girls in mathematics, then look at the debate about whether or not this should be a cause for concern, link this with mathematics' current role in the construction of masculinity and finally make some suggestions for an alternative approach to the teaching and learning of mathematics that might come closer to a social justice curriculum for all.

THE ACCESS OF GIRLS TO THE MATHEMATICS CURRICULUM

During the 1980s, substantial research evidence was accumulated about the mathematical performance of girls in school and their lower attainment and participation historically in public examination systems (Shuard, 1986; Isaacson, 1988; Hanna et al., 1990). There has been debate about the extent to which the underachievement is not 'real' but rather constructed (Walkerdine, 1989; Clarricoates, 1978) so that girls are positioned as 'successful but not succeeding' (Walden and Walkerdine, 1985: 82). Furthermore, there is evidence that in the UK the gap in performance in public examinations at 16 is closing (Department for Education, 1993: 10–11) although girls' underparticipation in mathematics is clear cut as soon as 'opting out' is permitted (Wilson 1991: 206–10). Consequently, at the most prestigious levels of attainment, mathematics remains largely a male preserve.

An extensive literature, from a variety of perspectives (Willis, 1996), has grown up attempting to explain the phenomenon. There are theories that focus on perceived characteristics of girls. It is suggested that girls tend to conform to the serialist model of thinking offered to them by their teachers in the primary school. Serialists move from certainty to certainty in small, ordered and well-defined steps. The claim is made that this disadvantages girls mathematically with respect to boys, who think holistically and have a versatile range of thinking strategies available: 'the level of uncertainty at which individuals are happy to work is a distinguishing characteristic between serialists and holists' (Scott-Hodgetts, 1986: 74). Alternatively, the concept of 'autonomous learning behaviours' has been employed to explain sex-related differences in mathematics:

> Autonomous learning behaviours are developed over a period of years and are learned as one is allowed, forced, or expected to do them. Greater participation in autonomous learning behaviours leads to greater development of autonomous learning behaviours which in turn leads to better performance on high cognitive level tasks.
>
> (Fennema and Peterson, 1985: 309)

This research proposes that both the internal motivational beliefs of boys and their external classroom experiences are likely to promote autonomous learning behaviours in boys rather than in girls when they are studying mathematics. However, the issue of 'autonomous learning behaviours' is not in itself straightforward: Leone Burton (1989) describes a group of girls she observed who displayed the autonomous learning characteristics of independence, persistence, choice and successful achievement but who did so in the context of proximity and approval, both supposedly functions of dependency rather than autonomy. In this case, 'the autonomy was a function of group rather than individualised action' (Burton, 1989: 182).

There is also evidence that teacher beliefs about females, males and mathematics have a detrimental effect on the learning of mathematics by girls and women (Fennema, 1990). John Pratt (1985) noted in his research into teacher attitudes that, although there was strong and near complete agreement that teachers should not stereotype school subjects, nevertheless, '[t]he attitudes of maths teachers suggest that girls' reluctance to study that subject . . . is unlikely to be recognised as a matter of concern by these teachers' (Pratt, 1985: 33). Systematic classroom observation in mixed classrooms reveals that small but significant differences with respect to student gender occur in the number of interactions that students have with their mathematics teachers (Leder, 1990). In addition, it is suggested that differences between girls and boys in achievement-related beliefs, and hence in the confidence brought generally to learning in the classroom, are provoked by differences in both the nature and frequency of positive and negative feedback from teachers; that boys and girls may provide different explanations and draw different implications from their successes and failures; and that 'mathematics appears to be an area that in general possesses those qualities that fit best with boys' achievement orientations' (Licht and Dweck, 1983: 103).

There are theories which depend upon biologically determined differences (discussed in Walkerdine, 1989: 8–9) which seem set for a revival: 'if not anatomy then evolution, X-chromosomes or hormones' (Rose, 1994: 18) will be discovered to be destiny. (I do not think they have found the gene yet for tidying up but I know already in whose genetic make-up it will be found to predominate.) In contrast, Gilah Leder (1986) concludes from her historical review that 'there is considerable historical evidence to indicate that many females valued exposure to mathematics, readily mastered its contents . . . and used the acquired skills most effectively within the bounds set by contemporary society' (Leder, 1986: 81). She goes on to point out that an 'unwillingness to pay the price extracted from those who conspicuously contravene cultural norms' (Leder, 1986: 83) may be a key feature in explaining the lower mathematical performance of girls after the beginning of adolescence and their underrepresentation amongst the highest mathematical attainers: with good reason (Isaacson, 1989), they are simply reluctant to succeed in the face of, at best, the discomfort, guilt and doubts about their femininity and, at worst, the unpopularity and ostracism that may follow success. Valerie Walkerdine has written of the contradiction and pain produced through the act of splitting – of being positioned like a boy and like a girl and having to remain 'sane'. A denial of the reality of difference means that the girl must bear the burden of her anxiety herself. It is literally not spoken.

(Walkerdine, 1985: 225)

Although not focusing on the mathematics curriculum alone, Máirtín Mac an Ghaill (1994) found in the school in which he conducted his research that '[t]here was much evidence of the constant pressure and surveillance that the young women were under' (Mac an Ghaill, 1994: 131). He records in particular the girls' descriptions of the boys' offensive behaviour (e.g. p. 132). Other researchers have also described how sexual language is used to intimidate and humiliate girls (Lees, 1987; Draper, 1993) and sexual violence and the threat of sexual violence are not uncommon (Kelly, 1989; Mahoney, 1989). Often, though not inevitably (Cornbleet and Libovitch, 1983; Rudduck, 1994), the response of girls is found to be not one of open protest but of 'withdrawal in a variety of unostentatious ways' (Spender, 1980b: 152). Typically, the girls' 'invisibility' strategy is effective and they become relatively anonymous, faceless and unknown. Julia Stanley found that many of the words used by teachers to describe quiet girls are highly pejorative:

'mouses', 'puddings' and 'boringly well-behaved girls', even contrasting them unfavourably with the 'more rewarding' tough lads who dominate classes by their bad behaviour and constant attention seeking. Girls' behaviour has been defined as a problem by reference to the masculine 'norm'.

(Stanley, 1986: 46)

There is a range of responses from teachers to the boys' strategies for establishing and maintaining dominance. At worst, male teachers may actively take part in similar sexual harassment of the girls in their classrooms (Herbert, 1989; Mac an Ghaill, 1994: 125–33). More commonly, 'misogynous male teacher discursive practices [act] as highly effective academic and disciplinary mechanisms in the policing of masculine boundaries' (Mac an Ghaill, 1994: 125), including those around the territory of mathematics, already overoccupied by men in secondary schools.

Finally, and offering insights linked to many of the above, there are those who look explicitly at the nature of the mathematics curriculum and the prevailing culture in specifically mathematics classrooms and find both relatively uncongenial to girls. Considering firstly the overt curriculum, it is noted that 'many more women than men see mathematics as neither relevant to their interests and experiences nor useful to them in their future lives and careers' (Barnes and Coupland, 1990: 73). (Open University (1986: 52–57) suggests practical ways in which teachers and school students can explore this issue.) Female images rarely occur in mathematics texts and when they do they are often ridiculous

(Northam, 1982). Experiences and interests which are characteristic of boys but unusual in girls are taken for granted: thus the 'cultural capital' (Bourdieu (1977), quoted and discussed in Giroux, 1983: 87–96) of the boys accumulates. In addition, where the mathematics is applied, it is to things rather than people. (For practical alternatives, however, see the 'packaging' of calculus undertaken by Mary Barnes and Mary Coupland (1990) and the Cabbage material, published by SMILE (n.d.), which contains twenty-two activities focused on the mathematics of textiles.) Considering secondly the prevailing culture in mathematics classrooms and prevalent teaching and learning styles,

> [t]he teaching methods used in mathematics can also create barriers to women's participation. We know that women express much less preference than men for competitive or individualistic approaches to learning and a greater preference for a co-operative mode. . . .. The traditional style of mathematics teaching is authoritarian and teacher-centred, and tends to encourage a competitive atmosphere.
>
> (Barnes and Coupland, 1990: 74)

A mathematics classroom in which girls might thrive is likely to be one in which learning takes place through interaction and co-operation, where group work and discussion are encouraged and validated, where experience, activities and ideas are shared, where individuals' contributions are welcomed and where creative and imaginative thinking is valued. (Isaacson (1990), Marr and Helme (1990), Morrow and Morrow (1995), and Rogers (1995) all detail practical strategies for achieving this.) Such mathematics classrooms, however, are rare. (Steven Downes (1994) describes a more common experience.)

We see, then, a systematic site of disadvantage for girls experienced within, and reproduced by, mathematics classrooms. It is not simply that girls are disadvantaged by sex role stereotyping and that therefore equality of opportunity will be provided by eliminating socialisation into passivity and subservience. Rather that they are oppressed and that the oppression is structural. The 'gender regime' (Kessler et al., 1985: 42) of mathematics classrooms, that is the pattern of practices which constructs femininities and masculinities and orders them in terms of prestige and power, militates against the involvement and achievement of girls. As well as by gender, individual girls are also located by class, 'race', sexuality and so on and these locations interconnect and affect each other. An additive model of oppression fails to caputre the complexity of how these different locations interrelate and how life is lived at any particular intersection. Class background, for example, will have a profound effect on how schooling is experienced by different girls (Kessler et al., 1985; Walkerdine and Lucey, 1989). Equally, overgeneralisation has led to some girls being rendered invisible and, as a consequence, the experience of black schoolgirls, for example, has been marginalised. Acknowledging the specificity of individual lives, the 'matrix of domination' (Collins, 1990: 225) and the differences between differently located girls and women, we can nevertheless still see gender as one key organiser positioning school students in secondary mathematics classrooms.

IS DIFFERENTIAL ACCESS TO MATHEMATICS A CAUSE FOR CONCERN? AND WHAT ABOUT THE BOYS?

It has been suggested that mathematics is a male fantasy searching for control, that the 'path to rationality, displayed best in mathematics, is a path to omnipotent mastery over a calculable universe' (Walkerdine, 1990: 23); and that 'this kind of thinking, to put it starkly, is destroying our planet and perpetuating domination and oppression' (Walkerdine, 1994: 74). As such, for those whose interest in ensuring equal access lies in a concern for social justice, mathematics is not something to which girls should be particularly encouraged to aspire nor should boys' attainment be uncritically endorsed. As I shall argue below, the question of what 'counts' as mathematics is not unproblematic (Verhage, 1990; Ernest, 1991; Harris, 1991; Restivo, 1992) and professional mathematicians, in one way or another all part of the hegemonic group, should not have a privileged right to settle the matter.

Nevertheless, there are considerable arguments in favour of taking the study of mathematics seriously. Firstly, it is pointed out that mathematics is currently a key entry qualification to positions of leadership in a technological world. Indeed, this could be exactly why girls are constructed as being 'naturally' not very good at maths and science.

> . . . Tomorrow,
> If weaving and cake making
> Are considered very important
> And those who want to get on in the world
> Need them as entry qualification
> Because they sort those who are capable
> From those who are not.
> Girls, it seems
> Will not.
> They will be 'naturally'
> Not very good at weaving and cake making
> When they are required
> For leaders.
>
> (Spender, 1980a: 128)

Secondly, 'mathematics is formatting our society. . . perhaps God did not organise the world according to mathematics but . . . [it seems] humanity has now embarked on just such a project' (Skovsmose, 1994: 43). Anyone involved at all with the world of education must realise just how common it is becoming to present information (often suspect and/or poorly analysed) numerically and then to use that as the basis for justifying policy. It is important for all our students, inasmuch as they are to participate in democratic citizenship, to have sufficient mathematical literacy to be able to understand the mathematical models being presented, to be aware of the preconditions of the modelling process which become hidden when mathematics gives it a neutral tone and to address the way that the existence of mathematical models affects fundamentally the context of social problem solving. (Skovsmose (1994: especially chapters 7 and 9) gives detailed, practical ideas about how to implement this project.)

Thirdly, it is *reason separated from emotion* rather than reason itself which has been the servant of gendered patterns of domination and the desire for mastery and control. It behoves any of us who wants to see a more just world to be suspicious of the fruits of reason but to argue instead for a caring responsible rationality (Rose, 1994: chapter 2). We need a mathematics and a way of knowing mathematics that supports the development of concern, connectivity, personal accountability and respect for the experience of the knower (Collins, 1990) alongside the development of reason: 'Just as rationality and autonomy are goals of the whole curriculum so should nurturance and connection be' (Martin, 1985: 197).

AN INCLUSIVE EPISTEMOLOGY OF MATHEMATICS

'In our culture the structured, plan-oriented, abstract thinkers do not only share a style but constitute an epistemological elite' (Turkle and Papert, 1990: 148). The kind of mathematics valued currently in educational institutions is formalist, abstract and bleached of context. It has been suggested that this represents a specifically male way of interpreting, thinking and knowing about the world. Other ways of thinking, knowing and learning exist. Carol Gilligan (1982), for example, has suggested that engaging with the concrete and contextual rather than reducing a given situation to an abstraction is at the heart of (women's) moral thinking. Mary Belenky, Blythe Clinchy, Nancy Goldberger and Jill Tarule in *Women's Ways of Knowing* (1986) describe what they term 'connected knowing' (p. 100), dependent on real talk and leading to the joy of intimacy with an idea. Geneticist Barbara McClintock has spoken of her intimate relationship with the objects of her study, of the need to 'hear what the material has to say' (Evelyn Fox Keller quoted in Turkle and Papert, 1990: 146).

> For McClintock, the practice of science was essentially a conversation with her materials. The more she worked with neurospora chromosomes (so small that others had been unable to identify them), "the bigger [they] got, and when I was really working with them I wasn't outside, I was down there. I was part of the system. I actually felt as if I were right down there

and these were my friends . . . .As you look at these things, they become part of you and you forget yourself".

(p. 146)

As with science, an inclusive epistemology of mathematics needs to acknowledge and respect such person-relatedness and the nurturing it implies of intuition and insight (Burton, 1995). Understanding the subjective meaning of mathematics for the meaning-making learners is of central significance in devising a mathematics curriculum which is inclusive.

> Maybe there are different approaches to mathematics, different ways to experience mathematics as meaningful, and different aspects of mathematics that make or do not make sense, and maybe mainly those ways are ignored and those aspects are unemphasised in the mathematics classroom that make females rather than males feel uncomfortable because of a lack of meaning. To turn away from mathematics in this view would be a decision of females who make fruitless efforts to create meaning out of what is going on. They would not be victims of gender-role expectations; they would like to live in worlds that make sense.
>
> (Jungwirth, 1993: 141–2)

Traditionally, mathematical knowledge is constructed as impersonal and external; it is presented as being stratified into hierarchies and also as appropriately 'delivered' through an educational system which is itself stratified. (Richard Noss (1990) has argued that the strengthening of such stratification was the main outcome intended by the imposition of the mathematics National Curriculum in the UK.) These two are linked: if students are encouraged not to rely on their own experience but to deny it and to accept in its place the knowledge and experience of experts, then the hierarchical structures are strengthened. In turn, existing patterns of inequality are strengthened (Spender, 1980a: 45). This stratification, the competitive hierarchies, the denial of personal knowledge, the lack of ownership, are all said to be antipathetic to the learning of women and girls (Rich, 1980; Spender and Sarah, 1989; Spender, 1989; Green 1992) and therefore need to be challenged in the construction of an inclusive curriculum.

In addition, however, other groups – for example, black and/or working class boys – whose perspectives are not part of the existing cultural hegemony are also not advantaged by a hierarchical and competitive epistemology which denies the validity of their own knowledge (Freire, 1972; Giroux, 1983; Gerdes, 1985). What is needed is an alternative epistemology which

> challenges all certified knowledge and opens up the question of whether what has been taken to be true can stand the test of alternative ways of validating truth.
>
> (Collins, 1990: 219)

138

If we are going to take social justice issues seriously, this will mean adopting classroom practices which are disruptive of some current constructions of masculinity, practices which some (young male) learners are going to find uncongenial (Willis, 1995: 192–5). These will include promoting a willingness to share ideas, making space for the ideas of others, supportive listening and less valorising of the individual and of individual success. It will also require working to uncover how the making of mathematics is bound up with the making of men and the making of women.

> Critical questions are what constitutes mathematics . . . what counts as valued knowledge, and how things came to be this way and how they are sustained. Such questions foreground relations between power and knowledge that exemplify the emancipatory position.
>
> (Johnston and Dunne, 1996: 61)

A curriculum which emphasises the historical and cultural roots of mathematics will support such questioning within, as well as of, the mathematics classroom. (Perl (1978), Alic (1986), Joseph (1991), Shan and Bailey (1991) and Nelson *et al.* (1993) all provide suitable starting points for such work.)

In short, we need a new epistemic strategy for mathematics which will discourage the production, damaging to the lives of both girls and boys, of those aspects of masculinity associated with domination whilst at the same time helping to realise the power of those who are not part of the hegemonic group – whether through, for example, gender, 'race', class or various combinations of these and other dominated sites. Such an epistemic strategy will not be based on any claims about ultimate truths,

> [nor] clothed in guarantees of any kind . . . [but] intimately related to the continuing struggles for social, political, and economic freedoms, and the freedom of individuals from the *authority* of one or a few parts of their selves and from external *authorities*.
>
> (Restivo, 1983: 141)

It will support us in the 'complicated and even messy enterprise' (Kenway *et al.*, 1994: 188) of working for gender equity in mathematics classrooms.

WHAT IS TO BE DONE?

I have argued elsewhere (Povey, 1996) that three key characteristics of a mathematics classroom predicated on such an epistemology will be that:

1   the learners make the mathematics;
2   mathematics involves thinking about problems;
3   difference and individuality are respected.

LIVERPOOL JOHN MOORES UNIVERSITY AVRIL ROBARTS LRC TEL. 0151 231 4022

In brief, the first implies the centrality of the students working together to produce as well as criticise meanings (Giroux, 1983), with the mathematics being co-constructed by a community of validators (Cobb et al., 1992: 594). The second reflects the understanding that a problem-centred curriculum involves the need to take risks, which is a precondition for imagining a different and more just world (Giroux, 1992: 78) and that posing and reposing problems helps uncover the linguistic assumptions hidden in their original formulation (Brown, 1986). Both of these suggest in turn the need to make room for students to move and breathe rather than to experience the current and increasing demands of performativity and patterns of surveillance. Finally, respect for difference and the individual presents a fundamental challenge to the 'feudal' (Tahta, 1994: 25) discourse of ability, a keystone of the current discourse of schooling in mathematics and under-pinning all its practices.

Attending to the surface phenomena of the curriculum will not, in itself, help us to promote social justice, although I have attempted above, wherever possible, to suggest pointers for good practice in this regard. Ensuring equal access to the secondary mathematics curriculum requires a fundamental shift in our thinking about how we come to know mathematics and what the strategies for embedding this new thinking in classroom practice might be (Povey et al., forthcoming). Without such a rethinking, mathematics, 'resonant of a powerful male, eurocentric culture which reifies its own perception of objectivity and reason, in an atmosphere promoting individualism and competition' (Burton, 1994), will continue to serve the interests of those who are currently dominant.

REFERENCES

Alic, M. (1986) *Hypatia's Heritage: a History of Women in Science from Antiquity to the Late Nineteenth Century*, London: The Women's Press.

Barnes, M. and Coupland, M. (1990) 'Humanising calculus: a case study in curriculum development', in L. Burton (ed.) *Gender and Mathematics: an International Perspective*, London: Cassell.

Belenky, M.F., Clinchy, B.M., Goldberger, N.R. and Tarule, J.M. (1986) *Women's Ways of Knowing: the Development of Self, Voice and Mind*, New York: Basic Books.

Bourdieu, P. (1977) *Outline of Theory and Practice*, Cambridge: Cambridge University Press.

Brown, S.I. (1986) 'The logic of problem generation: from morality and solving to de-posing and rebellion', in L. Burton (ed.) *Girls into Maths Can Go*, Eastbourne: Holt, Rinehart and Winston.

Burton, L. (1989) 'Images of mathematics', in P. Ernest (ed.) *Mathematics Teaching: the State of the Art*, London: Falmer.

—— (1994) 'Whose culture includes mathematics?', in S. Lerman (ed.) *Cultural Perspectives on the Mathematics Clasroom*, Dordrecht: Kluwer.

—— (1995) 'Moving towards a feminist epistemology of mathematics', in P. Rogers and G. Kaiser (eds) *Equity in Mathematics Education: Influences of Feminism and Culture*, London: Falmer.

Clarricoates, K. (1978) 'Dinosaurs in the classroom: the "hidden" curriculum in primary schools', in M. Arnot and G. Weiner (eds) *Gender and the Politics of Schooling*, London: Hutchinson.

Cobb, P., Wood, T., Yackel, E. and McNeal, B. (1992) 'Characteristics of classroom mathematics traditions: an interactional analysis', *American Educational Research Journal* 29: 573–604.

Collins, P.H. (1990) *Black Feminist Thought: Knowledge, Consciousness and the Politics of Empowerment*, London: Routledge.

Cornbleet, A. and Libovitch, S. (1983) 'Anti-sexist initiatives in a mixed comprehensive: a case study', in A. Wolpe and J. Donald (eds) *Is There Anyone Here from Education?*, London: Pluto Press.

Department for Education (1993) *Schools Update*, March, London: Department for Education.

Downes, S. (1994) 'Male order mathematics', *Mathematics Teaching* 148 (September): 20–1.

Draper, J. (1993) 'We're back with Gobbo: the re-establishment of gender relations following a school merger', in P. Woods and M. Hammersley (eds) *Gender and Ethnicity in Schools*, London: Routledge.

Ernest, P. (1991) *The Philosophy of Mathematics Education*, London: Falmer.

Fennema, E. (1990) 'Teachers' beliefs and gender differences in mathematics', in E. Fennema and G. Leder (eds) *Mathematics and Gender*, New York: Teachers' College Press.

Fennema, E. and Peterson, P. (1985) 'Explaining sex-related differences in mathematics: theoretical models', *Educational Studies in Mathematics* 14(3).

Freire, P. (1972) *The Pedagogy of the Oppressed*, Harmondsworth: Penguin.

Gerdes, P. (1985) 'Conditions and strategies for emancipatory mathematics education', *For the Learning of Mathematics* 5(1).

Gilligan, C. (1982) *In a Different Voice: Psychological Theory and Women's Development*, Cambridge, MA: Harvard University Press.

Giroux, H.A. (1983) *Theory and Resistance in Education: a Pedagogy for the Opposition*, London: Heinemann.

—— (1992) *Border Crossings*, London: Routledge.

Green, E. (1992) 'From empowering women to promoting girls: thoughts on feminist pedagogy from the women's studies classroom', in P. Boulton *et al.* (eds) *Ways and Meanings: Gender, Process and Teacher Education*, Sheffield: Pavic.

Hanna, G., Kundiger, E. and Larouche, C. (1990) 'Mathematical achievement of grade 12 girls in fifteen countries', in L. Burton (ed.) *Gender and Mathematics: an International Perspective*, London: Cassell.

Harris, M. (ed.) (1991) *Schools, Mathematics and Work*, Basingstoke: Falmer.

Herbert, C. (1989) *Talking of Silence: the Sexual Harassment of Schoolgirls*, Lewes: Falmer.

Isaacson, Z. (1988) 'The marginalisation of girls in mathematics: some causes and some remedies', in D. Pimm (ed.) *Mathematics, Teachers and Children*, London: Hodder & Stoughton.

—— (1989) ' "Of course you could be an engineer, dear, but wouldn't you rather be a nurse or teacher or secretary?" ', in P. Ernest (ed.) *Mathematics Teaching: the State of the Art*, Lewes: Falmer.

—— (1990) ' "They look at you in absolute horror": women writing and talking about mathematics', in L. Burton (ed.) *Gender and Mathematics: an International Perspective*, London: Cassell.

Johnston, J. and Dunne, M. (1996) 'Revealing assumptions: problematising research on gender and mathematics and science education', in L. Parker *et al.* (eds) *Gender, Science and Mathematics: Shortening the Shadow,* Dordrecht: Kluwer.

Joseph, G.G. (1991) *The Crest of the Peacock,* Harmondsworth: Penguin.

Jungwirth, H. (1993) 'Reflections on the foundations of research on women and mathematics', in S. Restivo *et al.* (eds) *Math Worlds: Philosophical and Social Studies of Mathematics and Mathematics Education,* Albany, NY: State University of New York.

Kelly, L. (1989) 'Our issues, our analysis: two decades of work on sexual violence', in C. Jones and P. Mahoney (eds) *Learning Our Lines: Sexuality and Social Control in Education,* London: The Women's Press.

Kenway, J., Willis, S., Blackmore, J. and Rennie, L. (1994) 'Making "hope practical" rather than "despair convincing": feminist post-structuralism, gender reform and educational change', *British Journal of Sociology of Education* 15(2): 187–210.

Kessler, S., Ashenden, D.J., Connell, R.W. and Dowsett, G.W. (1985) 'Gender relations in secondary schooling', *Sociology of Education* 58: 34–48.

Leder, G. (1986) 'Mathematics learning and socialisation processes', in L. Burton (ed.) *Girls into Maths Can Go,* Eastbourne: Holt, Rinehart and Winston.

—— (1990) 'Gender and classroom practice', in L. Burton (ed.) *Gender and Mathematics: an International Perspective,* London: Cassell.

Lees, S. (1987) 'The structure of sexual relations in school', in M. Arnot and G. Weiner (eds) *Gender and the Politics of Schooling,* London: Hutchinson.

Licht, B.G. and Dweck, C.S. (1983) 'Sex differences in achievement orientations', in M. Arnot and G. Weiner (eds) *Gender and the Politics of Schooling,* London: Hutchinson.

Lyell, K.M. (1881) *Life, Letters and Journals of Sir Charles Lyell, Bart,* Vol. 1, London.

Mac an Ghaill, M. (1994) *The Making of Men: Masculinities, Sexualities and Schooling,* Buckingham: Open University Press.

Mahoney, P. (1989) 'Sexual violence and mixed schools', in C. Jones and P. Mahoney (eds) *Learning Our Lines: Sexuality and Social Control in Education,* London: The Women's Press.

Marr, B. and Helme, S. (1990) 'Women and maths in Australia: a confidence-building experience for teachers and students', in L. Burton (ed.) *Gender and Mathematics: an International Perspective,* London: Cassell.

Martin, J.R. (1985) *Reclaiming a Conversation: the Ideal of the Educated Woman,* New Haven, CT: Yale University Press.

Morrow, C. and Morrow, J. (1995) 'Connecting women with mathematics', in P. Rogers and G. Kaiser (eds) *Equity in Mathematics Education: Influences of Feminism and Culture,* London: Falmer.

Nelson, D., Joseph, G.G. and Williams, J. (1993) *Multicultural Mathematics,* Oxford: Oxford University Press.

Northam, J.A. (1982) 'Girls and boys in primary maths books', in G. Weiner and M. Arnot (eds) *Gender under Scrutiny: New Inquiries in Education,* London: Hutchinson.

Noss, R. (1990) 'The National Curriculum and mathematics: a case of divide and rule?', in P. Dowling and R. Noss (eds) *Mathematics Versus the National Curriculum,* Basingstoke: Falmer.

Open University (1986) *Girls into Mathematics,* Cambridge: Cambridge University Press.

Patterson, E.C. (1983) *Mary Somerville and the Cultivation of Science, 1815–1840,* Boston: Nijhoff.

Perl, T. (1978) *Maths Equals: Biographies of Women Mathematicians,* Menlo Park, CA: Addison-Wesley.

Povey, H. (1996) 'Constructing a liberatory discourse for mathematics classrooms', *Mathematics Education Review*, (8): 41–54.

Povey, H., Burton, L., Angier, C. and Boylan, M. (forthcoming) 'Learners as authors in the mathematics classroom', in L. Burton (ed.) *Learning Mathematics, from Hierarchies to Networks*.

Pratt, J. (1985) 'The attitudes of teachers', in J. Whyte *et al.* (eds) *Girl Friendly Schooling*, London: Methuen.

Restivo, S. (1983) *Episteme 10: the Social Relations of Physics, Mysticism and Mathematics*, Dordrecht: Kluwer.

—— (1992) *Mathematics in Society and History: Episteme 20*, Dordrecht: Kluwer.

Rich, A. (1980) *Lies, Secrets and Silence*, London: Virago.

Rogers, P. (1995) 'Putting theory into practice', in P. Rogers and G. Kaiser (eds) *Equity in Mathematics Education: Influences of Feminism and Culture*, London: Falmer.

Rose, H. (1994) *Love, Power and Knowledge: Towards a Feminist Transformation of the Sciences*, Cambridge: Polity Press.

Rudduck, J. (1994) *Developing a Gender Policy in Secondary Schools*, Buckingham: Open University Press.

Scott-Hodgetts, R. (1986) 'Girls and mathematics: the negative implications of success', in L. Burton (ed.) *Girls into Maths Can Go*, Eastbourne: Holt, Rinehart and Winston.

Shan, S. and Bailey, P. (1991) *Multiple Factors: Classroom Mathematics for Equality and Justice*, Stoke-on-Trent: Trentham.

Shuard, H. (1986) 'The relative attainment of girls and boys in mathematics', in L. Burton (ed.) *Girls into Maths Can Go*. Eastbourne: Holt, Rinehart and Winston.

Skovsmose, O. (1994) *Towards a Philosophy of Critical Mathematics Education*, Dordrecht: Kluwer.

SMILE (no date) *Cabbage*, London: SMILE (written by Mary Harris and first published by her as part of Maths in Work).

Somerville, M. (1874) *Personal Recollections, from Early Life to Old Age*, London: John Murray.

Spender, D. (1980a) 'Educational institutions: where co-operation is called cheating', in D. Spender and E. Sarah (eds) (1989) *Learning to Lose: Sexism and Education*, London: The Women's Press (first published in 1980).

—— (1980b) 'Talking in class', in D. Spender and E. Sarah (eds) (1989) *Learning to Lose: Sexism and Education*, London: The Women's Press (first published in 1980).

—— (1989) *Invisible Women: the Schooling Scandal*. London: The Women's Press.

Spender, D. and Sarah, E. (eds) (1989) *Learning to Lose: Sexism and Education*, London: The Women's Press (first published in 1980).

Stanley, J. (1986) 'Sex and the quiet schoolgirl', in P. Woods and M. Hammersley (eds) *Gender and Ethnicity in Schools*, London: Routledge.

Tahta, D. (1994) 'Coming up to Russian expectations', *Mathematics Teaching* (146): March.

Turkle, S. and Papert, S. (1990) 'Epistemological pluralism: styles and voices within the computer culture', *Signs: Journal of Women in Culture and Society* 16(1): 128–57.

Verhage, H. (1990) 'Curriculum development and gender', in L. Burton (ed.) *Gender and Mathematics: an International Perspective*, London: Cassell.

Walden, R. and Walkerdine, V. (1985) *Girls and Mathematics: from Primary to Secondary Schooling*, Bedford Way Paper No. 24, London: University Institute of Education.

Walkerdine, V. (1985) 'On the regulation of speaking and silence: subjectivity, class and gender in contemporary schooling', in C. Steedman *et al.* (eds) *Language, Gender and Childhood*, London: Routledge.

—— (compiler) (1989) *Counting Girls Out*, London: Virago.

—— (1990) *Schoolgirl Fictions*, London: Verso.

—— (1994) 'Reasoning in a post-modern age', in P. Ernest (ed.) *Mathematics, Education and Philosophy: an International Perspective*, London: Falmer.

Walkerdine, V. and Lucey, H. (1989) *Democracy in the Kitchen: Regulating Mothers and Socialising Daughters*, London: Virago.

Willis, S. (1995) 'Gender reform through school mathematics', in P. Rogers and G. Kaiser (eds) *Equity in Mathematics Education: Influences of Feminism and Culture*, London: Falmer.

—— (1996) 'Gender justice and the mathematics curriculum: four perspectives', in L. Parker *et al.* (eds) *Gender, Science and Mathematics: Shortening the Shadow*, Dordrecht: Kluwer.

Wilson, M. (1991) 'Europe: an overview', in M. Wilson (ed.) *Girls and Young Women in Education: a European Perspective*, Oxford: Pergamon.

9

ACTION, EMBODIMENT AND GENDER IN THE DESIGN AND TECHNOLOGY CLASSROOM

Carolyn Dixon

INTRODUCTION

This chapter uses data from a research project conducted by the author during 1994–6 in Greenfield Comp., a state secondary school in the north of England (see Dixon, 1997b) to describe some of the ways that Year 9 students (13–14 years of age) engage with gender practices. An extensive literature on gender and resistance to schooling has acknowledged the commitments and interests at play in the gendered arena of the classroom. The starting point for this description is an attempt to reframe young people in school not only as 'learners' but as situated individuals with a life history of class, gender and ethnicity, and a psychology of desire and fear. In this view, they are, like us, accorded a wholeness and integrity that extends far beyond the coercive requirements of being a school 'pupil'.

While most of this chapter is concerned with detailed consideration of the classroom-based action of students, presented in 'episodes' (Quicke and Winter, 1994), the first section provides a brief theoretical overview of the research.

IDENTITY AND SCHOOLING

I have suggested that to start to understand student action from our own privileged position of (non-pupil) readers, we require to rethink student positioning within teacher texts; in effect, a suspension of the regulative ordering of young people in relation to official knowledge. In schools and other places, young people are working at the business of 'becoming somebody' (Wexler, 1992), and a distinct 'somebody' with commitments to a mediated gender order (Connell, 1987; Redman, 1996). The classroom is one (important) context in which the 'project of self' (Shilling, 1993) is undertaken, and a context in which inequalities of power are encoded in every aspect of official discourse, from knowledge and curriculum to

145

pedagogic practice. A range of accounts describe the functioning of broad categories of inequality of gender, class and race, and as Bates and Riseborough (1993) note:

> these are not disappearing but rather reappearing in new forms despite increasingly modernised structures of education and training. Contrary to the Majorite thesis, a classless society is not in the making.

In producing a 'new' account, it is not that such categories have lost their explanatory power, but rather that, in changing times, a complexity seemingly obscured by 'category' provides new insights into why 'the more things change, the more they stay the same' (Hill Collins, 1997). Both 'common sense' and critical readings of schooling suggest that, like us, students act in different ways in different places in school. Engaging with these meaningful differences is critical to understanding student commitments to particular patterns of oppressive or exclusive gendered behaviour:

> actors draw upon rules and resources in specific spatial contexts which are themselves ordered in ways which affect the production and reproduction of central features of our society such as gender and social class inequalities.
>
> (Shilling, 1991: 24)

Each of the student narratives told here takes place not only in a spatial and temporally located social and school history of curriculum and culture, but also within a number of individual life stories, each with its own trajectory. Throughout the daily exchanges of the classroom, and beyond, students and teachers construct particular meanings of gender, schooling and class. I hope to show that by putting to one side educational concerns about learning the official curriculum and by refocusing on the way students 'become somebody', our understanding of students, of gender, class and ethnic commitments (and, incidentally, of learning) is enriched.

THE BODY AND (CLASSROOM) SPACE

In this refocusing, I wish to maintain the centrality of the body in identity work. The corporeal or somatic is increasingly identified as a key site of social mediation (Morgan, 1993) and potential cultural transgression (Tate, 1997), yet is frequently overlooked in adult/teacher accounts of schooling.

> From the moment a child is born her or his body is defined, dichotomised, sexualised, rewarded, punished and socialised by others. The body can never be outside the symbolic order. At the same time, the symbolic order can never be disembodied.
>
> (Brittan, 1989: 73)

146

Just as 'all social interaction takes place in space, and it is impossible to conceive of social life outside spatial contexts' (Shilling, 1991) so all social life takes place between bodies, whether as present physical entities, or corporeally displaced by space or time. Interaction requires embodied subjects, and it is through the body that the 'self', whether conceived as unitary or multiple, comes to be 'in' the social world (Diprose, 1994). Our 'common sense' understandings of manner and social protocol tell us that places (space) are constructed by people (embodied subjects) through presence or absence, present, past, or in an anticipated future; that is, inhabited space and embodied subjectivities are mutually constitutive (it is in this sense that the term 'site' is used here). When it comes to schools, and school classrooms, such a relation is often refuted. In these places, student (and to some degree teacher) embodied subjects are dichotomised, as an educational ethic of high rationalism, 'the elevation of the mind', comes to regulate and control an ascribed 'natural' or animalistic body (Turner, 1996), with little regard to spatial context. Yet all learning requires somatic work, whether visual, aural, oral or the muscular work required in design and technology to shape and smooth materials. The body mediates an engagement with the social world. Under these circumstances, the disembodied, rational learner, a historically privileged form in modern western societies, is not an option, for rationalism is just one more way of 'dealing with' the body involving:

> the secularisation of culture, the erosion of superstition, the decline of magic, the intellectualisation of everyday life through the control and imposition of scientific reasoning, the calculation and regulation of bodies in the political interests of greater control and more efficiency, and the control of everyday life through the development of micro-bureaucratic techniques and practices.
>
> (Turner, 1996: 12)

The separation of 'mind' and 'body' in the educational project lies in the enlightenment origins of mass education, and the dominance of educational discourses of developmental psychology (see Walkerdine, 1989) and was still present in the way many teachers at Greenfield talked about students and teaching. As Diprose notes:

> In focusing on moral principles and moral judgement the assumption is that individuals are present as self-transparent, isolated, rational minds, and that embodied differences between individuals are inconsequential.
>
> (Diprose 1994: 18)

In practice, the classroom interactions of both male and female students at Greenfield was bound up with bodily difference, with body size, style, control and presentation. Within official discourses of schooling (and within most lessons observed), bodies, in so far as they are acknowledged as present, are considered disruptive. They required constant surveillance, regulation and control ('sit in your place, don't wander, stop tapping'), for it is the (student) body that expresses most readily and easily those things that have come to be read as resistance to school: boredom, disinterest, physical tiredness and hostility.

ACTIVELY MAKING THE CLASSROOM

This chapter also represents an attempt to understand classroom processes, for in 'changing times', the individual classroom may be a key site for work around social injustice for many teachers (in contrast, for example, to a past decade of school- and union-based working parties and large-scale pedagogic innovation). A view-point that is concerned with the micro-processes of classroom gender practice locates the teacher as a key agent in regulating and reproducing (or contesting and transforming) the gender order of the classroom. In this reading, in contrast with a reductionist account of social reproduction, teachers can 'make a difference'.

In constructing the classroom as a specific temporal and spatial site for the embodied work of identity, bodies and the spaces they occupy become centred. Morgan (1993), writing about male social practice, notes the way certain social spaces allow, and give rise to, particular forms of men's action. Such spaces would include publicly legitimate sites, such as the battlefield and the sports arena, and other 'informal' sites such as the street, where male embodiment is associated with particular practices. These 'sites of bodily power' (Morgan, 1993: 76) are numer-ous. Indeed, the presence of male action itself is constitutive of such a site, although some spaces may permit a greater sense of acting with the body, or embodiment, than others. Sites are contested and contradictory, and the design and technology workshop, like other spaces in school, is such a site. 'Sites of bodily power', whether constructed through repeated use, through shared cultural narratives, or through the resonance of mythic constructions of spatially located action (Measor and Woods, 1984), as in 'gang' territories, do not determine gendered action. The ways students engage with particular discourses of gender and sex-uality vary, mediated not only by the congruence of other social narratives, but also by personal projects of embodied fear and desire. The episodes included here do not represent or characterise, but rather illustrate the complexity of differentiated ways of 'dealing with' the body. From this flows the imperative for this type of analysis, for different ways of 'dealing with the body' may have implications for future forms of embodiment. In an institutional world structured by long tradi-tions of social inequality, different strategies and commitments have implications both for a student disruption of the gender order in Greenfield classrooms, and for the sorts of futures young people in this study may build.

The episodes considered here were all 'transcribed' from video footage of students in design and technology (D&T) lessons at Greenfield, supplemented with student and teacher interviews, classroom observation and student analysis of the video record.

While the D&T department at Greenfield cannot be characterised by a strong commitment to curriculum innovation, neither is it very traditional. There are no 'woodwork' and 'metalwork' teachers here, and all the teachers describe themselves rather in pedagogic terms, as facilitative or 'child-centred'. However, it remains a site of conflict as different teacher values compete for dominance (Dixon, 1997b).

From its inception in April 1988, National Curriculum technology has undergone continual transformation, as the tensions between a range of interest groups were, and still are, played out in the construction of a curriculum subject (Layton, 1995; Medway, 1992). By the time the research period started, in September 1994, a 'final version' was working its way through into schools. The absence of Statutory Attainment Testing at Key Stage 3 allows teachers to focus on Key Stage 4 and GCSE, as the point at which their interpretations of the Standing Orders are tested in practice. Consequently, at Greenfield, it is still largely the examination syllabus which drives curriculum construction. Changes in the Standing Orders (summarised in Layton, 1995) have had little impact, except to allow the restitution of prior practices. As Layton notes, these changes took place in the context of an ongoing workload dispute, a perceived 'overload' in curriculum change (Layton, 1995: 111) and, for many teachers, increased insecurity about their posts, either within the reconstructed technology curriculum (Paetcher, 1993; Paetcher and Head, 1996), or more generally within the context of the shrinking education budgets of local authorities. All except one of the teachers involved in the study argued that National Curriculum requirements were pushing them (reluctantly) back towards the reproduction of a traditional craft/technical curriculum.

Johnny: domination and the controlled body

Johnny is a white, male student highly regarded by his peers and rarely 'in trouble' with teachers. Through bodily style and the development of a personal narrative of indifference to the localised and general requirements of the school, he works at the business of 'being cool'. Johnny, like many other male students at Greenfield, is 'one of the lads'.

Episode

Ivan and Johnny are at a workbench, Ivan seated, Johnny leaning forward, his weight supported on one arm. They are talking. Johnny points at Ivan, then as Ivan raises his hand, grabs his wrist with one hand, without shifting his weight off his other arm. He holds Ivan's wrist as Ivan tries to free it by twisting/raising his arm, and holds his arm at an uncomfortable angle as he talks to Ivan. There is little sign of any aggressive intent in his face (they are talking about going out that evening). Johnny's face is close to Ivan's and he sustains eye contact as Ivan continues to try and release his arm without rising from his seat or using his other hand.

Johnny shifts his focus from Ivan, and releases his hand, and it is as if the incident had not happened.

Johnny and Ivan's friendship appears marked, in the classroom, by such encounters, in which Johnny produces displays of overt domination which Ivan does not seriously resist (see Dixon, 1996). With the power of initiation and closure, Johnny controls such episodes, moving fluently from crudely aggressive postures to friendly exchange, in a refined performance of 'self-control': control of his temper, physical strength and 'potential' to dominate through pain. Such exchanges repeatedly position Ivan as the dominated and passive object of Johnny's more active masculinity.

Particular male social practices (or masculinities) invoke particular forms of embodiment, and such 'warfare' and fighting classroom interactions offer the possibility of public validation of a dominant form of masculinity: being 'hard' but being 'in control' (Canaan, 1991). Through these repeated combative moments of domination, Johnny, and others like him, are able to construct a personal narrative of identity in which the body is required to perform a continual display of emotional distance and the rejection of intimacy. In this task, all the physical and cultural resources of the workshop are drawn upon and transformed, as guns and knives are improvised out of tools and materials in momentary or extended sword fights, machine gunning and grenade throwing. While, at Greenfield, these passing exchanges appeared to be the territory of 'all boys', and for Johnny and others came to signify a personal project of embodied, exaggerated, 'hyper-masculinity', other male students may have a different investment in the gender order, and so be engaged in a different construction of the male body.

Philip and Daniel; rational selves, untrusted bodies

Philip and Daniel are committed to academic success although they, like other boys, 'mess about' in lessons ('let your hair down, have a bit of fun'). They were keen to point out the parameters of this: disturbing a good relationship with the teacher, annoying or hurting others, and not achieving, were all reasons for them to stop behaving disruptively. Refusing the strong football culture of the school, they cannot fail to recognise their distance from 'the lads', and their 'outsider' status as they report being frequently hit, kicked, or spat upon as they move around the school. Not only are such boys positioned by others as weak and cowardly, they are also considered naïve, foolish, they lack 'nowse' (common sense), although they are considered 'clever' academically.

(Goody goodies) . . . they can't do anything. They can't play football. They concentrate on the rubbish lessons. In PE, they can't kick a ball or 'owt . . . they get in 'way, en you're afraid to tackle them in case you hurt them . . . (in a whining voice) . . . 'Sir . . . he's hit me!'

Boys who don't play any football are boring . . . . Them that don't do any
sport like . . . say . . . 'I can't do it – it hurts my back' and all that, well half
of them haven't ever done it. They won't try it.

These 'others', the 'clever swots' who 'can't kick a ball' are constructed by 'the
lads' in a comic strip parody of 'the wimp', effete, cowardly, unwilling to try things
out, weak and fragile. The refusal of a particular masculine embodiment threatens
the legitimacy of the dominating body as a naturally derived, and thus incontest-
able, form. Both Philip and Daniel assert, in limited ways, their identity as 'boy',
and through this assertion of *gender*, a social identity, they create the fictional
possibility of being 'a lad'. Their 'non-lad' position becomes, then, a matter of
choice; they could be as others, but reject it, although they simultaneously recognise the 'low peer status' that rejection brings.

In such a rejection, not through a supposed physical deficit but through the
elevation of an alternative, rationalistic male practice, Philip and Daniel 'call up'
violent exclusion and domination. Surprisingly perhaps, they are not labelled
'queer', a term in regular and indiscriminate use at Greenfield, and largely meaning
'stupid'. They are beyond this laddish banter. They are 'just fuckin' girls'.

I think some people think less of us . . . . Oh yes, because we don't play
football that much'

It's not so much the pressures of school, homework, it's the pressures of
other kids. I mean, they'll come up to you, they'll smack you in the face.
they'll kick you . . . for no reason – just stupid!

walking past them in the corridor, and they'll wind you in the stomach,
then trip you over, kick you in the thigh and legs to give you 'dead legs' or
whatever.

Their gender constantly disputed, they claim an identity as 'sensible pupils' with an
'adult' understanding of the school (the 'lads' are described as 'kids'). Although
this identity has little peer legitimacy in school, and brings with it further consequences, it is not contested as *their identity*. It is however, an identity constantly
under attack. In the face of these direct assaults from their peers, Philip and Daniel
have developed strategies that create 'safe spaces' in which the work of self can be
nourished.

PHILIP: We have a group of friends who we hang out with.
DANIEL: I mean, we go to the library, we do us homework, we help our friends,
each other . . . . They're who we can talk to.
PHILIP: You can let your guard down. With other kids, I think you've got to keep
your guard up, but with your friends, and in a nice atmosphere, you can let
your guard down.

151

Fortunately in D&T lessons Philip and Daniel were with their friends and felt in a 'nice atmosphere'. Here, they agreed, they could 'be ourselves', and undertake the 'unguarded' work of self.

While still operating with notions of naturalism, unlike Johnny, for whom the body is a source of power and public affirmation of self, Philip and Daniel construct their masculine bodies as deficit in relation both to girls and to the rationalism of the school.

PHILIP: I think the girls are a bit neater, most of the time, than boys. Like, they'll . . . once they've finished with the drill, or a handsaw, they'll put it away, where we'll leave it on the desk 'til somebody else uses it' . . . . We're like – Oh, we've got to rush this, rush through this, get the idea and make the box.

While affirming their gender location as male, this and other comments were offered as critique rather than plaudit, a recognition of the gendered nature of their own perceived failure. Their self-knowledge does not, in this context, create the possibility of self-transformation. In fact, in this area, Philip and Daniel achieve lower grades than many of 'the lads', for despite a curriculum rhetoric of analytic process (Medway, 1992), rushing, making and completing are rewarded. In the classroom, and to their peers, these students appear to fail, for despite extensive evidence of engagement with the design process (these students submitted A4 ring-binders of research and analysis, unlike Johnny's single crumpled sheet), both students are left with unassembled bits and pieces of ambitious designs. Philip and Daniel are 'trapped' by their acceptance of the official curriculum discourse, they want to 'design' better, yet the classroom, and available forms of masculinity, do not allow them to do this.

Computers also offer the possibility for participating in and validating male social practice. They can be seen to denote technicity and a form of masculinity located in workplace hierarchies, the 'modern hero' of late capitalist management systems (Morgan, 1992: 89). Few of the boys I spoke to had computers at home, although some had 'games stations', and while boys clearly dominated the equipment in school, few had any specific knowledge or interest. Johnny and others spent much time trying to corrupt the hard drives on the machines, reconfiguring, or simply copying 'tricks' that allowed their name, or some succinct epithet, to be repeated on a rolling screen. In contrast, Daniel and Philip work on computers at home, in lessons and in lunch breaks, producing a school newspaper and word-processing assignments. Engaging with 'new technologies' sustains a self-construction as 'ordinary boys', while also recognising and legitimating the distance between their masculine identity and that of 'the lads'. Through their use of computers, their positioning of 'the lads' and their acceptance of the school's values of 'achievement', they engage with a discourse of class mobility which elevates command over others, through the medium of technological command.

The development of new technology, especially at its more sophisticated levels, may provide opportunities for the demonstration of other features of masculinity, this time to do with the manipulation of things, and perhaps, indirectly, people.

(Morgan, 1992: 96)

However, most of what Philip and Daniel spoke of was not an assertion of their masculinity, but a story of protecting the self. That is, a 'protecting' from the aggression, physical violence and exclusion of 'the lads' (and some girls), and 'protection', through 'friendship' with teachers, from the alienating processes of schooling, which, it has been argued, in some senses, produce 'the lads' (Willis, 1977; Connell, 1989; Mac an Ghaill, 1994). That the alternative, white, masculine identity sought for by these two boys is not viable at Greenfield is noted by Philip himself, as he explains that they have 'only two more years to go':

PHILIP: You hear of 13 and 14 year olds committing suicide, and I can perfectly understand that. It isn't right. It shouldn't ever happen, but I can perfectly understand it. . . . It's not so much the pressures of school, homework, it's the pressure of other kids.

LIFE AT THE MARGINS; GIRLS SURVIVING 'D&T'

As Campbell (1993: 211) notes, the way men and women deal with difficulty in their life differs dramatically. For many girls at Greenfield, D&T was not a 'site of bodily power', but rather a site of marginalisation and physical domination. In the technology workshop, girls sat at the edges of the room in areas away from machinery and equipment and, unlike 'the lads', they were easily moved when their place was needed by others. In those rooms with both workbenches (with vices) and tables, they sat almost exclusively at the tables. Similarly, equipment, and especially the machine tools, were used predominantly by boys. In general, girls would stand quietly and wait for the boys to finish, or walk away. While boys' activity could be characterised in relation to both masculinity and resistance to schooling, girls did not comply, but neither did they directly challenge it. Rather, they found a range of ways around it, strategically contesting aspects of male practice while negotiating the demands of femininities. These 'coping' strategies are themselves an investment in particular gender orders, and have implications for the types of future narratives of self that girls construct.

Marginality and exclusion from equal participation in workshop activity is sustained not only by the practices of male students, but also by teacher interactions, which confirm the appropriateness of female deference. Just as combative interactions run throughout an analysis of male classroom interaction at Greenfield, girls' interactions with others are characterised by brief and ongoing moments of 'willing' and imposed deferral.

Girls have been traditionally taught that fulfilling other people's needs is more important than rewarding their own desires. They have been encouraged to deny and suppress their own inner needs and, as a consequence, have not been able to develop an authentic sense of entitlement for their desires. Hence they will not be able to experience themselves as people with entitled wants, feelings and needs.

(Weeda Mannak, 1994: 17)

Narette

Narette is one of two black female students in Mr Hepworth's group. Born in The Gambia, she spent her early years in Tobago, and has lived in the UK since the age of 6, passing through school with the same students she is with now. She is a competent and imaginative design student who attempts ambitious and distinct designs.

Episode

Students are required to 'design and make a container (from wood)' for their own use, and Mr Hepworth, the teacher, is working with Sarah, but surrounded and watched by five other girls. This is the group with whom Narette often works. She waits quietly, occasionally leaning forward and pushing her work into view, but fails to attract his attention. As he leaves the group, she and Alli (another girl) call 'Sir', and Alli follows him as he moves away. She talks to his back as if he were attending to her, and when he fails to respond, repeats her question in a louder, more insistent tone. It 'works', because he turns and answers her, and she moves away. Other girls in the group then start calling 'Sir', until he tells them not to shout at him. He returns to assist Sarah again.

Donny approaches the group, and moves beside Narette, talking to her. He leans and takes her work from the table, talking about it in a high pitched squeaky voice. 'Oh, what's this . . . mmm . . . very interesting. . . . I made this.' Annoyed, Narette takes it from him, stepping back, and quickly Donny slips into her place, leaning forward, and shouting his own question. Mr Hepworth stops work, and answers him, then stands up. Narette holds her work out in front of her at arm's length, with an audible 'Sir, can you have a look at mine?' He returns to work on Sarah's box, and she lowers her arms, turns and, having waited in total over eight minutes, moves away.

A position is being created here, both by Mr Hepworth's gendered response which privileges Donny's needs, and by Donny's intervention, in which the needs of girls are subordinate to those of boys. The 'gender-appropriate' responses of the girls, their reluctance to vocalise as loudly as Donny and their willingness to wait allow this positioning to exist, but do not necessarily assure their compliance. In talking about this episode after watching it on video, the girls involved discussed a range of strategies used by girls and boys to gain teacher help. Their comments show that, once again, discursive positions (in this instance, that of deferred need as a dimension of femininity) are sometimes accepted yet 'internally resisted', 'accommodated' to achieve other ends, and sometimes publicly contested (Anyon, 1983). Narette expresses her dissatisfaction with the teacher, employing ideas about 'fairness' but stopping short of articulating them, while Nichola and Lorraine went on to discuss their own strategies for gaining attention.

NARETTE: I was so bored . . . just waiting for Sir. I was bored . . . and Sir . . . isn't very. . . 'cus I'd been waiting round for him ages, then other people. . . . And Alli is still following him, but she had the sand-papering to do.

NICHOLA: That's what I used to do like. I used to carry around my box, sanding it still, even if it were really smooth, so I had summit to do, to be getting on with my work . . . so I'd be able to get Sir, like 'Sir! Look! I've done it.'

CD: Would you take turns? Say he helped you Lorraine, would you say 'Nichola's before me?'

LORRAINE: No. Usually I go stick it in his face.

CD: Are there ways of asking him?

LORRAINE: I just go 'Sir! Can I do . . . ? or 'Have I done this?' . . . whatever. . .

NICHOLA: Keep on at him, then he goes 'Stop curling your lip'.

LORRAINE: Yeah . . . Don't give in.

They were also able to anticipate Donny's strategy of distracting Narette by being 'stupid . . . silly voice and that . . . snidey' in order to take her place, but pointed to the difficulties faced by the teacher. While Nichola believed that Mr Hepworth should, and would, tell him off and 'make him go to back – proper place', Lorraine explained:

Yeah, but if he said to him 'Do you mind?', he'd put a silly voice on and get summit else . . . like 'No, I don't mind . . . this is my baby-sitter for tomorrow night' or summit, and still . . .

The episode provides an instance of both how positions available to girls are constructed by others (Mr Hepworth and Donny) and how they are differently taken up, transformed or rejected. This is not about a decontextualised moment in which, for decentred subjects, 'anything is possible', for in taking up (compliance), transforming (accommodation) or rejecting (resistance), the girls here bring the full force of their life narrative to bear. Narette does not ultimately reject deference, despite her strong sense of injustice.

I'm not bothered really, 'cus sometimes I feel I want like I want some help, when he wants to help me, but . . . I'll go away . . . wait.

155

'Help' is not an entitlement here, but dependent on an arbitrary feeling of goodwill of the teacher ('wanting to help'). In her words, even her *feeling* of need is reliant on another (the teacher) initiating by wanting to help her. Her need is transformed into the fulfilment of another's needs. Narette cannot do what Nichola or Lorraine do, she is not as them, just as they are not as each other, but an individual with another life story.

> Part of the tenacity of gender is its personal individuality: to understand and address fully any individual's gender identity requires investigation of a unique confluence of personal and cultural meaning.
>
> (Chodorow, 1995: 524)

For Lorraine, the deferral of need through waiting and losing turns has its rewards in the space it creates for other action.

> He's a nice teacher. Any other Design teacher'd not let us talk. He lets us walk around. Not like a lesson where you've got to be sat on your chair all the time. I like what we're doing now – painting and drawing, 'cus we can talk at the same time, especially when we're painting. I like talking.

Although deferral means losing out in terms of assistance, it means more time for talking, more privacy, less 'teacher scrutiny' and so can be tactically accommodated so long as it does not interfere with Lorraine's own classwork aims. As she has shown, she feels she has sufficient strategies ('I go and stick it in his face') for gaining help when necessary.

Nichola has a more explicit agenda of resistance. While she also employs a range of accommodative practices to make life in the classroom more personally satisfying, she is also engaged more strongly with issues of justice. She is generally critical of the lack of a visibly fair system:

> Sometimes, it's really . . . 'cus everybody else needs his help as well as you, but you'll be waiting there sometimes, someone'll come and jump in front of you.

Later, she makes the same point, but 'for' Narette, and then offers her support:

> I don't like people pushing in, especially if someone's there first. If you were there . . . I'd have given him a punch back.

Throughout, she was highly critical of Donny, and keen to show how Narette persisted in trying to get the teacher's attention, and ultimately she offers the possibility of physical resistance as a way of challenging not only 'unfairness', but the specific unfairness of this positioning in relation to Narette. In a class with only three Afro-Caribbean pupils, Narette's ethnicity cannot be disregarded.

Nichola recognises the specificity of Narette's life narrative, and that certain actions are not available to her; she offers to act in her place.

Nichola and Sarah: dealing with harassment

[resistance] . . . is often a defensive action [no matter how creative] that is aimed not at transforming patriarchal or other social structures, but at gaining a measure of protection within these.

(Anyon, 1983)

Nichola is 'a laff'. She is tall, very conscious of her appearance, and rightly proud of her sense of humour. She 'hangs around' in lessons with a group of five girls and the one black male student in the class, Leroy, and as a group they are often told off for laughing and talking too much. The teacher, Mr Hepworth, talked of her 'innocent little smiles' when he told her off, implying her conscious use of an 'exaggerated femininity' (Skeggs, 1991). She enjoys technology, and considers herself good at it.

> I chat a lot. I walk around, but I always get on with the work and in the end it always comes out as a good result.

She has varied work aspirations: a combat soldier, until 'lads all said "It's not a woman's job like" and that'. When she was younger, she was going to become a model, an aspiration she now considers stupid. At the moment, she is thinking about being a PE teacher. She used to 'hang around' with two white boys, Peter and Donny, but does not any more because Leroy, now her closest friend, dislikes them.

Episode

The project is to 'design a telephone', and Nichola has produced a design with which she is very pleased. Moving around the class to canvas opinion on its merits, she approaches Peter and Donny to ask Peter. He is slow to respond and then answers. Nichola is about to move around him to the next bench when he stretches out his arms as if to hug her. She moves away but is against the chalkboard, and so cannot avoid him. He reaches and grabs her wrist, pulling her down over his shoulder to the desk. She leans forward on her elbow, where he has pulled her and asks Donny what he thinks but as she does this Peter puts his arm around her waist. She looks sharply and simultaneously he removes his hand and rises from his seat. Nichola reaches over to pinch his backside, but he flaps his hands and pulls his sweatshirt down to cover himself while 'backing off'. She turns away and holds up the design for Ruby and

Lorraine to see, leaving Pete standing watching her. He slowly returns to his seat.

Peter, unlike Johnny, frequently interacts with girls in lessons and is active in 'trying out' the physical domination of girls. He often touches girls, and especially the group of which Nichola is a member as they can 'take a laff'.

PETER: We're only messing about . . . they know we're only joking really. . . . I'm always messing with Sarah.

Sarah talked about Peter, and about how she felt.

SARAH: It gets on my nerves . . . . It didn't at first, but when he carries on wi' it. . . . I was getting on with my work (*laughs*), and if you take no notice of him, he doesn't do it again. . . . They just want you to retaliate.

Often, the girls in this group do as Sarah does – they 'ignore' it – but in this instance, Nichola acts differently. Peter's 'offer' of an embrace, seated and looking up, calls upon a discourse of 'mothering' which Nichola sometimes adopts, hugging and holding Peter close, actions which are sexually ambiguous (see Dixon, 1997a). However, on this occasion Nichola refuses to comply, and so Peter resorts to a more direct attempt at the imposition of his desire. Perhaps feeling confident because Nichola seems at first to 'ignore it', he tries to extend his physical domination, holding her waist, but instantly realising the failure of that action as Nichola rises and retaliates. In a symbolic reversal of objectification, she tries to pinch his bottom. Peter has either to accept this reversal or to take a defensive stance. He is compelled by events to recognise Nichola's greater height, reach and strength. He is positioned, for a moment, as an unwilling object, in a reversal of embodied power relations of domination. That Nichola is able to close this episode, by turning and walking away, reinforces this momentary reversal, while ensuring that it remains 'amicable'. Both she and Peter can assimilate or reject this moment in the story they tell of their lives. For Nichola, it is a taste of what it is to be an agent, one whose body offers sensations associated with the exercise of power. For Peter, it offers a momentary loss of male power. Nichola's brief creative disruption of the gender order (as it is mediated by their two bodies in daily practices) creates the possibility for Peter to examine those sensations of 'lost power', and so consider his gender practices. For Nichola, the feeling of these momentary reversals and disruptions, the way they affirm the sensation of 'being someone', can be carried forward in further encounters with Peter and Donny. Further, unlike Sarah's response, Nichola's resistance is a public display. She is seen to have 'won'. Peter is seen to be defensive, wrong footed, unable to exercise the masculine identity he seeks.

Sarah's response of 'ignoring it', it could be argued, deepens the alienation of 'body' and 'self'. In the extreme of this separation, the body becomes distant, an object to be violated, because subjectivity, 'self', resides elsewhere; it is not touched. It is constructed as inside, quiet, able to separate and 'cut off' in the absence of a body which can act for it in the world. As the work of girls and women who self-harm (i.e. purposefully injure themselves, e.g. by incision or burning) reminds us, that separation must be worked at, enforced through the rigorous control and denial of corporeality. Cutting or burning the body is a manifestation of the need to preserve that separation and so resolve the violence done to the body by others: 'If you take no notice of him, he doesn't do it again'. Of course, Peter, and others, do it again and again, because with it they achieve a sensation of embodied power; they achieve 'manhood'. 'Taking no notice' becomes a way of coping with routine violation of the body, but a way that constructs the self as a silent observer of the act. There is no silent promise of future action, only the promise of further denial.

Nichola's response affirms the idea of an autonomous self as one able to act upon the world, and act with the body (Davies, 1990). She is able to use the 'only messing around' context of these interactions to dominate Peter physically, and later, by tickling him, something he dislikes, calls up his 'child/non-adult' position-ing of earlier exchanges. So Nichola is able to introduce the position offered as a position of subjugation earlier, 'mother', and transform it into a position of not only psychological, but public and physical domination. In these small, local and specific disruptions of the gender order, and the creation of moments of challenge, girls like Nichola 'survive' the positioning of dominant discourses of femininity, and maintain a sense of self as agent. The pressures within the classroom are substantial. As Alison Jones points out, in a situation in which you are always marginal, the choice is not between 'being liberated' and 'being oppressed'.

> Rather it is a choice between being 'Okay' and 'normal' or being 'weird', between being on the margins, or in the centres – albeit the marginalised centres reserved for women.
>
> (Jones, 1993)

However, it appears that very few girls are able to survive Greenfield with a more sustained rejection of dominant femininities, without becoming 'weird' or socially ostracised.

CONCLUSION

Different gendered forms of embodiment 'both affect and in turn are affected by the contexts in which they occur' (Shilling, 1991), but as the work of Johnny, Philip, Daniel, Narette, Sarah and Nichola shows, there is no predetermined or uniform pattern to the ways individuals build these contextually available practices into a sustained narrative of the 'somebody' they are and can become. In and out of school, young people engage with a diverse range of gender practices, but within school, and within the particular context of the D&T workshop at Greenfield, these practices do not always provide viable survival strategies. For Philip and Daniel, and for Sarah and Narette, these practices violate the autonomy of the self. 'Buying into' the dichotomy of mind/body, through continued practice, has differing implications for these students that relate to their positioning in broader power relations. For Philip and Daniel, this period of violent abuse is made bearable by the promise of future (masculine) technocratic status. For Narette and Sarah, disembodiment offers a momentary refusal of violation, but without a promise of future power, and only the promise of 'more to come'. For Nichola and Johnny the body provides its own rewards, in the 'buzz' or 'frisson' of acting powerfully with the body, acting as an 'agent' in, and maker of, the social world (Davies, 1990); yet for them also, such corporeal power sits respectively in differing trajectories of resistance and domination.

I have quoted Bates and Riseborough, writing in the context of youth and inequality in the UK, and Hill Collins talking about the situation of African–American women in the USA, to make the point that, for many educators, the past two decades seem to have been about surface change and structural stagnation. While things may 'look better', many educators are aware that, for 'most kids', the future looks much the same (or worse) than it did in the 1970s. Yet in some ways, pessimism about the possibility of social justice is unjustified, for as we can see, it is not that 'nothing is happening'. 'Gender', 'class' and 'race' are being constantly transformed through the contradictory and creative work of these students. The central task of a pedagogy committed to addressing issues of social injustice and power is to intersect these transformations, recognising the differently embodied work of students. Through an active, public deconstruction of the teacher and student body, teachers can produce the possibility of a different classroom, a place in which Narette is seen and heard, Philip and Daniel don't feel they have to 'keep their guard up', Sarah and Nichola have the possibility of directly challenging sexual harassment and still being 'a laugh', and Peter and Johnny and 'the lads' have the opportunity to examine critically the 'somebodies' they are becoming. The imposition of a National Curriculum may not have aided this work, but neither has it closed the door on it, for the continued presence of students in schools ensures that classrooms remain a place of hugely creative conflict over social power.

REFERENCES

Anyon, J. (1983) 'Intersections of gender and class', in S. Walker and L. Barton (eds) *Gender, Class and Education*, Farnborough: Falmer.

Bates, I. and Riseborough, G. (eds) (1993) *Youth and Inequality*, Buckingham: Open University Press.

Brittan, A. (1989) *Masculinity and Power*, Oxford: Blackwell.

Campbell, B. (1993) *Goliath: Britain's Dangerous Places*, London: Methuen.

Canaan, J.E. (1991) 'Is doing nothing just boys' play?' in S. Franklin *et al.* (eds) *Off-Centre: Feminism and Cultural Studies*, London: HarperCollins.

Chodorow, N.J. (1995) 'Gender as a personal and cultural construction', *SIGNS* 20(3): 516–44.

Connell, R.W. (1987) *Gender and Power*, Cambridge: Polity Press.

—— (1989) 'Cool guys, swots and wimps: the interplay of masculinity and education', *Oxford Review of Education* 15(3): 291–303.

Davies, B. (1990) 'Agency as a form of discursive practice: a classroom scene observed', *British Journal of Sociology of Education* 11(3): 341–61.

Diprose, R. (1994) *The Bodies of Women: Ethics, Embodiment and Sexual Difference*, London: Routledge.

Dixon, C. (1996) 'Having a laugh, having a fight: masculinity and the conflicting needs of self in Design and Technology', *International Studies in Sociology of Education* 6(2): 147–66.

—— (1997a) 'Pete's tool: identity and sex-play in the design and technology classroom', *Gender and Education* 9(1): 89–104.

—— (1997b) 'Being, becoming and belonging: gendered identity work in the Design and Technology classroom'. Ph.D. thesis, University of Sheffield.

Hill Collins, P. (1997) 'The more things change, the more they stay the same: African-American women and the new politics of containment', Address to Annual Conference, British Sociological Association, York, England.

Jones, A. (1993) 'Becoming a "girl": post-structuralist suggestions for educational research', *Gender and Education* 5(2): 19–31.

Layton, D. (1995) 'Constructing and reconstructing school technology in England and Wales', *International Journal of Technology and Design Education* 5(2): 89–118.

Mac an Ghaill, M. (1994) *The Making of Men. Masculinities, Sexualities and Schooling*, Buckingham: Open University Press.

Measor, L. and Woods, P. (1984) *Changing Schools*, Milton Keynes: Open University Press.

Medway, P. (1992) 'Constructions of technology: reflections on a new subject', in J. Beynon and H. Hughes (eds) *Technological Literacy and the Curriculum*, Lewes: Falmer.

Morgan, D.J.H. (1992) *Discovering Men: Critical Studies in Masculinity 3*, London: Routledge.

—— (1993) 'You too can have a body like mine', in S. Scott and D. Morgan (eds) *Body Matters*, London: Falmer.

Paetcher, C. (1993) 'Power, knowledge and the Design and Technology curriculum', PhD thesis, King's College, London.

Paetcher, C. and Head, J. (1996) 'Power and gender in the staffroom', *British Educational Research Journal* 22(1): 57–69.

Quicke, J. and Winter, C. (1994) 'Education, cooperation and the cultural practices of assertive girls', *International Studies in Sociology of Education* 4(2): 173–90.

Redman, P. (1996) 'Empowering men to disempower themselves: heterosexual masculinities, HIV and the contradictions on anti-oppressive education', in M. Mac an Ghaill (ed.) *Understanding Masculinities*, Buckingham: Open University Press.

Shilling, C. (1991) 'Social space, gender inequalities and educational differentiation', *British Journal of Sociology of Education* 12(1): 23–44.

—— (1993) *The Body and Social Theory*, London: Sage.

Skeggs, B. (1991) 'Challenging masculinity and using sexuality', *British Journal of Sociology of Education* 12(2): 127–39.

Tate, S. (1997) 'Making your body your signature: weight training and transgressive femininities', Paper presented to Annual Conference, British Sociological Association, York, England.

Turner, B. (1996) *The Body and Society*, 2nd edn, London: Sage.

Walkerdine, V. (1989) *Counting Girls Out*, London: Virago.

Weeda-Mannak, W. (1994) 'Female sex-role conflicts and eating disorders', in B. Dolan and I. Gitzinger (eds) *Why Women? Gender Issues and Eating Disorders*, London: Athlone.

Wexler, P. (1992) *Becoming Somebody: Towards a Social Psychology of School*, Bristol: Falmer.

Willis, P. (1977) *Learning to Labour. How Working Class Kids Get Working Class Jobs*, Farnborough: Saxon House.

Part II

GENDERED CHOICES
POST-16

10

THE GENDERED LANDSCAPE OF POST-COMPULSORY ROUTES

Lorna Unwin

INTRODUCTION

This chapter examines the extent to which the post-compulsory routes open to young people form a gendered landscape. It considers the implications of such a landscape for both the young people themselves and the professionals who provide them with careers education and guidance.

It has become a truism, at the end of the 1990s, to state that young people face a bewildering set of choices once they have completed the compulsory stage of their education. In essence, those choices are contained within the following five routes:

1   Continue in full-time education in school, sixth-form college or further education college; this route further divides into academic and vocational tracks.
2   Leave full-time education to seek employment (full-time or part-time work).
3   Leave full-time education to enter a government-sponsored training scheme.
4   Leave full-time education for a mixture of part-time further education and part-time work.
5   Leave full-time education but do not participate in any further education, training or mode of employment.

To say that young people 'choose' between these routes is, of course, highly contentious for, in many cases, the act of choosing falls to someone other than the young person or is, at least, heavily influenced by one or more adults associated with the young person. For example, in relation to choosing whether or not to remain in full-time education, a young person's choice may be affected as follows: parents might decide which 'A' levels their child should pursue; a school might refuse to let a pupil stay in its sixth form thus forcing an application to a local college; and a school may persuade a student to take a GNVQ course rather than 'A' levels. Where a young person has decided to try and find employment, it is the employers who will decide the extent to which that choice of route can be fulfilled or whether, for example, a young person should be offered training under the Modern Apprenticeship initiative (see Unwin and Wellington, 1995).

In attempting to make their choices, all young people are constrained by the culture of the society in which they live, the aspirations of the adults with whom they interact, the economic climate, and the ability of education and training organisations to provide them with the opportunities they desire. This chapter explores the extent to which young people's gender acts as a further constraint on their ability and opportunity to make decisions about their future beyond compulsory schooling. To that extent, the chapter is particularly concerned with exploring the 'structural and situational influences', as defined by Banks *et al.* (1992) which impact on young people's decision making. It does, however, also consider the extent to which young people can exercise *agency* in their decision making and so exert some control over their lives.

QUALIFICATIONS, PARITY AND SEPARATE TRACKS

Despite the seemingly neat categorisation of post-compulsory routes listed above, the reality behind those routes can be confusing and is certainly complex. It is not the intention of this chapter to debate the origins and meanings of the academic/vocational divide which still shapes the structure and curricular content of both compulsory and post-compulsory education (see Pring, 1995). However, it is worth noting here that both boys and girls are affected by the divide from the early stages of their school careers. Society's view of whether young people are 'academic' or 'practical' in terms of their aptitude and level of intelligence still echo the Platonic distinctions which divided people into philosopher kings (gold level), auxillaries or merchants (silver level) and artisans (bronze level) (see Green, 1990).

In modern terms, this is reflected most clearly in the occupational divisions between professionals, technicians and operatives, and, until the establishment of comprehensive schools, with the 1944 Education Act's concept of grammar, technical and secondary modern schools. And, in crude curricular terms, we now have a post-16 qualifications structure which mirrors those divisions: 'A' levels (for the academically able); GNVQs (for those in the middle); and NVQs (for those who work best with their hands). These divisions can, of course, be overcome. Hence, young people with GNVQs are entering higher education whilst some young people with 'A' levels have chosen to join the Modern Apprenticeship where they will work towards NVQs related to their occupational area. Interestingly, and perhaps, in time, of great significance, the academic/vocational divide no longer maps onto a divided system of institutions. In the late 1990s, a young person could study for 'A' levels, GNVQs and NVQs in a school sixth-form, a sixth form college or a further education (FE) college. Similarly, NVQs at Levels 4 and 5 now form part of the curriculum in some universities, and young people on Modern

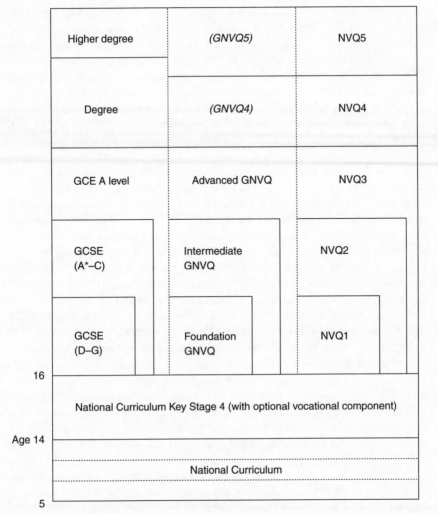

Figure 10.1 The NVQ framework
Source: P. Huddleston and L. Unwin (1997) *Teaching and Learning in Further Education*, London: Routledge

Apprenticeship may be studying for GNVQs and extra GCSEs (e.g. in a modern foreign language) as well as NVQs with their employer.

Since the introduction of NVQs (SVQs in Scotland) in 1986, the UK has had a national qualifications framework which purports to give 'parity of esteem' to the academic and vocational qualifications which it embraces (see Figure 10.1). An Intermediate GNVQ is, therefore, said to be equivalent to four GCSEs (grades A–C) and to an NVQ at Level 2, whilst an Advanced GNVQ is said to be equivalent to two 'A' levels and to an NVQ at Level 3. Unfortunately, the UK interpretation of

167

what constitutes the academic and the vocational has always valued the academic, which is said to have depth and rigour and involve considerable mental ability, over the vocational where 'doing' is seen to be more important than 'knowing'. This contrasts with the approach taken by the UK's European neighbours, notably France and Germany, who offer young people the opportunity to follow an academic or vocational route which is regarded as being equally demanding. The French vocational *baccalaureat* programme and its German equivalent, the *Abitur*, both involve students in taking a range of general education classes including mathematics, a foreign language and a humanities subject alongside the specific vocational subject (see Green and Steedman, 1993).

Whilst the promotion of 'parity of esteem' might appeal to notions of equity and fairness and act as an important motivating device for schools and colleges who want to encourage young people to take their courses, in reality the concept of 'parity' is a myth. To say this does not imply a belief that the Platonic categorisations were correct, but is based on empirical evidence from the world of education and employment which shows that people with academic qualifications still have greater access to further and higher education, to higher paid jobs, and to positions of status within society. A recognition that the myth of parity of esteem is dangerously false is clearly important for all young people. For young women, who still face discrimination in the labour market, a realistic awareness of the ways in which the qualifications structure operates outside educational institutions is vital.

Evidence of the myth of 'parity of esteem' comes from Robinson's analysis of the relationship between qualifications and earnings in the UK between 1993 and 1995 (Robinson, 1997). He found that people with academic qualifications earn more than those with vocational qualifications and, significantly, that earnings do not respect the national qualifications framework. Robinson shows that the framework's notion of equivalences, based on levels (i.e. four GCSEs are equal to an NVQ Level 2), does not translate into earnings as someone with four GCSEs will actually earn a similar amount to someone with an NVQ Level 3. In other words, at each level, academic qualifications produce earnings similar to those for vocational qualifications one level higher. Evidence from the Youth Cohort Study supports Robinson in that it found that at ages 23/24, young women's earnings were higher if they had remained in full-time education (see Payne, 1995).

Robinson's thesis that academic qualifications produce better returns has implications for women who, as Felstead *et al.* (1995) have shown, do not have equal access to vocational qualifications in the workplace unless they are in a female-dominated occupational sector such as clerical/secretarial, personal services (e.g. hairdressing, retailing) or healthcare (e.g. nursing, childcare). Robinson argues that this disparity could be an 'equal opportunities red herring' given that academic qualifications actually provide greater economic leverage than their vocational counterparts. The recent trend for girls to perform better than boys at GCSE and in some 'A' level subjects, therefore, may give young women access to more opportunities in the labour market as well as academic empowerment (see SCAA, 1996). And Robinson's thesis would suggest that girls would do well to concentrate on achieving a decent set of GCSEs before embarking on a vocational route.

Educational 'parity' can also be challenged in terms of the status afforded to 'A' levels as against vocational qualifications. The widening of the post-16 curriculum, particularly in schools through the introduction of GNVQs in 1991, has been a major factor in encouraging more young people to remain in full-time education. However, research suggests that teachers have steered their 'brightest' pupils towards 'A' level and filled GNVQ classes with those youngsters who, given improved labour market prospects, would normally have left school at 16 (see Higham et al., 1996). It should be noted that research is also beginning to show that many young people, particularly those with poor GCSEs, have benefited from the more learner-centred pedagogical approach of the GNVQ and have felt it has allowed them to demonstrate their academic as well as their vocational potential. Despite its progressive nature and its contribution to the broadening of the post-16 curriculum, the GNVQ merely diverts young people (and to some extent teachers too) to another track.

The long-awaited unification (see Spours and Young, 1997) of the post-16 curriculum has yet to happen, though in Scotland the implementation of the *Higher Still* proposals will move much more firmly in the direction of bridging the academic/vocational divide (see Raffe, 1997). Under Higher Still, 16 year olds in Scotland will be able to take any combination of forty- or eighty-hour units (usually grouped into 160-hour courses) in a range of academic and vocational subjects available at five levels. The same assessment and certification procedures will apply to both academic and vocational subjects and students may take courses at different levels at the same time. According to Raffe (1997), this system, though still in its infancy and with room for improvement, has significant advantages over the post-16 system in England and Wales:

> Instead of dividing students and allocating them to parallel tracks, it provides a single ladder for all students; it also caters for the diversity of students by allowing them to start climbing at different rungs on the ladder, to climb it at different speeds and to progress either vertically or horizontally.
>
> (Raffe, 1997: 185)

THE GENDERED LANDSCAPE

Issues around 'parity of esteem' affect both boys and girls, but their rates of participation *vis-à-vis* the different routes can help us gain a better picture of the gendered nature of post-compulsory education and training. We have already seen that girls are overtaking boys in terms of academic achievement up to the age of 18, but we know from other chapters in this book that many subjects at 'A' level are gendered in terms of their pupil profiles. Vocational qualifications, which reflect the organisation and character of the world of work, are, necessarily, even more gendered than their academic counterparts. One reason why this could be said to be a matter of concern is that the increase in the numbers of young people remaining in full-time education after 16 has resulted in many of them taking vocational qualifications (largely GNVQs); consequently the stereotypical divisions of the world of work are being further entrenched in schools and colleges.

Young people's images of jobs, careers and the concept of 'work' are formed very early in life. Francis (1996), in her study of 7–11 year olds in a London primary school who discussed views of their future occupation, found that 'many girls chose powerful, high-status jobs' but:

> a binary gender dichotomy appears to remain between the type or attributes of jobs chosen by girls and boys, with more girls opting for artistic or caring occupations, and boys choosing more scientific or sporting jobs. Moreover, few children chose jobs which are traditionally performed by the opposite sex.
>
> (Francis, 1996: 57)

In their study of male and female trainees on Youth Training in Devon and Cornwall, Hodkinson et al. (1996) found some evidence to support Gaskell's (1992) claim that young women relate their choice of job to their future roles as wives and mothers though, for some women, such thoughts only surfaced once they had moved closer to taking on domestic responsibilities, for example moving in with a boyfriend. Hodkinson et al.'s study suggests that young women do exert much more *agency* in their decision making than Gaskell's work maintains. However, their study also points out that when young women choose to enter a traditionally male occupational sector, they have to fight against sexist attitudes from fellow workers, fellow students and employers.

Breaking down the initial barrier is particularly hard for girls and boys if they are not supported by the adults in their lives. In her study of women graduates who entered non-traditional jobs in the technical professions (science and engineering), Devine (1994: 72) found that, although their parents had been supportive, these women had faced hostility from non-specialist teachers and careers advisers, 'regarding their choice of degree and subsequent occupation on the grounds that it was an inappropriate job for a woman'. Jenny Ozga's collection of personal accounts of women in educational management shows the difficulties they face resulting in the decision by many women to reject management because 'the price is too high'. Sadly, such decisions mean that the very institutions (schools, colleges, universities) which could offer support and inspiration to female students have limited numbers of female role models (Ozga, 1993: 9).

Much of the empirical research which has examined young people's decision-making processes related to careers, training and qualifications has been qualitative, and often ethnographic in its methodological approach. As Bates and

Riseborough (1993) point out, this means that the young people who have been studied are located across a large number of settings and contexts. The research can, therefore, present us with very rich accounts of individual young people, or present us with a profile of young people in a specific area, but it would be dangerous to overgeneralise those findings for all young people. In her study of 16–18 year old girls on a YT course in 'caring' and on a BTEC National Diploma course in fashion design, Bates (1993a; 1993b) analyses the social, domestic and economic restrictions operating at local level against which these girls had to make their decisions. Detailed awareness of such restrictions and their impact on young people's attitudes and concepts should, ideally, be developed by all those responsible for guiding and advising young people about their post-16 choices.

In their study of post-16 destination patterns in Derbyshire, Fergusson and Unwin (1996) found that even within one English county, there were distinctly different cultural and socio-economic influences affecting young people's choices. For example, in one small town, the nature of local industry meant there was still a steady supply of jobs for 16 year old boys regardless of their academic achievement. Boys from the local comprehensive school were, therefore, attuned to the idea of leaving school well before the time came for them to make that decision.

Examination of the state-sponsored training route (YT and Modern Apprenticeship) for school leavers, unsurprisingly, also reflects the gendered world of work. It should be pointed out here that this route is now open to 16 to 25 year olds making it an option for young people who have remained in full-time education until 18 or even to university graduates (see Huddleston and Unwin, 1997). Much has been written about the problems of YT and its predecessors in terms of lack of quality and its potential to exploit young people. Whilst some would argue that YT has its share of decent schemes offering trainees real jobs with reputable employers and the chance to achieve vocational qualifications, the statistics show that, on the grounds of equal opportunities, it has done nothing to help young people break out of stereotypical job patterns.

Modern Apprenticeship (MA), launched in 1994, and aiming to provide a higher status work-based route, is also dividing males and females into traditional sectors. By mid 1997 there were some 70,000 apprentices on the MA, two-thirds of whom are male and predominantly white. Female apprentices are located in traditional female sectors such as childcare, retailing, hairdressing and hotel and catering, whilst male apprentices dominate in sectors such as engineering, chemicals and steel (DfEE, 1996). Advocates of the MA would argue that it has raised the status of the work-based route through its insistence that young people work towards a minimum of NVQ Level 3 (in contrast to Level 2 on YT), that they acquire Key Skills (usually by achieving GNVQ Units) and that they are directly employed rather than being on the books of a training provider. Whilst its curriculum content and employment conditions may be laudable, the MA has, as yet, done little to advance the cause of both men and women who want to enter non-traditional areas of work. By segregating female apprentices into what Payne (1991) has called the 'narrow range of occupations traditionally regarded as "woman's work"', it has condemned them to the less well-paid jobs which offer less scope for advancement. However, as Brine argues in Chapter 11, there is little point in directing women into areas of work in which their chances of promotion are even more limited.

Whilst YT and the MA can help us gain a picture of the gendered landscape of the youth labour market, we have to remember that significant numbers of young people leave school to enter jobs which are unconnected to the state-sponsored training schemes, and many will have been working part-time for at least the last two years of their period in full-time education. Again, local conditions play a key role here in determining the extent to which young people can gain experience of the world of work and the extent to which that experience will be determined by gender. One of the main employers of part-time youth labour is the retail industry whose supermarkets and shops rely heavily on school and college students (males and females) in the evenings and at weekends when the other main source of labour for retailers, married women, want to take time off. Unwin's (1995) research on young people in Cheshire found that both girls and boys were working an average of twelve hours per week in supermarkets for which they received relatively good rates of pay. Whilst equality of opportunity appears to be in operation for students who choose to work part-time, the industry takes a different view when it comes to its relatively small numbers of full-time staff. Ashton *et al.* (1990) show that the armies of part-time married women and students are managed by a highly trained core of largely male employees.

Whilst part-time work does provide young people with important financial support and with useful employment-related key skills, it also inducts them into a complex set of structures and behavioural attitudes, many of which have gendered origins. Discussions of the relationship between part-time work and full-time education tend to concentrate on the argument that students should be able to make use of their employment experiences in their studies, particularly if they are on vocational courses. There is, of course, some merit in suggesting that because part-time work forms a considerable part of many young people's lives, it is counterproductive for schools and colleges not to draw on this experience. Perhaps of greater importance, however, is that teachers and careers guidance profes-sionals should create opportunities for young people to discuss and analyse their work experience in order to develop a more sophisticated understanding of how the labour market is constructed and the implications of its structures for career and FE decision making. Part of that discussion might focus on the limitations of part-time work which, though it may appear attractive to a 16 year old (flexible hours, relatively good pay), offers little in the way of security or occupational advancement. For young women, such a discussion might help them look beyond their domestic horizons which could be dangerously entrenched through part-time work which brings them into contact with older women who are fitting their job around home and family.

The youth labour market is also characterised by its role in the informal economy where young people are often willing to work long hours and move from job to job, and are less concerned than more mature adults about health and safety regulations and other legislative matters which govern jobs in the formal economy. Fergusson and Unwin's (1996) study of Derbyshire found that boys in inner city Derby were leaving school, often part way through Year 11, to work on local building sites on a daily contract basis. This is an underresearched field both in terms of the academic literature and from the point of view of the agencies who provide advice and guidance to young people. Griffin (1993), for example, reminds us that the sex industry is a significant source of informal employment for both girls and boys. A realistic picture of their local labour market in all its manifestations should be available to all young people and needs to be understood by the adults who provide them with advice and guidance.

IMPLICATIONS AND POSSIBLE ACTION

There is no shortage of research focusing on young people's decision making, much of which suggests that *structure* rather than *agency* is the more dominant imperative. Young women are thought to have limited horizons unless they are products of single-sex grammar schools where they are taught to believe they can achieve just as much if not more than men (see e.g. Deem, 1984). Careers officers will recount frustrating conversations with legions of girls who want to beome nursery nurses or hairdressers, yet admit that there are jobs available in these sectors. University admissions' tutors bemoan the lack of female applicants to science and engineering courses but do not stop to question how well they support women on such courses or the extent to which the courses themselves might project a macho culture. Young men and boys have now become a cause for concern because they are falling behind their female peers in the academic race. One explanation for this is that in some areas of the country, they have little hope in gaining meaningful employment and so cannot see any point in working hard at school.

The gendered landscape of post-compulsory education and training presents a considerable barrier to young people who want to exert some *agency* in their lives and, at the same time, creates a major problem for those charged with advising young people about post-16 choices. Young people often make pragmatic decisions based on their knowledge of local and, sometimes, national conditions in education and employment. They may know more than the adults who try to advise them. Yet, those pragmatic decisions may only be appropriate in the short term and may lock the young person into a straitjacket they find hard to escape. The challenge, therefore, is to find a balance between respecting young people's images and knowledge of the different options presented to them, and attempting to enourage young people to explore less safe or unusual alternatives.

To some extent, young people break down barriers and bring reality to the otherwise rhetorical pronouncements of policy makers. When GNVQs were launched in 1992, the policy makers stated that they hoped they would secure

LIVERPOOL
JOHN MOORES UNIVERSITY
AVRIL ROBARTS LRC
TEL. 0151 231 4022

entry to higher education as well as being attractive to employers. By 1996, 180,000 GNVQ registrations were recorded, covering 20 per cent of the cohort (DfEE, 1996). In signing up for GNVQ courses in such large numbers, young people have forced higher education institutions to begin recognising them as appropriate entry qualifications. Similarly, on the MA, young women have gained apprenticeships in non-traditional sectors with companies such as Rover Cars, ICI and British Steel, and young men are working in childcare organisations. But such breakthroughs have to be sustained and mechanisms put in place to ensure young people do not have to continue their fight for recognition having already had the courage and tenacity to challenge traditional barriers.

REFERENCES

Ashton, D., Maguire, M. and Spilsbury, M. (1990) *Restructuring the Labour Market*, London: Macmillan.

Banks, M. *et al.* (1992) *Careers and Identities*, Milton Keynes: Open University Press.

Bates, I. (1993a) 'A job which is "right for me"?', in I. Bates and G. Riseborough (eds) *Youth and Inequality*, Buckingham: Open University Press.

—— (1993b) ' "When I have my own studio . . . ": the making and shaping of "Designer Careers" ', in I. Bates and G. Riseborough (eds) *Youth and Inequality*, Buckingham: Open University Press.

Bates, I. and Riseborough, G. (eds) (1993) *Youth and Inequality*, Buckingham: Open University Press.

Deem, R. (1984) *Co-education Reconsidered*, Milton Keynes: Open University Press.

Devine, F. (1994) 'Gender segregation and labour supply: on "choosing" gender a-typical jobs', *British Journal of Education and Work* 6(3): 61–72.

DfEE (1996) *DfEE News 213/96 Participation in Education and Training by 16–18 year-olds in England: 1985–1995*, London: Department for Education and Employment.

Felstead, A., Goodwin, J. and Green, F. (1995) *Measuring up to the National Training Targets: Women's Attainment of Vocational Qualifications*, Centre for Labour Market Studies, University of Leicester.

Fergusson, R. and Unwin, L. (1996) 'Making better sense of post-16 destinations: a case study of an English shire county', *Research Papers in Education* 11(1).

Francis, B. (1996) 'Doctor/nurse, teacher/caretaker: children's gendered choice of adult occupation in interviews and role plays', *British Journal of Education and Work* 9(3): 47–58.

Gaskell, J. (1992) *Gender Matters from School to Work*, Buckingham: Open University Press.

Green, A. (1990) *Education and State Formation*, Basingstoke: Macmillan.

Green, A. and Steedman, H. (1993) *Educational Provision, Educational Attainment and the Needs of Industry: A Review of the Research for Germany, France, Japan, the USA and Britain*, Report No. 5, London, National Institute for Economic and Social Research.

Griffin, C. (1993) *Representations of Youth*, Cambridge: Polity Press.

Higham, J., Sharp, P. and Yeoman, D. (1996) *The Emerging 16–19 Curriculum Policy and Provision*, London: David Fulton.

Hodkinson, P., Sparkes, A.C. and Hodkinson, H. (1996) *Triumphs and Tears: Young People, Markets and the Transition from School to Work*, London: David Fulton.

Huddleston, P. and Unwin, L. (1997) *Skills, Stakeholders and Star-gazing: the Relationship between Education, Training and the Economy*, London: Further Education Development Agency (mimeo).

Ozga, J. (ed.) (1993) 'Introduction: in a different mode', *Women in Educational Management*, Buckingham: Open University Press.

Payne, J. (1995) *Options at 16 and Outcomes at 24: a Comparison of Academic and Vocational Education and Training Routes*, Youth Cohort Report No. 35, Sheffield: Department for Education and Employment.

—— (1991) *Women, Training and the Skills Shortage*, London: Policy Studies Institute.

Pring, R. (1995) *Closing the Gap: Liberal Education and Vocational Preparation*, London: Hodder & Stoughton.

Raffe, D. (1997) 'The Scottish experience of reform: From "Action Plan" to "Higher Still"', in A. Hodgson and K. Spours (eds) *Dearing and Beyond, 14–19 Qualifications, Frameworks and Systems*, London: Kogan Page.

Robinson, P. (1997) *The Myth of Parity of Esteem: Qualifications and Earnings*, Working Paper 865, Centre for Economic Policy, London School of Economics.

SCAA (1996) *GCE Results Analysis*, London: School Curriculum and Assessment Authority.

Skeggs, B. (1988) 'Gender reproduction and further education: domestic apprenticeships', *British Journal of Sociology of Education* 9(2): 131–50.

Spours, K. and Young, M. (1997) 'Towards a unified qualification system for post-compulsory education: barriers and strategies', in A. Hodgson and K. Spours (eds) *Dearing and Beyond, 14–19 Qualifications, Frameworks and Systems*, London: Kogan Page.

Unwin, L. (1995) *Staying the Course. An Investigation of Non-Completion Rates in South and East Cheshire*, Middlewich South and East Cheshire Business–Education Partnership.

Unwin, L. and Wellington, J. (1995) 'Reconstructing the work-based route: lessons from the Modern Apprenticeship', *Journal of Vocational Education and Training* 47(4): 337–52.

11

'EQUAL OPPORTUNITIES' WITHIN THE POST-COMPULSORY SECTOR

Training for undereducated, unemployed women

Jacky Brine

> In the (European) Community, the proportion of people of normal
> school-leaving age who leave the education system with a secondary
> qualification is 42%, against 75% in the United States of America
> and 90% in Japan. . . . There is a direct connection between this
> problem and the problem of *the failure of education, which is a
> particularly widespread factor of marginalization and economic and social
> exclusion.*
>
> (EC 1993a: 118, original emphasis)

This quotation is taken from the European Commission's *White Paper: Growth,
Competitiveness, Employment*, the key European policy document of the early 1990s.
It shows the Commission's concern with the problem of undereducation,
unemployment and social exclusion, themes which are developed throughout
the ensuing White Papers of *Social Policy* (EC, 1994) and *Education and Training*
(EC, 1995a), and which are central to this chapter; for my focus here is on the
unequal *outcomes* of compulsory schooling. These unbalanced outcomes relate to
class, race and physical or learning disability, as well as to gender. For many years I
taught unemployed, generally undereducated, adults and young people, before
turning my attention to related research.

Not only do many young people leave school with no, or few, qualifications, but
increasing numbers of girls and boys are excluded from state schooling. The post-
school, longer term consequences of undereducation on working class black and
white girls are considered in this chapter. Girls leaving school at the end of Year 11,
with no or few qualifications, may find paid employment. Given their lack of
qualifications, skills and experience, such employment is likely to be in the service
industry. It is likely to be very low paid, to have very little opportunity for further
training or promotion, and to have very little security (Social Europe, 1993; 1994).

They may also join the government's Youth Training programme; they may continue their education through a local college; or they may be unemployed. Some young women will become pregnant, and then marry, or bring up their children with a partner, or as lone mothers. There are other 'illegal' choices which young unemployed women might make. Nevertheless, all of these routes could lead the girls, a few years later, to the unenviable state of long term unemployment.

The increase in unemployment across the European Union has been influenced by shifts in demography, by the European Single Market, by the construction of other economic blocs and by the political and economic changes in Central and Eastern Europe. Most importantly, it has been influenced by the ubiquitous impact of 'new technology' throughout the service industry, the financial sector and, importantly, the manufacturing sector: a change in the means of production equal, as European President Jacques Delors stated, to that of the industrial revolution (EC, 1987a; 1993a). Although the impact of these changes has not been confined to black and white people of the 'working classes', or to low and undereducated people, or people with disabilities, it is, nevertheless, these social groups that represent the largest categories of the long term unemployed, with intense concentrations found in particular regions and particular areas of cities (EC, 1995b). Across all the countries of the European Union, including the UK, there are social groups and particular geographical areas where there is mass long term, and even generational, unemployment. Recent reports, including the UK's National Child Development Study (Bynner, 1996), the Council of Europe (1992), and the OECD (1992) have all shown that the undereducated and those with low educational attainment are most likely to be the long term unemployed. Reports also show that the long term unemployed are most likely to experience poverty and to become, in the European Commission's terms, 'socially excluded' (EC, 1994). This concept of 'social exclusion' refers to the 'exclusion' of particular social groups from economic and social life and includes women from the white and black working classes, women with physical and learning disabilities, chronically ill women, women migrants and immigrants.

I use the term 'undereducated' deliberately, firstly to signal a deeper educational consequence than that indicated by 'low or underqualified' – a consequence that relates to the educational 'process' as well as to quantifiable outcome – and secondly, to distinguish it from definitions and statistical indicators of functional illiteracy. Moreover, as Michael Apple argues (Apple, 1996), education is not a passive player in this economic and social context, but institutionally constructs and maintains this group-differentiated impact, whilst accepting, at the same time, that individual schools, colleges and teachers 'make things happen' for individuals, classes and schools. Despite all the best efforts of individual teachers, schools or colleges, social groups have unequal access to education, and given the economic and social context within which it takes place, education leads to, and maintains, 'unequal' outcomes.

I address two major concerns within this chapter: first, that of gender and class, and second, the implications of the European training policy on long term unemployed women in the UK.

Social and economic class has a direct and problematic relationship to the actual degree of unequal access to compulsory education within the UK, and leads, at the end of compulsory schooling, to 'unequal' outcomes, which are further compounded by the power-related differences of race, gender, physical or learning disability. I am concerned with the late twentieth century long term consequences of the 'unequal' outcomes from compulsory education on black and white women from the working classes. I deliberately use the plural to refer to the numerous economic and social differences between those in employment (traditional and contemporary 'working class' employment: permanent, temporary, casual, formal and informal) and those unemployed (and engaged in informal paid work, unpaid work, 'illegal' work, voluntary work, education, training, other pursuits and activities).

Whilst I am equally interested in the 'agency' of policy makers, educators and students, and in the ways in which we find spaces and gaps to exercise our agency, nevertheless these struggles of resistance and agency actually signal the power-supporting structures and processes of education, which are themselves contextualised by their European economic and social context. In this chapter, I accept the individual meritocratic exceptions, but then discount them as exceptions which prove the general rule that reflects the power relations between social groups.

In considering the implications of European Union policy on the training and subsequent employment opportunities for undereducated, long term unemployed women in the UK, I focus on two of the European Commission's policies: the European Equal Opportunities Programmes and 'Objective 3' of the European Social Fund (ESF) and on the interplay between them. Woven throughout the chapter are the UK government's published interpretations of European policy.

I try, where possible, to 'translate' the language of European policy, but there still remain unavoidable direct references to texts and concepts. Although the language of European policy is often dense and obscure, I struggle with it, searching for the gaps, the silences and the slight textual movements which signify shifts in policy. For it is these slight textual shifts which consequently affect the education and training provision, the opportunities and choices available, and the arenas for agency and struggle of unemployed women.

I begin by sketching the origins of the ESF and of the European interest in 'equal opportunities'. I follow this with a critical overview of the reforms of the ESF and their implications for unemployed women. I then focus on the Commission's Equal Opportunities Action Programmes, concentrating on their influence upon the training policy of the ESF. In the conclusion, I explore the lack of class and race analysis inherent in the Equal Opportunities Action Programmes, and the implications of this for ESF-funded training for undereducated, long term unemployed women.

THE ESF AND THE EUROPEAN INTEREST IN
EQUAL OPPORTUNITIES

The major source of funding for training unemployed women and men in the UK is the ESFund. The ESF is one of the four Structural Funds of the European Union. This was set up under Article 123 of the Treaty of Rome (EC, 1957) with the purpose of supporting the vocational training and retraining of workers. Of specific concern is Objective 3 of the ESF (ESF/3). Until 1993, ESF/3 related to the training of long term unemployed people aged over 25, and since then also to unemployed people aged under 25. ESF/3 includes a special section and budget allocation towards unemployed *women*, currently referred to as the 'pathway' for equal opportunities for men and women – the EO-pathway.

Until 1994, ESF/3 carried a distinct budget for training women. From 1994, the specific EO-pathway 4 is increasingly interpreted as meaning the single-sex provision for men as well as women. It is, however, interesting to contextualise this discrete gendered funding within the overall ESF/3 budget. For example, the EC budget for 1990–2 allocated 239 MECU to 'specific schemes to assist women encountering difficulties on the labour market'. At today's rate of exchange of 1.38 ECU to the pound, 239 MECU is £173 million. Although this appears a very large sum of money, this 239 MECU was only 5.8 per cent of the total 4,020 MECU allocated to Objectives 3 and 4 of the ESF (EC, 1990a: 38–9). The total allocation from the Structural Funds to all objectives for this period was 60,315 MECU (p. 13). The 239 MECU allocated to women was therefore just under 0.4 per cent of the total funding allocation available. This means that European women are only gaining specifically gendered access to a very small portion of the total funding available to us. Of the cake, or perhaps, more accurately, from the bakery, unemployed, undereducated women get the crumbs. From the Commission's point of view, the entire ESF budget, in total, is a mere 7 per cent (approximately) of all Commission funding (EC, 1990a). Furthermore, the specific allocation for the training of women is, as just shown, an extremely small part of that 7 per cent. Within the overriding economic concern of the European Union, the budget allocated to training unemployed, undereducated women could be seen as little more than tokenistic. Nevertheless, conversely, ESF/3-funded training for women represents, within the UK, relatively well-funded provision, with allocations for childcare and travel expenses built in. Yet, this much needed resource, to individual training providers, is little more than one small budget 'line', 0.4 per cent of the total budget available from the combined Structural Funds.

The ESF/3 explicit provision for women has been directly influenced by the European discourse of gendered equality. This equality discourse is also rooted in the Treaty of Rome. Article 119 refers to equal pay between men and women, and the basis for its inclusion was economic, the aim being to ensure that free competition was not distorted by the employment of women at lower rates than men for the same work (EC, 1978: 1). The immediate impact of Article 119, whatever its motive, was that it required Member States to implement it. Subsequently, Article

119 provided the route for all the equality directives. Both founding Articles, 119 and 123, are directly connected to the prime European economic goal of establishing a 'perfect market situation': of making the EU a major economic force in the world, able to compete with the USA and Japan (EC, 1975; 1976; 1987b; 1990a; 1992). This economic emphasis on the potential labour force is a major influence behind the European Commission's education, training, and equal opportunities policies.

A major site for the European location of the discourse of equal opportunities has been the Action Programmes for the Equal Opportunities of Women and Men. The first programme ran from 1982 to 1985; the second from 1986 to 1990; the third from 1991 to 1995; and the current fourth programme from 1996 to 2000. The Action Programmes provide an overall direction, a 'mission statement' of priorities for action and funding which act as an interpretative filter for the practical implementation of relevant legislation and primary policy statements. These Programmes are 'Recommendations' and, as such, carry no legal force. Whilst they indicate the European Commission's point of view, their apparent intention behind related legislation, they nevertheless generate questions concerning the strength of the Commission's actual commitment to gendered equal opportunities: questions of tokenism; questions of possible containment and femocratisation of feminist activity within the Commission's Equal Opportunities Unit, such as that described by Hester Eisenstein (1991); and questions of subsequent Member State interpretation of Commission policy.

Allowing for the extensive critique implied within these questions, the Action Programmes have, nevertheless, attempted to ensure women's right of access to funded training provision, to increase their opportunities within the labour market, whilst at the same time meeting the Commission's prime requirement of economic growth. This raises yet another issue, which I have considered elsewhere (Brine, 1992): that which questions the extent to which training can increase opportunities within the labour market – or to put it another way, how many women gain paid employment related to, or as a result of, ESF/3-funded training.

THE REFORMS OF THE EUROPEAN SOCIAL FUND

Although the first Equal Opportunities Action Programme only came into effect in 1982, the ESF has operated since the early 1960s. As I have discussed in detail elsewhere (Brine, 1995), significant shifts in European training policy have been reflected in the major reforms of the ESF in 1971, 1977, 1987 and 1993. There are two themes of significance to this chapter, which run through the Reforms of the ESF: first, the decentralisation of power to individual member state governments, and second the policy reforms relating directly to unemployed women who have, since 1971, been a designated 'group' for ESF/3 training.

Firstly, the decentralisation of power. Prior to the 1977 Reform, the ESF had been administered directly by the Commission, but this second Reform established a national system of administration and the Department of Employment (DE) acted as the UK managing body. This Reform enabled Member State governments to consider European-funded training as part of their own national employment/training policy, and the DE was now able to filter individual applications in the light of national-government-led policies. Furthermore, as will be seen later in this chapter, the DE, now the Department for Education and Employment (DfEE), is itself a major recipient of ESF funds. The process of decentralisation of control has continued, and subsequently has been strengthened by the 1987 Reform. This Reform allowed Member State governments to determine, within the Commission's objectives, their own priorities for funding. The latest, 1993, Reform continues the process of decentralisation and subsidiarity in which Member State governments agree with the Commission a detailed 'Plan' for the use of ESF/3 from 1994 to 1999 (DE, 1993a).

I turn now to the policy reforms relating directly to unemployed women. The first Reform of 1971 introduced the system of Priorities and Guidelines through which funding for certain social groups was to be prioritised over others: significantly, 'women' were specified as one of these 'groups'. The 1977 Reform increased the importance of this system of Priorities and Guidelines. The Reform identified two separate priorities related to training for women: one addressing occupational underrepresentation and the other hierarchical underrepresentation, (Morgan-Gerard, 1980). However, full funding was allocated only to the first priority, occupational underrepresentation. The 1977 Reform's main eligibility criteria for women were that they:

1   be aged over 25;
2   have lost jobs, never worked, or wish to return to work after a break;
3   have no or inadequate qualifications – that is, are unskilled or semi-skilled (EC, 1981: 2).

At this time, ESF/3 training is focused on undereducated women, and although equal high priority is given to training in traditional male occupations as is given to training for new jobs, training related to hierarchical underrepresentation is given a lower priority and stands little chance of gaining funding.

The meaning of this is that working class, unemployed, undereducated women were 'encouraged' out of training for advancement in traditional occupational areas, for instance textiles or clerical work, where they might have re-entered the labour market at a 'higher' position – with correspondingly higher pay and status and possible influence. Instead, training has been directed towards new jobs (mainly through setting up co-operatives and other enterprises), or towards occupations of underrepresentation. From the 1977 Reform, European policy and European interpretations of that policy have continued to prioritise training for occupations of underrepresentation – occupations such as plumbing, brick-laying and other occupations related to the building renovation and construction industries. Simultaneously, they have neglected hierarchical underrepresentation (Brine, 1992).

THE ACTION PROGRAMMES FOR EQUAL OPPORTUNITIES FOR WOMEN AND MEN

Five years after the significant 1977 Reform of the ESF, the First Equal Opportunities Action Programme (1982–5) came into operation. Its influence is evident in the Commission's key decision of 1983, which reinforced the importance of the Guidelines and Priority system and that unemployed women were to be targeted for training (EC, 1983: 2). The decision stated that:

> The Social Fund supports programmes specifically to help women aged over 25 to find new jobs, especially in the fields of computers, electronics and office work. It also helps women to find jobs in industries where they are traditionally under-represented, or more qualified jobs in industries where women are frequently employed.
>
> (EC, 1984a: 9)

The First Action Programme's influence is also evident in the *Council Recommendation regarding the Promotion of Positive Action for Women*, (EC, 1984b). A Recommendation is the Commission's actual point of view but, unlike a Directive, it does not hold any legality. This particular document recommends that Member States:

> 1b) . . . encourage the participation of women in various occupations in those sectors of working life where they are at present under-represented, particularly in the sectors of the future, and at higher levels of responsibility in order to achieve better use of all human resources.
>
> (p. 34)

> 4) . . . diversification of vocational choice, and more relevant vocational skills, particularly through appropriate vocational training . . . encouraging women candidates and the recruitment and promotion of women in sectors and professions and at levels where they are under-represented, particularly as regards positions of responsibility.
>
> (p. 35)

> 8) To make efforts also in the public sector . . . particularly in those fields where new information technologies are being used or developed
>
> (EC, 1984b: 35)

This Recommendation, in 1984, was concerned with *present* underrepresentation, particularly in the *sectors of the future*, which are those related to the growth and impact of new technologies; and also, significantly, equally concerned – at this stage

– with hierarchical underrepresentation. This generates the question of why, given this clear Recommendation, the subsequent interpretations of the 1977 Reform and later ESF Reforms and Guidelines have so prioritised occupational under-representation and, simultaneously, neglected hierarchical underrepresentation, increasingly marginalising and vaporising training related to 'new', information and computer technology.

The Second Equal Opportunities Action Programme (1986–90) had an even greater effect on ESF/3-funded training for women. This Action Programme recommended actions which encouraged women towards 'an equal level of parti-cipation in employment linked with new technology' (EC, 1985: 9).

> Applications to the ESF were to offer training for 'jobs for women in occupations in which they are under-represented (which often implies the use of new technologies)'.
>
> (EC, 1985: 23)

This emphasis on 'occupations of underrepresentation', with only an adjunct to new technology, influenced the applications of the time – many of which, like the Commission, simply appended new technology training to the main skill area. Furthermore, it also influenced subsequent interpretations of policy as it was this reference to underrepresentation, rather than that of new technology, that was adopted and developed within the ESF/3 system of Guidelines and Priorities.

The third ESF Reform in 1988 fell in the middle of the Second Equal Oppor-tunities period. Unemployed women were eligible for ESF/3-funded training only if they were thought to encounter *particular difficulties* on the labour market – clarified as those unemployed women with no, or few, qualifications or other 'marketable' skills: those women who are more often of the white and black working classes, rather than the generally better educated, usually white, middle classes. The policy no longer mentions 'underrepresentation' or 'traditional or 'new technology', but, in accordance with the principles of subsidiarity, merely specifies the parameters within which individual Member State governments could reflect their own national training and employment policies.

The Third Action Programme (1991–6) refers back to the Second Action Programme and reiterates the need for measures which will encourage women towards occupations of underrepresentation (EC, 1990b). It states the need for an increase in both participation (i.e. the *numbers* of women employed in such occupa-tions) and the level of contribution (i.e. women's *hierarchical* position within those occupations), especially contributions related to decision making. The Third Action Programme continues the emphasis on occupations of underrepresenta-tion and, significantly, despite stating this need to increase the *level* of contribution, pays no attention to hierarchical underrepresentation within traditional female occupations, for example occupations within the textile industry.

Significantly, the Second Action Programme's emphasis on new technology is now absent, or at least submerged beneath the broader concept of occupational underrepresentation: the Third Action Programme's generalisations have replaced the Second Action Programme's recommendations relating to specific aspects of training. The Second Action Programme had emphasised underrepresentation and new technology. New technology is now missing, and the omission has made it easier for Member States to make a broader interpretation of intentions than would otherwise have been possible. Moreover, the supposedly non-gender-specific reports during this time make progressively less mention of women – in some cases vaporising them away altogether in their continued reference to the male worker (EC, 1990c). This has happened despite the Commission's own Recommendation of November 1987 (Social Europe, 1989a), and the findings of the European Toledo Seminar of 1989 where the need for training in the 'occupations of the future' such as new technology was stressed (Social Europe, 1989b). Instead, the Third Action Programme emphasises training for local employment initiatives and for women setting up their own enterprises or co-operatives, and as Janet Hannah has shown, the risk involved in this is considerable and success is rare (Hannah, 1989).

From its general statement regarding occupations of underrepresentation, and its emphasis on new enterprises and co-operatives, the specific focus of concern in the Third Action Programme is on 'atypical' working patterns, 'quality' of work and sexual harassment. Whilst these concerns are rightly included in the Action Programme, it nevertheless makes no acknowledgement of the economic necessity of paid employment, nor does it acknowledge the hierarchical underrepresentation of women, nor does it show any awareness of class, race or disability differentials or power relations between women, and nor does it refer to information, computer or 'new' technology. I believe that these are crucial omissions in a document which functions to influence policy intention, interpretation and implementation.

In 1993, part way through the period covered by the Third Action Programme, the Commission published its *Regulation for the Community Structural Funds 1994–1999* (EC, 1993b), in which there is an even tighter concentration of ESF/3 policy and funds onto priority groups and regions. The Regulation also demands that ESF/3 comply with the 'observation of the principle of equality of opportunity between men and women' (EC, 1993b: 29). And, yet again, the Action Programme provides for the promotion of

> equal opportunities for men and women on the labour market especially in areas of work in which women are under-represented and particularly for women not possessing vocational qualifications or returning to the labour market after a period of absence.
>
> (EC, 1990b: 40)

It is in the Fourth Equal Opportunities Action Programme (1996–2000) that the policy effects of the 1993 Regulation appear. The main aim of the Fourth Action Programme is to integrate gender equality into Community, national, regional and local policies, including those relating to training and the labour market. The

Fourth Action Programme points out that within ESF/3, the demand for equal opportunities applies to *all* funded training. It sees education and training as powerful tools for stimulating desegregation of the labour market and although it does not refer specifically to training in information technology, it expresses its concern with the gendered effects of teleworking. Although the Third Action Programme's shift away from specific training strategies continues, the Fourth Action Programme's occasional statement continues the Second Action Programme's emphasis on those 'occupations and sectors of activity where women are traditionally under-represented' (EC, 1995c: 8). It also continues the definite shift, begun in the Third Action Programme, towards mainstreaming gender-based equal opportunities, stating its first objective as being

> to promote the integration of the equal opportunities for the male and female dimension in all policies and activities,

and, as its third objective,

> to promote equal opportunities for men and women in a changing economy, especially in the fields of education, vocational training and the labour market.
>
> (EC, 1995c: 39)

The Commission's policy intention during the 1990s has been to mainstream gender-based equal opportunities, whilst at the same time maintaining some discreet provision. However, European-funded research, conducted in 1996 into the British ESF-funded training for unemployed women, showed that 'equal opportunities' are *not* being mainstreamed (Brine, 1996). Moreover, whilst the specific 'equal opportunities' provision of the EO-pathway is being overwhelmingly interpreted by providers as being 'the one for women', the DfEE is increasingly emphasising the fact that 'single-sex' provision applies to either women *or* men 'returners' to the labour market, and also that men as well as women can benefit from training geared towards sectors or occupations where they have been traditionally underrepresented. Not only does the DfEE emphasise, in this way, the potential of ESF/3 funding for single-sex training for men as well as for women, but it also continues the practice of inserting *traditional* before 'underrepresentation':

> Training opportunities and motivational coaching will also be offered for both women and men seeking work in sectors or occupations in which their gender has been *traditionally* under-represented where this is in accordance with the Sex Discrimination Act 1975.
>
> (DE, 1993a: 70, emphasis added)

This emphasis on *traditional* underrepresentation is subsequently reinforced by the 1994 Guidelines, in which this statement now reads:

Training opportunities and motivational coaching **must** be offered for both women and men seeking work or self-employment in occupations in which their gender has been traditionally under-represented where this is in accordance with the SDA 1975.

(DE, 1993b: 14, emphasis in original)

As well as stressing 'must', the reference to 'sectors' of underrepresentation has been omitted, leaving only traditional *occupational* underrepresentation.

The UK government, in its recent document submitted for Commission approval of the UK ESF policy (DfEE, 1996), makes numerous gender-based equal opportunities statements, referring often to the *principle* of equal opportunities. However, such statements are immediately omitted from the 1994 Guidelines which are distributed within the UK to 'sector managers' such as the Further Education Funding Council (FEFC), the National Council for Voluntary Organisations (NCVO), and the National TEC Council (N-TEC), and to individual training providers. Within these UK ESF Guidelines, the only remaining explicit statement of 'equal opportunities' is that referring to the discreet gendered provision of the EO-pathway. The following year, the 1995 Guidelines supplement this by including a further general criterion which funding applications must meet (DE, 1994). This general criterion statement refers almost exclusively to the equal opportunities policies of the training organisations themselves and says almost nothing explicitly about the actual training being offered, or its relationship to the labour market.

This continual reshaping of the Regulation's demand for the mainstreaming of equal opportunities is, in the UK 1996 Guidelines, further manipulated and marginalised. An earlier statement relating to other possibilities within ESF/3 for single-sex training has been removed (DfEE, 1995), referring only to the ring-fenced gendered training of the 'equal opportunities' Pathway. Rather than being mainstreamed, 'equal opportunities' between women and men is, by 1996 within the UK, effectively marginalised into the specific 'equal opportunities' Pathway.

CONCLUSION

In this chapter I have traced the development of European equal opportunities policy and its impact on the training policy of the ESF/3, and, in the light of UK government reinterpretation of policy, I have considered the impact of the policy on the training and employment opportunities of undereducated, long term unemployed women. In my overview of the Reforms of the ESF, I detailed the development and relationship of the two major themes underpinning this chapter: the decentralisation of power onto individual Member State governments, and the policy Reforms which relate directly to unemployed women. Emerging from this account is an understanding that there is a definite lack of class, or race, analysis within the Equal Opportunities Action Programmes, and that, when compounded by the interpretations of the UK government, this policy limits the training, and

186

hence employment opportunities of undereducated, long term unemployed women.

A recent Commission Recommendation on access to continuing vocational training stated: 'Problems faced by women in gaining access to employment are largely attributable to their limited access to vocational training' (Official Journal, 1993: 38).

It is possible that some of the problems faced by women in gaining access to employment *might* relate to their having limited access to vocational training. However, the reports referred to in the introduction to this chapter strongly suggest that problems in gaining access to employment relate far more closely to the structure of the labour market and, consequently, to structural unemployment. These 'problems' also relate to the continuing gendered, class and race power relations which are embedded in and maintained by the structure of the labour market (Social Europe, 1993; 1994; van Doorne-Huiskes *et al.*, 1995). In the latter half of the twentieth century, structural unemployment (and underemployment) have been influenced by shifts in demography, by global capitalism and the construction of other regionalized blocs, by political change across Eastern and Central Europe, and by the widespread impact of 'new' technology.

Marquand (1990) refers to current rapid technological changes as being the latest 'Kondratiev wave'. She defines a Kondratiev wave as a long cycle of economic activity developing from a technological change and creating a disjuncture between the technology and the social and political organisation of the society. Yet, despite the Commission's Recommendation of 1984, which prioritised training related to new technology, the ESF/3 policy, in general and in the UK in particular, has increasingly marginalised and vaporised such training. The Third Action Programme (1991–5) makes no reference to information, computer or 'new' technology – a crucial omission in a document which functions to influence policy intention, interpretation and implementation. Throughout this time of great change, and great opportunity, class for class, and race for race, men have retained their economic power over women (OECD, 1994; van Doorne-Huiskes *et al.*, 1995).

Within the UK, the government's interpretation of ESF/3 policy has ensured that working class women have been encouraged into areas of traditional occupational underrepresentation, such as the manual skills of the construction and building renovation industry. Women entering these occupations are unlikely to disrupt the hierarchies of entrenched male power existing in these industries. Cockburn (1987) and Brine (1992) have both observed that young and adult women trained in manual skills are actively encouraged into newly feminised areas, such as wrought iron work in engineering or wooden toy making in carpentry, which effectively takes women out of direct competition with men. This means that the hierarchy of male power is maintained in the areas of traditional male skills, into which these women are being encouraged. At the same time, the lack of training or higher qualifications in women's traditional skill areas equally effectively maintains the hierarchy of male power there. The lack of class and race analysis discernible throughout the Action Programmes becomes even more

187

apparent in this Third Action Programme. The Action Programmes point towards the consistent positioning of working class unemployed women against that of working class men: the inequality to be addressed is 'gender' based.

Underrepresentation is a crucial concept within the 'equal opportunities' discourse. Within the Equal Opportunities Action Programmes and the ESF it has two relationships: first, *occupational* underrepresentation, and not *hierarchical*; second, occupational underrepresentation defined in relation to the occupational dominance of working class *men*. The discourse does not appear to address the positioning of working class women against that of middle class/educationally privileged *women*; it is never positioned against middle class *men*. 'Inequality' for working class, undereducated women is, I would argue, as related to class as it is to gender, and unless 'equal opportunities' policies address this, then policies, such as the ESF, will be weakened by its omission.

The emphasis within the current Fourth Action Programme is on the mainstreaming of gendered equal opportunities across all Commission policies and actions. At the same time the British interpretation of ESF policy stresses that 'equal opportunities' relates to men as well as women. The UK government has shown little regard for the *spirit* of mainstreaming gendered equal opportunities. There is, within the UK, a definite process of marginalisation of gender-based equal opportunities and hence a marginalisation and a limitation of the training provision for undereducated, unemployed women. A similar trend of marginalisation is also identifiable within Germany (Brine, 1996). This process of marginalisation was evident in interviews conducted in the UK with key personnel in the FEFC, the NCVO, and N-TEC (Brine, 1996). The majority of interviewees made a general assumption firstly, that provision for women was through the specific gendered allocation of the EO-pathway; secondly, that this EO-pathway represents the Commission's concerns with equal opportunities and underrepresentation; thirdly, that any reference to equal opportunities and underrepresentation relates as much to specific provision for men as for women. There is a danger that the mainstreaming of equal opportunities within ESF/3 is being interpreted to mean the mainstreaming of the specific EO-pathway. This means that instead of mainstreaming the whole of ESF/3 to allow for equal opportunities for women, it is the existing meagre provision for women, the EO-pathway, which is being mainstreamed to enable 'equal opportunities' actions for men. Therefore, the rest of ESF/3 is effectively maintained for traditionally 'male'-defined and male-targeted provision. Of all the sector managers, it was only the voluntary sector which attempted to ensure a definite spread of women across the whole of ESF/3. Reinforcing the marginalisation of gender-specific provision is the government's continual emphasis on *traditional* occupational underrepresentation. This particular emphasis on 'traditional' is also evident in research from Belgium and the Netherlands (Brine, 1996).

This specific gendered provision of the EO-pathway must be retained, for without it, it is highly unlikely that there would be any women-only provision. However, the EO-pathway has been heavily restricted in its usefulness by the narrow definition of the Sex Discrimination Act (SDA). Defined in terms of traditional occupational underrepresentation this provision continues to be narrowly interpreted either into those trades related to the construction and building renovation industries, or towards low level application of new technology. An amended SDA, where the emphasis is no longer on traditional occupational underrepresentation but on positive action, directly addressing the structural disadvantage of women within the labour market, could, and hopefully would, create far more choice within a supportive women-only environment.

The mainstreaming of equal opportunities across ESF/3, and consequently the provision for women, currently appears very poor. The question is not simply of how many women are being trained, under which particular pathway of ESF/3, but of a closer analysis of the women actually receiving training (race, disability, poverty, age, etc.), the type and level of training, and the immediate and long term 'outcomes' from that training – employment related, personal and educational. The mainstreaming of provision for women cannot be achieved simply through expecting women to fit in with the existing provision for men, as was suggested by some interviewees (Brine, 1996). The needs of domestic responsibilities must be built into all provision so that women, men and children can benefit. However, the EO-pathway is not enough: mainstreaming is the only way in which women can gain access to the widest possible range of provision and the EO-pathway must be an addition to that, and not an alternative. Sector managers and training providers should be required to show that between 40 and 50 per cent of their beneficiaries, across all of ESF/3, are women. It is only by having the widest possible choices that undereducated, long term unemployed women can increase their choices, and chances, within the labour market. Yet, to reiterate the crucial point, ESF/3 will *not* in itself create jobs and all training provision must be seen within the wider framework of structural unemployment and the widespread changes in demography and production referred to at the beginning of this chapter. And, finally, to refer back to my opening quote from the Commission's *White Paper on Growth, Competitiveness, Employment* (EC, 1993a), the inherent inequality in the fact that 42 per cent of Europeans (girls and boys) are leaving school with no secondary qualification implies not only that pupils are not being educated for employment, but also that, realistically, given the high probability of unemployment for these pupils, neither are they being educated for unemployment. The perennial argument surrounding the role of education to work must now adapt to the equally important question of the role of education to unemployment, for the harrowing fact is that many young people are leaving school un- and undereducated, and ill-prepared for either employment or long term unemployment.

REFERENCES

Apple, M. (1996) *Cultural Politics and Education*, Buckingham: Open University Press.

Brine, J. (1992) 'The European Social Fund and the vocational training of unemployed women: questions of gendering and regendering', *Gender and Education*, 4(1–2): 149–62.

—— (1995) 'Educational and vocational policy and the construction of the European Union', *International Studies in Sociology of Education* 5(2): 145–63.

—— (1996) *Integration of Women into the Labour Market within the Framework of ESF Objective 3 in the United Kingdom*. Full Report including Supplementary Reports from Belgium, Netherlands, Luxemburg and Germany, presented to the European Commission, August.

Bynner, J. (1996) 'Gendered skill development', Paper presented to the Skills Focus National Conference, Bristol.

Cockburn, C. (1987) *Two-track Training: Sex Inequalities and the YTS*, London: Macmillan.

Council of Europe (1992) *The Unemployment Trap: Long-term Unemployment and Low Educational Attainment in Six Countries*, Strasbourg: Council of Europe Press.

Department of Employment (1993a) *The European Social Fund: a Plan for Objective 3 in Great Britain: 1994–1999*, London: DE/ESF Unit.

—— (1993b) *European Social Fund: Guidance for 1994 Applications: Objective 3*, London: DE/ESF Unit.

—— (1994) *European Social Fund: Guidance for 1995 Applications: Objective 3*, London: DE/ESF Unit.

Department for Education and Employment (1995) *European Social Fund Guidance for 1996 Applications: Objective 3*, London: DfEE/ESF Unit.

—— (1996) *The European Social Fund: A Plan for Objective 3 in Great Britain: 1997–1999*, London: DfEE/ESF Unit.

van Doorne-Huiskes, A., van HOOF, J. and Roelofs, E. (eds) (1995) *Women and the European Labour Markets*, London: Paul Chapman.

Eisenstein, H. (1991) *Gender Shock: Practising Feminism on Two Continents*, Sydney: Allen & Unwin.

European Commission (1957) *Treaty of Rome*.

—— (1975) *The Evaluation of Vocational Training*, Luxembourg: OOPEC.

—— (1976) *Vocational Guidance and Training for Women Workers*, Luxemburg: OOPEC.

—— (1978) *Background Report 21st July: Encouraging Equality for Women: the Community Record*, London: European Commission.

—— (1981) *Women of Europe Supplement 6: Women and the European Social Fund*, Brussels: European Commission.

—— (1983) *Council Decision 77009/83 dated 21 June 1983*, Brussels: European Commission.

—— (1984a) *European File 2/84: the European Social Fund: a Weapon against Unemployment*, Brussels: European Commission.

—— (1984b) *Council Recommendation of 13 December 1984: Promotion of Positive Action for Women*, Brussels: European Commission.

—— (1985) *Equal Opportunities for Women: Medium-term Community Programme: 1986–1990: COM (85)801*, Brussels: European Commission.

—— (1987a) *New Forms and New areas of Employment Growth: a Comparative Study*, Luxemburg: OOPEC.

—— (1987b) *Implementation of the Equality Directives*, Luxemburg: OOPEC.

—— (1990a) *Annual Report on the Implementation of the Reform of the Structural Funds: COM(90)516, 1990*, Luxemburg: OOPEC.

—— (1990b) *Equal Opportunities for Women and Men: the Third Medium-term Community Action Programme: 1991–1995: COM (90)449*, Brussels: European Commission.

—— (1990c) *European File 5/90: Education and Training in the Approach to 1992*, Brussels: European Commission.

—— (1992) *European Social Fund: Community Support Framework 1990–92: Objectives 3 & 4: United Kingdom*, Luxemburg: OOPEC.

—— (1993a) *White Paper: Growth, Competitiveness, Employment: the Challenges and Ways Forward into the 21st Century*, Luxemburg: OOPEC.

—— (1993b) *Community Structural Funds 1994–1999: Regulations and Commentary*, Luxemburg: OOPEC.

—— (1994) *European Social Policy: a Way Forward for the Union – a White Paper*, Luxemburg: OOPEC.

—— (1995a) *White Paper on Education and Training: Teaching and Learning: Towards the Learning Society*, Luxemburg: OOPEC.

—— (1995b) *Employment in Europe 1995*, Luxemburg: OOPEC.

—— (1995c) *Fourth Medium-term Community Action Programme on Equal Opportunities for Women and Men 1996–2000 (OJL 335: Council Decision of 22 December 1995)*, Brussels: European Commission.

Hannah, J. (1989) 'Worker co-operatives as a response to unemployment: the impact upon participants', Ph.D. thesis, Newcastle-upon-Tyne Polytechnic.

Marquand, J. (1990) 'The fifth Kondratiev and the last frontier: vocational education and training research priorities for the 1990s', *British Journal of Education and Work* 3(3): 79–84.

Morgan-Gerard, F. (1980) *Equal Opportunities and Vocational Training: Catalogue of Training Innovations in the EC Member States*, Berlin: CEDEFOP.

OECD (1992) *Adult Illiteracy and Economic Performance*, Paris: OECD.

—— (1994), *Women and Structural Change: New Perspectives*, Paris: OECD.

Official Journal of the European Communities (1993) *OJL 181: Council Recommendation of 30 June 1993 on Access to Continuing Vocational Training, (93/404/EEC)*, Brussels: European Commission.

Social Europe (1989a) *Supplement 8: Activities of the Commission of the European Communities in the Fields of Education, Training and Youth Policy during 1987 and 1988*, Luxemburg: OOPEC.

—— (1989b) *Supplement 3: The Toledo Seminar on the Evaluation of Community Policy on Equal Opportunities for Women and Men: Outlook for 1992*, Luxemburg: OOPEC.

—— (1993) *Supplement 3: Occupational Segregation of Women and Men in the European Community*, Luxemburg: OOPEC.

—— (1994) *Supplement 4: Wage Determination and Sex Segregation in Employment in the European Community*, Luxemburg: OOPEC.

Part III

GENDERED SCHOOLING AND DIFFERENTIAL ACHIEVEMENT

12

MAKING SENSE OF THE 'GENDER GAP' IN EXAMINATIONS AT GCSE

David Jesson

Public interest in the ways that boys and girls respond to schooling has been a feature of the (English) educational system at least since the period of the Taunton Commission's (1868) work on endowed schools. At that time there were some 840 'endowed schools', the great majority of which (820) applied their endowments solely towards the education of boys. One of the recommendations of the Commission, taken up in the Endowed Schools Act, sought to broaden educational provision by interpreting bequests for the education of 'children' as referring equally to girls as to boys. The response to the Act was not wholeheartedly positive, however, and when political direction changed shortly thereafter, responsibility for implementing the Act was downgraded to the Charity Commissioners which effectively emasculated the more radical, interventionist, thrust that had been intended.

The recommendations of the Taunton Commission were related to 'fair allocation of resources' and did not specifically propose the setting up of entirely new girls' schools, although, in practice, this was largely what occurred. Since that time the benefits of educating boys and girls separately have been often debated with much heat, but often with very little light. Both sides of the argument are plagued by 'idiosyncratic samples . . . and particularly the inadequate control for preexisting differences' (Marsh, 1989). Thus we still do not know, for example, whether there *are* genuine educational advantages or disadvantages to be gained for either gender in the provision of single- or mixed-sex schools. Indeed, the argument has often been settled, in practice, by fashion rather than by enquiry; by conviction rather than by evidence. It is only recently that it has become possible to examine some of the elements of the relative differences between boys and girls in order to explore the extent to which 'gender' differences, rather than those due to 'ability' or 'social background', for example, make a *difference* to the progress and final levels of achievement of pupils in schools. This *de facto* lack of evidence has not inhibited repeated claims being made on behalf of single-sex schools that their pupils 'do better' than those who attend other types of school. That the agenda in the mid to late 1990s has changed markedly from that which prompted the Schools Council Programme 3 on 'Reducing Sex-differentiation in Schools'is evidenced by concern, regularly expressed, that it is boys rather than girls who may be at a 'disadvantage'.

In this chapter we start by looking at evidence supplied in the yearly publication, by the Department for Education and Employment (DfEE), of School Performance Tables. The performance tables (DfEE, 1992; 1993; 1994; 1995; 1996) provide information on a school by school basis, showing the percentage of pupils achieving particular 'levels' of GCSE performance. These figures show clearly that girls' schools appear to get better results than all others. We then turn to the outcomes for individual *pupils* and use this as a starting point to explore whether the apparent 'advantage' is sustained when we look at the performances of individual pupils. This is followed by an exploration of some of the subjects which pupils study in school, and of their rates of entry and performance within them. The chapter concludes by summarising the evidence presented about gender differences in performance at 16+ and links this with developing sources of information about comparative outcomes of schooling which are becoming increasingly available through international studies.

THE NATIONAL PICTURE OF SCHOOL PERFORMANCE

School data was investigated to determine the gender balance of the 3,000 or so schools who supplied data for performance tables over a five-year period. We chose only those schools listed in DfEE records as 'Comprehensive', since it was assumed that these would form a broadly comparable group of schools. The omission of 'Selective' schools meant that we used information from around 84 per cent of schools listed in the tables. Many of those omitted were independent schools, but a number of maintained grammar schools were also excluded by this strategy.

Of the schools in our sample, around 5 per cent were *boys-only* comprehensives; 4 per cent were for *girls*, leaving over 90 per cent as 'mixed' comprehensive schools.

Figure 12.1 shows the percentage of pupils in each school type who achieved the 'benchmark' qualification of five or more 'higher grade' (grades A* to C) GCSE passes. Each school type provided examples of performance across a wide range of outcomes as indicated, but at almost every stage a consistent picture emerged of single-sex girls' schools (the upper line) outperforming both 'mixed' (the middle line) and single-sex boys' schools (the lower line). It must be emphasised, however, that whilst we have no *guarantee* that the schools compared actually served comparable communities of pupils (apart from gender), the consistency of the 'advantage' of girls' schools is marked at almost all levels.

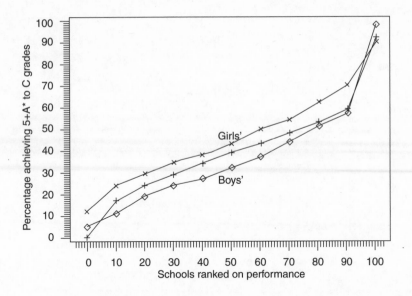

Figure 12.1 Examination results for girls', boys' and mixed comprehensive schools (data from Performance Tables, 1992–5)
Note: The middle line shows the performance of all pupils in mixed (co-educational) schools

Given that where single-sex *comprehensive* schools exist it is likely that they need to *co-exist* with other schools serving the 'other' gender, it seems likely that Figure 12.1 compares pupils who come from broadly similar backgrounds. We could, perhaps, have compared single-sex schools within a given locality, but by their very nature these schools are not very common and it seemed more appropriate to make these comparisons at a national level. This macro comparison constitutes our first 'evidence' of differences in performance between gender-differentiated schools' outcomes.

THE 'LOCAL' SITUATION – GENDER AND PERFORMANCE IN ONE GROUP OF SCHOOLS

Over the years many groups of schools (often all or most of those in particular local education areas) have collected information about the performance of individual pupils. We have utilised some of this information in Figure 12.2, which shows the examination results for some thirty or so schools. In Figure 12.2 we have taken the opportunity of tracking the performance of the (approximately equal numbers of) girls and boys separately for each school. Schools have been ordered on the overall average number of 'good' GCSE passes, and the average performance for the girls and boys has been plotted on the same graph.

197

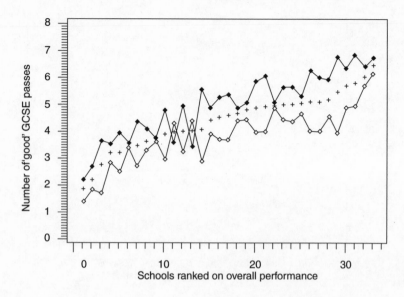

Figure 12.2 Examination results for girls and boys in mixed schools (performance data published in 1996)

Note: The line containing solid squares refers to girls' performance in each school, the lower line to boys'; the middle line (+) shows the average school performance

In Figure 12.2 the 'gap' between girls' and boys' performance in each school is measured by the vertical distance between the diamond shapes in the diagram. In general it appears that girls outperform the boys in the same school, but with some interesting exceptions. In three schools there appears to be almost no difference in performance, whilst in a further two boys achieve *higher levels* on average than girls. On the other hand there appear to be one or two schools where the 'gap' between girls' and boys' performance is much wider than is common elsewhere.

Looking at schools' performance in this way certainly suggests that there may be some 'innate' tendency for girls to outperform boys in GCSE examinations, but there are also some indications that the extent to which this 'difference' is apparent may depend upon the school which pupils attend. Is it possible, for example, for schools to act to 'close the gap' between pupils? And are there risks that some schools may (inadvertently, one hopes) act so as to widen the differential? A first reading of Figure 12.2 suggests that all three of these observations have some factual basis in the actual results presented.

HOW DO 'VALUE-ADDED' CONSIDERATIONS AFFECT THE 'GENDER GAP'?

In order, however, to go further in our investigations it is important to bring a further factor into the comparisons. We have access to the 'prior attainments' of

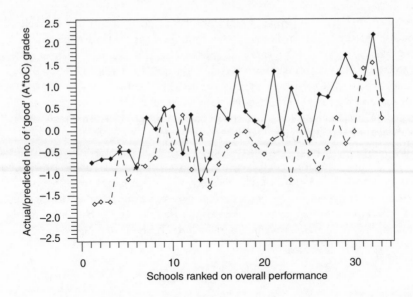

Figure 12.3 Examination results for girls and boys in mixed schools: difference between actual and predicted performance in each school

Note: The solid line refers to girls' performance in each school, the lower line to boys'

the pupils attending these thirty or so schools, and so can use these to 'iron out' any differences in pupils' outcomes which are related to their differing starting points. We have used a measure of pupils' prior attainments to correlate with their GCSE performance; for all pupils this correlation was relatively high (around 0.7), and was similar for both girls and boys taken separately. We used this measure to calculate a simple prediction model which gave an estimate of the number of 'good' GCSE passes each pupil would obtain, based on the relationship between 'prior attainment' and 'GCSE outcome' available from the data. This 'predicted outcome' was then compared with pupils' *actual achievements* and the average of this difference for each pupil was calculated for each school, and then for each gender within each school. The results are shown in Figure 12.3 which reports the results for girls (full diamonds) and boys (open diamonds) for schools in the same order as that utilised in Figure 12.2.

In Figure 12.3 the overall indication is that, for most schools, girls' performance is higher than boys'. In twenty six of the thirty-three schools, girls 'do better' than boys. However, the three schools we noted in Figure 12.2 where boys and girls appeared to perform equally are still shown to be providing similar outcomes once their pupils' prior attainments have been taken into account. A *further* two schools also give similar indications – suggesting that, overall, in five schools there was little or no 'gender gap' in performance. These schools may, of course, achieve this outcome by having lower than expected achievements for girls, and they would be obvious candidates for more exploratory follow-up by case studies as has been identified in Harris and Russ (1995). Even more interestingly, the two schools which showed boys 'doing better' than girls in their performances before account was taken of prior attainment, still appeared in this category even after this characteristic has been taken into account – suggesting that in these schools the tendency for girls to outperform boys has been reversed.

Thus, although there appears to be clear evidence of girls' performance being *in general* higher than boys', it is also apparent that this may be substantially affected by the *particular school* which a pupil attends. In around a quarter of the schools in our sample, there are indications that the generally observed 'advantage' for girls does not apply. In a more extensive study reported by Schagen (1996) it was found that in as many as one-third of schools there was no significant advantage of girls' over boys' performances. We cannot unfold this part of the story any further here, but would direct readers to the references to case-study approaches in which this situation has been more systematically explored (European Congress on Educational Research, 1996).

INDIVIDUAL PUPIL PERFORMANCE – THE ROLE OF GENDER

Whilst it is true that schools remain the major focus for the public *reporting* of performance, it is obvious that such performance is the sum of the achievements of the individual pupils within them. We have taken the opportunity of changing our focus on performance from the number of 'good' grades obtained at GCSE, to the

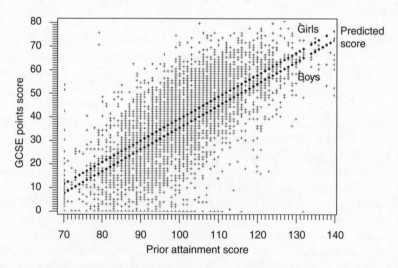

Figure 12.4 GCSE performance in 1996 for 5,000+ pupils, showing differential in favour of girls

total number of *points* which pupils achieve from the examinations they take. This allows *every* examination taken by pupils to contribute to their measure of performance rather than only those in which achievement was at grade C or above.

In Figure 12.4 we have plotted the GCSE points score for each pupil (A* = 8, A = 7, B = 6 . . .) against their prior attainment score. We have also plotted the 'best fit' lines for the scores of girls and boys separately.[1]

In Figure 12.5 we have sought to show the underlying situation of girls' and boys' GCSE performance by plotting their results independently. Girls' results are shown as full diamonds, boys' by open diamonds. A first inspection of Figure 12.5 suggests that the 'wave' of full diamonds takes up more of the upper half of the diagram, whilst in the bottom half the open diamonds predominate. This gives some indication, however crudely, that the performance of girls is generally higher than that of boys. The patterns of 'gender-differentiated' performance are summarised in the two parallel lines running from bottom left to upper right in Figure 12.5 – these show that at each level of prior attainment there is a clear tendency for girls to achieve higher scores than boys – and that this differential is around four GCSE points.

This is the evidence which has so far been missing from our discussion. In Figures 12.4 and 12.5 we have compared the GCSE outcomes for individual pupils at each level of prior attainment score; these have allowed a *prediction* of the average performance at GCSE for each pupil. When these predictions are separated into those for girls and those for boys, the girls' predicted scores are seen to be uniformly higher than those for boys.

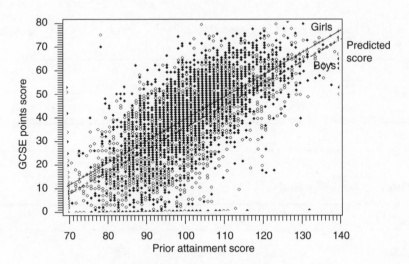

Figure 12.5 GCSE points scores achieved by pupils in 1996 plotted agianst prior attainment by gender

Note: Solid diamonds refer to girls' performance, open diamonds to boys'

WHAT FACTORS CONTRIBUTE TO GIRLS' ENHANCED PERFORMANCE AT GCSE?

Entry to GCSE examinations

Option choices for subjects later to be examined at GCSE are available to all pupils on an identical basis. Pupils take similar numbers of courses in Years 10 and 11, but not all pupils who *take the course* for a particular subject are *entered for that GCSE* examination. In Table 12.1 we show the percentage of pupils, by gender, who took each number of GCSE examinations in 1996.

In Table 12.1 the pattern of entries shows that on average girls enter for more GCSE examinations than boys, and that this is particularly marked for entries at the higher levels; over 80 per cent of girls enter for nine or more examinations, but only 70 per cent of boys do so. This differential entry may go some way to 'explain' the enhanced performance levels of girls, but we can check this by comparing the 'average grades' achieved by pupils at each entry level – obtained by dividing their total points score by the number of examinations entered. This information is provided in Table 12.2.

Table 12.2 shows that for most entry levels, the 'quality' of performance by girls was higher than that for boys. Only at the very lowest and the highest entry levels did the performance of boys surpass that of girls; over the great majority of entry profiles the advantage was still clearly with the girls.

Table 12.1 The number of GCSE examinations entered in 1996; boys' and girls' results presented separately

Entries	0–5	6	7	8	9	10	11+	Avge
Girls	6	2	3	8	53	26	2	8.7
Boys	9	3	6	12	48	19	3	8.3
Overall	7	2	5	10	51	22	2	8.5

Table 12.2 The average number of GCSE examinations entered for girls and boys

Entries	0–5	6	7	8	9	10	11+
Avge Pts/Entry							
Girls	0.9	2.0	2.6	3.2	4.8	5.1	5.2
Boys	1.1	2.0	2.4	3.1	4.4	4.7	5.3
Overall	1.0	2.0	2.5	3.2	4.6	4.9	5.2

Attendance over years 10 and 11

One factor that seriously reduces pupils' capacity to benefit from the curriculum as delivered by the school is their actual *receipt* of it. Missing school for whatever reason is likely to cause additional difficulties for pupils in seeking to respond to the diverse demands of their various courses.

The group of schools which we are using as a test-bed for information about differential performance routinely collected 'Attendance' information for the purposes of in-school monitoring. This data has been made available for all 5,000 pupils – and thus allows an investigation of the incidence and effects of patterns of attendance on GCSE performance.

We divided pupils into four groups on the basis of their attendance patterns: the lowest quarter; those with attendance patterns up to the average for all pupils; those with attendance patterns above the average for all pupils; and those with the highest attendance records. (Because of the 'clumping' of the data it was not possible to construct groups of absolutely equal size; the 'best' attendees were those with the 'best' 20 per cent of attendances, the other groups were slightly larger.) We have presented the breakdown of these groups by gender in Table 12.3. Similar results were reported by Schagen (1996)

One surprising observation to arise from Table 12.3 is the extent to which girls' attendance levels are *lower* than boys'. On average there are more girls with 'below average' and 'low' attendance levels (58 per cent) compared with just 50 per cent for boys. Counterbalancing factors exist for 'above average' and 'high' levels.

No explanation of this phenomenon is attempted here; we are more interested in the impact which attendance levels have on examination performance, but it is a facet of gender response to schooling which has not, to date, received very much attention. In Table 12.4 we show, on average, the GCSE scores for pupils in each of the attendance categories we have identified above.

Table 12.4 shows the disadvantage which pupils experience when they attend less rather than more frequently. The average GCSE score for pupils in the 'low' attendance category is just over half that of pupils who attend most regularly. But of even more interest is the extent to which the 'disadvantage' of girls is not as great as that of boys with similar attendance patterns: at every attendance level, girls appear to do substantially better than boys, and, although the difference

Table 12.3 The percentage of girls and boys in each of four 'attendance rate' groups

Attend group	Low	Below average	Above Average	High
Girls	29	29	26	16
Boys	24	26	28	21
Overall	27	27	27	19

Table 12.4 The GCSE points achieved by girls and boys in each of the four 'attendance rate' groups recorded in Table 12.3

Attend group	Low	Below average	Above average	High
GCSE points				
Girls	28	43	46	48
Boys	21	35	39	43
Overall	25	39	43	45

narrows slightly for those who attend most regularly, it represents a substantial gender differential in favour of girls.

It would, of course, be possible to speculate about the causes of such differences, but without further investigation of this situation it would seem premature to do more than simply report these findings without comment. Tables 12.3 and 12.4 do appear to offer somewhat contrasting views of the situations in which girls and boys find themselves. Boys attend 'better', but appear to gain less from their attendance than girls, and the deficit attached to 'poor' attendance appears to disadvantage girls rather less than it does boys.

Characteristics of, and performance in, individual subject areas

With the advent of the National Curriculum there is much greater consistency in the subjects studied by pupils in Years 10 and 11, both within and between schools. The 'common core' subjects of English, mathematics and science are studied by all pupils along with a modern foreign language and aspects of technology. This situation contrasts sharply with that reported as short a time ago as 1992 where, particularly in the sciences and modern languages, there was considerable differentiation by gender in entry rates (Stobert *et al.*, 1992).

A more recent examination of this situation has found much greater convergence of entry rates, although, it must be added, with differentials now occurring not so much in the *subjects being 'taken'* in Years 10 and 11, as between the numbers of those actually *entered for* the relevant examinations. Table 12.5 gives the national percentages of pupils in core subjects who entered for GCSE examinations (all e.g. DFE, 1994).

In the 'core' subjects of English and science the rate of non-entry was surprisingly high – well over one in ten of all pupils did not enter for GCSE examinations in these subjects. But, as we have seen elsewhere, the situation was more extreme for boys than for girls; their proportionate entry was *always below* that of girls and in mathematics over one in six boys was 'not entered' for the examination, compared with around one in eight for girls.

THE 'GENDER GAP' IN GCSE EXAMINATIONS

Table 12.5 The rate of GCSE entry in the major subjects and combination of subjects for girls and boys

Subject	per cent entry	per cent entry
	Female	*Male*
English	92	87
Mathematics	87	83
Science	89	87
Modern language	74	62
Eng./Maths/Sci.	84	82
Eng./Maths/Sci./Mod. Lang.	71	59

There was one other subject where comparable and consistent figures are relatively easy to obtain: modern foreign languages. (We have included European studies in the 'modern foreign language' category, since this is an option which some schools offered for some of their 'less able' pupils.) In this subject substantial proportions of pupils were *not entered* for examination; two out of five boys were excluded from an assessment for which, we assume, the National Curriculum had ensured that they studied.

We have no evidence about possible reasons for such a substantial drop-out in this subject area, but it was apparent from some of the school-based analyses which we have carried out over the last few years that the decision to omit pupils from 'modern foreign languages' examination entry was heavily dependent on the school which a pupil attended. Schools differ substantially in the decisions which they made about entry to modern languages examinations: in some there was a uniform entry rate for boys and girls, differing, however, in the 'average entry rate' between schools; in others there was very sharp differentiation with girls' entries outnumbering boys' by more than 20 per cent. In one school, over a half the girls were entered for a modern foreign languages examination, whilst less than a quarter of boys were similarly involved.

These observations go some way to substantiate the findings quoted above of a general differential in favour of girls in entry policy – the evidence from Table 5 above, and the practices of some schools, show clearly that entry decisions are not simply 'school-dependent' but 'subject-dependent' as well.

Subject 'pass rates'

Over the past few years, the Department for Education (more recently the Department for Education and Employment) has published comparative information on the pass rates for the Year 11 cohort in a range of GCSE subjects (DFE, 1994). We present some of these in Table 12.6.

Table 12.6 The upper part of the table shows the success rates for girls and boys – the foundation GCSE subjects and their combinations. The lower part shows the success rates for girls and boys in other GCSE subjects (the number base here is the number entering each exam)

Subject	Achieved	A* to C	Achieved	A* to G
	Female	Male	Female	Male
English	63	45	92	86
Maths	42	42	84	80
Science	40	40	86	83
Maths/Sci.	34	34	80	77
Eng./Maths/Sci.	32	29	80	76

	Per cent of entry with			
	A* to C		A* to G	
	Female	Male	Female	Male
Mod. Lang.	50	39	97	95
E/M/S/ML	37	32	94	93
Geography	53	47	95	96
History	56	50	97	97
Art/design	59	42	97	94

In the common core subjects of mathematics and science, the differential in performance at the 'higher' levels (those achieving grades A* to C) between boys and girls is relatively small, even though, as we have seen, there were considerable differences between them in their overall entry rates. Results in English reflected a totally different situation, however, with girls' performance massively outclassing boys'. In fact, the differential in English language examination outcomes between girls' and boys' performance is probably wider than in any other subject in the curriculum.

The lower half of Table 12.6 shows the different outcomes in subjects where the entry rates were different for girls and boys. We have taken account of this in presenting the results by showing the *percentage of entries* achieved within the A* to C and A* to G pass categories. It is in the former, denoting 'high quality' assessment of outcome performance, that girls' results show substantially higher levels than boys'.

From the evidence presented in Table 12.6 we conclude that 'gender equality' in examination entry and performance is still very far from being achieved across a wide range of the subject areas for which pupils traditionally study. It is only in science and in mathematics (for which the issue of gender equality was addressed by the Cockcroft Report, 1982) that we see anything approaching a gender-neutral set of outcomes.

Interestingly, part of the remit of the Cockcroft Committee was to address the perceived *underachievement* of girls in mathematics at the end of the 1970s and early

1980s. This it did by recommending reforms both to the content and method of examination of the subject, and since that time, whilst achievement in mathematics has improved all round, the improvement in girls' performance has been at a higher rate than boys.

Similar tendencies may also be apparent in the development of courses for 'double science', which is now the predominant mode of study designed to meet National Curriculum science requirements. Before its implementation, there were considerable imbalances in both the take-up and performance in the component parts of the science curriculum. More boys took physics and chemistry than girls; the reverse was true in the biological sciences. It was difficult, therefore, to obtain an *overall view* of performance in science by gender, since the individual examinations had different profiles and entry rates, and, indeed, many pupils took no science examinations at all. What is clear from the figures as we present them now is that double science appears to provide a gender-neutral set of outcomes at GCSE. And in this, along with mathematics, it differs markedly from many other subjects which pupils study in the school curriculum.

SUBJECT PROFILES FOR ENGLISH, MATHEMATICS AND DOUBLE SCIENCE

Recent work on the performance of girls and boys in the 'common core' subjects of English, mathematics and double science was reported in Jesson (1996). Figures 12.6, 12.7 and 12.8 show the 'most likely' GCSE grade awarded in each of these subjects to pupils who had specific Key Stage 3 scores.

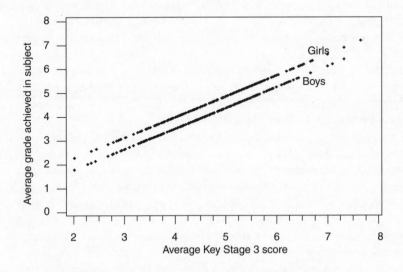

Figure 12.6 GCSE performance: characteristics of English related to KS3

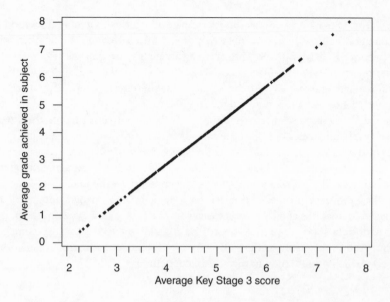

Figure 12.7 GCSE performance: characteristics of mathematics related to KS3

In Figure 12.6 there are two lines separated by around three-quarters of a grade point reflecting the English grades achieved, on average, by girls (upper line) and boys (lower line). The figure gives a very clear indication of the 'advantage' which girls experience in the 'progress' made in English compared with their male counterparts. The role of the Key Stage assessment is to ensure that as far as is possible, it is only the performance of those pupils who start at similar 'starting points' that is compared. On this basis it is clear that girls make greater progress than boys in English – or that, more provocatively, girls find English easier than boys.

Figures 12.7 and 12.8 show the situation as far as performance in GCSE mathematics and double science is concerned. In these subjects there appears to be *no* differentiation by gender in the outcomes achieved, or, put slightly differently, girls and boys make similar progress from similar starting points.

Two interesting consequences flow from further consideration of the situations represented in Figures 12.6, 12.7 and 12.8, one of which is indicated by Figure 12.9 which combines the information from the English and mathematics diagrams.

In Figure 12.9 the line linking performance in mathematics to Key Stage 3 starting points is lower than the line showing girls' performance in English for pupils of 'average or lower' Key Stage 3 scores. For the relatively small group of girls with 'higher' Key Stage 3 scores, the grades achieved in mathematics first approach and then exceed those for English. Thus, adapting the language used above, we may say that for many girls mathematics appears 'harder' than English. For boys the story is slightly more balanced, in that at lower 'starting points' boys

208

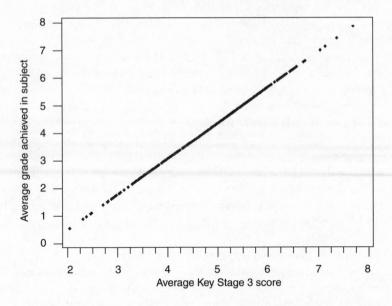

Figure 12.8 GCSE performance: characteristics of double science related to KS3

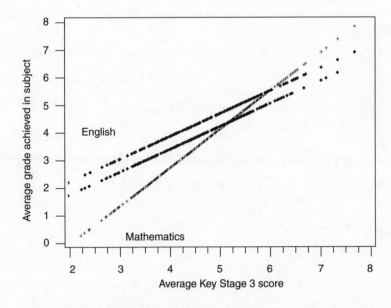

Figure 12.9 GCSE performance: relationship between English and maths
Note: The upper line of solid diamonds relates to girls' performance in English; the lower line of solid diamonds relates to boys' performance in English; and the third line (+) relates to girls' and boys' performance in mathematics

'do considerably better' in English than in mathematics, and yet 'do better' in mathematics increasingly as they have higher Key Stage 3 'starting points'. In practical terms, of course, Figure 12.9 emphasises the different characteristics of these two subjects as far as gender-differentiated performance is concerned.

The second consequence is indicated in Figure 12.10, which shows the GCSE results for one particular example school in mathematics, and indicates that, in this school, many more girls (results shown as open diamonds) than boys (results shown as asterisks) achieved grades which were *below* those that their peers obtained elsewhere.

This finding should be of considerable import, in so far as it indicates potential for considerable improvement in the performance of substantial numbers of pupils. That, in this case, these underperforming pupils happen to be girls suggests a priority for investigation and consideration of what actions might be appropriate to redress the situation.

In issues such as these, the question of gender differentiation in performance is seen to be subsumed under the wider heading of tackling school improvement. In this area, access to information in a form similar to that presented in this section may have a crucial role to play in identifying pupils (and perhaps even teaching groups) for whom the indications are that similar pupils 'do better' elsewhere. It offers collegial groups of schools opportunity to share strategies which deliver greater success, and so benefit all by raising overall levels of achievement. This is clearly a task which calls for a mix of the type of quantitative information presented here alongside qualitative evaluation of the associated practices which may have

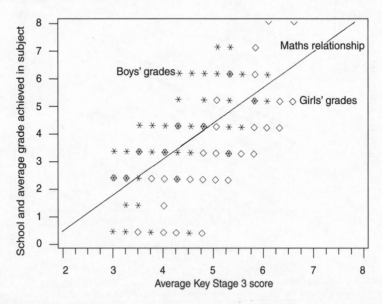

Figure 12.10 GCSE performance gender differences in one school's mathematics department

had some role to play in bringing about the differences between performance which we observe.

SUMMARY AND CONCLUSIONS

The broad range of evidence that we have presented in this chapter confirms the widely held view that girls achieve at higher levels than boys in a wide range of schools and in different subjects. However, we have noted that there do appear to be schools which act in such a way that performance differentials are reduced – and, in some cases, reduced by enhancing the performance of boys rather than by limiting that of girls.

The existence of such schools has only recently come to light through the widespread introduction of 'value-added' investigations of school (and pupil) performance. One example of such a study was reported by Jesson (1966); many others are coming 'on stream', in particular those emerging from the NFER 'QUASE' project,[2] and others available through YELLIS[3] (based at the University of Durham). In effect, schools whose performance is evaluated in this way pose very interesting challenges to those where more conventional (at least in 1990s terms) outcomes occur.

A number of studies of schools such as these are currently under way, seeking to align qualitative investigations of schools' policies and actions to set alongside the quantitative evidence[4]. As yet, this way of working is too novel to have provided anything more than very sketchy accounts of what specific actions schools might take to redress any gender imbalance that might be implicit in their examination results. However, given the need for every school to set targets for their own internal 'improvement' in forthcoming performance, it would be very surprising if this issue were not very high on the agenda of the majority of schools. Most schools, as this chapter has shown, conform to a stereotypical account of gender-differentiated performance in favour of girls. Is this to be the 'model' for the future, or are there hopes that actions can be taken to eradicate this evidence of underperformance? If action (like the Cockcroft Report's emphasis on 'girl-friendly' mathematics) directed to reversing perceived 'inequities' in the system worked in the late 1970s and early 1980s, is there any reason to suppose that it cannot happen again?

One view of *any* differential in performance is given by Reynolds (Reynolds and Stringfield, 1996; Reynolds, 1996): that its upper level sets an achievable target for what *all* can achieve. On this basis, there would appear to be considerable advances which might accrue in schools' performance if they were able to bring the performance levels of their male pupils up to that of their female counterparts. Whether or not this proves to be possible is at best, at this stage, a speculation, but the issue is sufficiently challenging to have set in train a fresh round of activity mirroring that which occurred in the late 1970s and early 1980s when it was considered necessary to address the imbalance between girls' and boys' performance which, at that time, appeared to favour boys.

Reynolds' account of what is routinely expected of *all* pupils in schools, say in Taiwan, contrasts very sharply indeed with the levels of performance to which the English education system has grown accustomed. The gender differential debate is only part of this enquiry, but it is one which has clear dimensions and considerable promise of delivering substantial dividends in improved (and improving) levels of performance.

NOTES

1 Figure 12.4 is a scattergraph where each '+' represents the GCSE score of one or more pupils, the parallel lines show the 'best estimate' score for pupils of given prior attainment, the upper line shows the estimate for girls, and the lower line full diamonds shows the same for boys.
2 QUASE project (Quantitative Assessments in Secondary Education). Information available from NFER, The Mere, Upton Park, Slough, SL1 2DQ.
3 YELLIS project (Year 11 Information Service). Information available from Centre for Educational Management, School of Education, University of Durham.
4 See, for example, the ESRC-funded 'Improving Schools Project' based at Homerton College, Cambridge, under the directorship of Professor John Gray.

REFERENCES

Department for Education (1994) *Statistical Bulletin* 7/94.
Department for Education and Employment (1992–6) *Secondary School Performance Tables*, London: DfEE.
European Congress on Educational Research (1996) Symposium Papers, Seville.
Harris, A. and Russ, J. (1995) *Pathways to School Improvement*, Sheffield: Employment Department.
Jesson, D. (1996) *Value Added Measures of School GCSE Performance*, London: HMSO.
Marsh, H.W. (1989) 'Effects of attending single-sex and co-educational high schools on achievement, attitudes, behaviours and sex-differences', *Journal of Educational Psychology* 81 (1): 70–85.
Mathematics Counts (1982) *Report of the Committee of Inquiry into the Teaching of Mathematics*, London: HMSO.
Reynolds, D. (1996) *Schools as High Reliability Organisations*, University of Newcastle-upon-Tyne.
Reynolds, D. and Stringfield, S. (1996) 'Failure-free school is clear for take-off', *School Management Update, Times Educational Supplement* 19 January: 10–12.
Schagen, I. (1996) 'Male/female differences at the end of compulsory education in England and Wales', Paper presented at the European Congress on Educational Research, Seville.
Stobart, G., Elwood, J. and Quinlan, M. (1992) 'Gender bias in examinations: how equal are the opportunities', *British Educational Research Journal* (3): 261–76.

13

GENDERED RELATIONS BEYOND THE CURRICULUM

Peer groups, family and work

Máirtín Mac an Ghaill and Chris Haywood

LIVERPOOL
JOHN MOORES UNIVERSITY
AVRIL ROBARTS LRC
TEL. 0151 231 4022

INTRODUCTION

Sex-role socialisation, which held together a multitude of projects as diverse as changing school texts, and establishing gender fair teaching styles, non-traditional role models, unbiased careers advice and girl-friendly schools was seen to have a lot to answer. . . . The simplicity of the portrayal of the processes of learning and gender identity formation, its assumptions about the nature of stereotyping, its somewhat negative view of girls as victims had all contributed to the creation of particular school based strategies.

(Arnot, 1991: 453)

Recent media reports have highlighted a major concern among parents, teachers and government officials about boys' low academic achievement and its links to increased alienation and anti-social behaviour (OFSTED, 1996; Carvel, 1996; Bennett, 1996). In response to the emerging thesis of boys' underachievement, the dominant media explanation suggests that these findings are evidence of equal opportunities having 'gone too far' and making schools less 'boy-friendly'. Educationalists have responded to this concern by locating the dynamics of underachievement primarily in relation to available role models, curriculum content, teaching styles and classroom management. However, such responses remain disconnected from contemporary social theory, and fail to acknowledge that schooling processes are intricately connected to a broader field of power relations. In light of the continued failure of educationalists to go beyond examining gender as a technical variable or effect, this chapter argues that there is a need to view pupils' gender identity formation critically as a dynamic process. More specifically, it is suggested that a wider focus that incorporates young people's peer groups, changing family forms and developing local labour markets, highlights a broader impetus in the making of pupils' gender identities.

FROM SEX ROLE SOCIALISATION TO DECONSTRUCTING SEX/GENDER IDENTITIES

Until recently, discussions on gender issues and schooling have concentrated on femininity and girls' schooling. Masculinity has been assumed to be unproblematic and continues to remain relatively absent from mainstream educational research. However, where boys' and girls' schooling experiences are considered, there is a tendency to use sex-role theory. Such theories have a history in the disciplines of social psychology and anthropology and suggest that men and women are culturally specific social constructions. They emphasise the historical variability of gender identity as opposed to the fixed nature of biology. A number of writers, such as Connell *et al.* (1982), Wolpe (1988) and Davies (1989), have persuasively presented the case against biologically based and sex role socialisation theories. They suggest that these theories are inadequate in explaining the complex social and psychological processes involved in the development of gendered identities. It is suggested that sex role approaches often take for granted a definition of femininity and masculinity, which are implicitly assumed to be ahistorical and unitary categories. However, work by Butler (1990) has illustrated how our understanding of the very social divisions based on biological differences is socially and historically contingent. They argue that the biological differences between the sexes are a consequence of the interrelationships between various social scientific and physical science disciplines. In effect, sex role theory sets up a false dichotomy between nature and culture. As a consequence, educational research often identifies different genders on the basis of biological differences. However, as Butler (1993: 28) suggests: 'Even as the category of sex is always re-inscribed as gender, that sex must still be presumed as the irreducible point of departure for the various cultural constructions it has come to bear.'

Alongside setting up a false dichotomy between sex and gender, sex role theories assume that gender divisions contain predictable and hierarchical relations of power. Power in this sense is mediated through ordered binaries. This means that males and females exist in unequally structured oppositions, and as a result, power is differentially refracted according to their sex. For instance, traditional feminist accounts of schooling and gender assume that masculinity and femininity are products of rational subjects occupying power relations located in patriarchal social structures. As Kessler *et al.* (1985) argue, in placing power at the centre of an analysis of masculinity, it is important to comprehend fully the complexity of its dynamic within institutional cultures. The conceptual difficulties involved in moving beyond monocausal explanations that employ a dualistic model of power are highlighted in the attempt to explore the complexities and contradictions of the interplay between aspects of social power such as class, age, sexuality, gender and 'race'/ethnicity.

The suggestion that there are a range of subject positions that may be occupied within different contradictory discourses is useful in understanding the local cultural production and reproduction of specific pupil masculine and feminine identity formations (Henriques *et al.*, 1984; Walkerdine, 1991). Rather than consider schools as mechanically reproducing gender identities, schools may be seen as active agents in the making of teacher and pupil femininities and masculinities. In this way, the official and hidden curricula do not merely reflect the dominant role models of the wider society, but actively produce a range of femininities and masculinities that are made available in local schooling arenas for pupils collectively to negotiate and inhabit within peer subcultures. As Wolpe (1988: 11) points out in relation to gender and power: 'differentiated forms of male power can only be accounted for by analysis which takes into consideration the specific conditions that give rise to these situations'. Contemporary modes of pupil masculinities and femininities are portrayed as highly complex and contradictory, displaying power, violence, competition, a sense of identity, and social support. We suggest that there is a need to move away from categorical theories, which emphasise that gender/sex relations are shaped by a single overarching factor. Rather, we suggest that these relations are multi-dimensional and differentially experienced and responded to within specific historical contexts and social locations. Consequently, gender/sex categories can be seen to be shaped by and shaping the processes of colonisation, of racism, of class hegemony, of male domination, of heterosexism and other forms of oppression. In short, gender can be seen as a crucial point of intersection of different forms of power, stratification, desire and subjective identity formation (Fanon, 1967; Mac an Ghaill, 1994b). In the following section we wish to re-engage sex role theory, by suggesting that a combination of more recent social and cultural theorising and a refocus to include broader social relations beyond the curriculum can offer insights into the possible dynamics in the development of pupils' gender identities.

PEER GROUP GENDERED/SEXUAL CULTURES

Peer group cultures have long been identified as of central importance within the educational process. In *Life in School*, Hammersley and Woods (1984: 3) note that:

> There can be little doubt that pupils' own interpretations of school processes represent a crucial link in the educational chain. Unless we understand how pupils respond to different forms of pedagogy and school organisation and why they respond in the ways that they do, our efforts to increase the effectiveness, or to change the impact of schooling will stand little chance of success.

For Brake (1980: 36) these cultures emerge as 'attempts to resolve collectively experienced problems arising from contradictions in the social structure, and that they generate a form of collective identity from which an individual identity can be achieved'. Applying his argument to the area of gender relations within schools, it may be argued that peer group cultures are key school-based mechanisms through which different femininities and masculinities are developed and lived out. In this section, we concentrate on the underresearched area of female peer groups. However, it is important to see masculinity not simply as complementary to femininity which, in doing so, tends to reinforce perceived unitary conceptions and 'natural' binary differences. At the same time, this section introduces the underresearched area of sexual cultures, suggesting that it has strategic importance in understanding the gendered nature of peer group cultures.

Early feminist work argued that a determining feature of girls' education was male-orientated schooling. It has been argued that the formation of female peer groups is highly contingent on the relationships between females and males. Feminist empiricists such as Lees (1986; 1993) have tried to locate the dynamics of female peer cultures by examining various forms of gendered abuse. Lees (1993: 16) argues:

> Gaining an identity as a young girl involves forming an identity – a sense of self – in opposition to the depiction of girls as sex objects, in opposition to the characterisation of the idea that women are no more than sexual beings.

In this way, sexual reputations become a significant arena wherein girls can accomplish social credibility. Also Halson (1989), carrying out research with 14 year old, white, lower middle class girls in a co-educational school, has linked their experience of sexual harassment with broader structural sources of social power. Their position of powerlessness is seen to derive from an organised/normalised structured relation between men and women, leading Halson to conclude that female and male interactions in the school: 'are both a product of and a reproduction of power differences between women and men' (1989: 142). In these accounts the formal curriculum exists as part of a broader structure of patriarchal power. However, other studies have suggested that examining the dynamics of female peer group cultures may involve moving away from masculinity as a central organising aspect.

Social class has been identified as a dynamic in girls' gender identity formation. McRobbie's (1978) early work suggested female peer groups celebrated a 'culture of femininity' that involved articulating class-based modes of being female. She argues that femininity was primarily created and reinforced outside school, usually in the girls' bedrooms. Mirroring explanations of male peer groups such as Willis (1977), and Corrigan (1979), McRobbie suggests that working class female peer groups could be identified through their oppositional activities to the school. In contrast middle class girls were more likely to take up the official institutional school ideology that cultivated passivity and conscientiousness. Importantly, the dynamics of working class female opposition to school was linked through form-ing steady relationships with men that resulted in marriage. Griffin, (1985) in her study, has suggested that the dynamics of female peer group cultures could not be contained within the cultural nexus of anti- or pro-school attitudes, friendship patterns and future job aspirations. Rather, she argues that certain gendered categories such as 'good girls' and 'trouble-makers' intersect differential class locations, making particularities of different females less distinct.

Aggleton (1987) has made an interesting contribution to this debate. He argues that accounts which suggest pupils' school-based responses to schooling as the key dynamic for the organisation of peer group relations may be exaggerated. Rather, he suggests that culturally acceptable and non-culturally acceptable practices articulated in schools can be identified as part of more general organising princi-ples evident within the home. He bases his analysis on a non-commercial, middle class female, subcultural group who rejected traditional working class femininities based upon marriage and reproduction. At the same time, this peer group also rejected conventional middle class understandings of females in further education and the assumption that they were there to access employment in nursing or secretarial work. According to Aggleton, this particular group of middle class females transported shared values in the home, those of autonomy and effortless achievement, into the school arena. The values were also shared and promoted by their parents, suggesting that young female subcultural styles reflected and articu-lated an intergenerational culture which was evident in the school. Similarly, Mac an Ghaill's (1994a) study of female peer group cultures in Parnell School suggests the existence of class-based differences within groups of females. Importantly, rather than seeing the formation of these peer groups as being reducible to the specific dynamics of the formal curriculum, it was the broader collective experi-ence of social deprivation, mass unemployment and shared communities outside the school, which contextualised the social formation of these particular female subcultures.

One important development in understanding gender in schools has been to reconceptualise gender peer groups as sexual cultures (Kehily and Nayak, 1996; Haywood and Mac an Ghaill, 1997). Most work that considers sexuality in peer groups tends to do so through a framework of gender. By this, we mean that sexuality tends to be located as a simple empirical category, alongside areas such as work or the family. A shift to a notion of sexual cultures involves not only inverting the interrelationship between sexuality and gender, but also imploding gender as *the* primary analytical category. This implosion allows other forms of social power such as 'race'/ethnicity, age and class to be considered as constitutive aspects of peer group cultures. For instance, other work with which we have been involved has charted the emergence of different cultures in educational sites based upon the consumption of popular cultural forms, homophobia and misogyny (Mac an Ghaill, 1994a). In this way, the differences between males were marked by their access to and taking up of particular heterosexual styles. Such styles were also used to demarcate class location and in some instances different English ethnicities. Alongside the consequence of creating a differentiation between young men, sexual cultures can also be seen as unifying groups of men and women.

Many accounts of sexuality within schools appear to emphasise the intense pressures upon different genders to conform to particular sexual practices (Lees, 1986; Jones and Mahoney, 1989). Haywood (1996) was able to observe pupils both inside and outside the classroom. Key places outside the curriculum, such as house parties, allowed males and females to share sexual experiences and knowledges. Importantly, this ethnography highlights how knowledge collected outside the curriculum informed gender relations within the curriculum. For instance, many spaces beyond the curriculum allowed groups of males and females to develop and embellish their sexual knowledges. These knowledges were often transported back into the curriculum. One effect of this developed knowledge was for some students to displace the school's demands for high levels of academic achievement, in favour of a more sophisticated and active heterosexuality.

One important aspect of work on peer group cultures has been to challenge accounts that tend to equate *female* with *gender*. Furthermore, given the diversity of class locations, ethnicities and investments in different sexualities, the meanings that surround male/boy and female/girl are no longer predictable.

FAMILY AND SCHOOL INTERRELATIONS

Further possible influences in the formulation of pupil identities can be located in the rapid change in the organisation of family life, that includes the increase in mother-headed lone families and the changing material conditions of local labour markets. It is important to stress that it is the interplay between a number of sites, involving family/kinship relationships, peer networks, media representation, and school and workplace experience that provides a filter through which gender identities are culturally produced and reproduced. The current diversity of English family forms makes it difficult to conceptualise the interrelationship between pupils' school experiences and their home lives (Robinson, 1988). Connell *et al.*'s (1982: 73) formulation is helpful in exploring complex sets of intergenerational class and gendered relations. In their study of the relationship between home, school and student peer groups in Australia, they make the important point that

> families are not closed universes but places where larger structures meet and interact . . . We do not mean to suggest that families are simply pawns of outside forces any more than schools are. In both cases, class and gender relations create dilemmas (some insolvable), provide resources (or deny them), and suggest solutions (some of which don't work), to which the family must respond in its collective practice.

Most of the work linking the school and the home with reference to gender issues has concentrated on young women and girls (Harris *et al.*, 1993). Nava (1984; 1992) has written how, for girls, against a background of 'labouring in the home, pleasing and serving others, their girlhood merges into womanhood'. Feminist accounts have reported the wide range of experiences of the domestic division of labour in girls' homes (Griffin, 1985; Cockburn, 1987; Smart, 1992). They provide much evidence of the unfair burden of females 'managing things and people in their homes' compared with males who merely tend to 'help out'. There is also discussion in the texts of the extra burdens young women and girls are presently experiencing with the increase in lone-parent, mother-headed families. It is important to stress here the different generational responses to the disruption of conventional forms of domestic femininity and masculinity, with a tendency for the younger generation to be more assertive in challenging traditional expectations. Of particular significance here is the generation of girls and boys who have been brought up by feminist mothers (Aggleton, 1987; Mac an Ghaill, 1994a). A further important element which has been underexplored is the impact of class and ethnicity on the girls' differentiated experiences of home life (Mirza, 1992). A major difficulty for female pupils is that teachers refuse to acknowledge both the different range of representations of domesticity in the arena of the home and the relationship between the gendered nature of domestic responsibilities (i.e. house work) and school work (Harris *et al.*, 1993).

In contrast, until very recently, little was written concerning boys' schooling and the domestic division of labour, that was assumed to be unproblematic. Hollands (1990: 10) is an important exception to this trend. He suggests that 'the power position within the working class household is crucial in forming masculine identities'. More specifically, he is critical of earlier studies of English male youth cultures for failing to explore the significance of the domestic sphere in the transition of boys into adulthood. In a study of school masculinities, Mac an Ghaill (1994a) found that in interviews with working class and middle class male pupils, parents were frequently mentioned as influencing their orientation to schooling. He reported on the cultural continuity between middle class parents and schooling, suggesting that working class parental affirmation and legitimation of schools' authority was more complex and diverse. For example, there was no predictable, mechanistic, intergenerational links between parents' and their sons' evaluation of schooling. Parents who were actively supportive of the school sometimes produced anti-school male pupils, and parents who appeared indifferent or hostile to school sometimes had academic-orientated sons. Equally important in shaping parents' relations with schools are memories of their own schooling. As Connell *et al.* (1982: 166) found: 'working-class people are often injured, insulted and disempowered by their experience with schools'. Such experiences may explain some fathers' ambivalent and contradictory support for their sons' education, in 'pushing them to get on', while having severe doubts about the value of academic knowledge (Mac an Ghaill, 1994a).

Importantly, alongside increasing numbers of teenage mothers, there is evidence to suggest a growth in the numbers of young men becoming teenage fathers. At present, theorising the dynamics of teenage men's motivations through a conceptual framework tends to begin with the family unit (Lerman, 1986). Studies on masculinities by Brittan (1989) and Morgan (1992) have suggested that the family has traditionally been a significant resource that men use to make their masculinities. Other studies have suggested that entrance into fatherhood is a mark of manhood, a defining moment in boys' rites of passage. Current research that we are carrying out has indicated that male teenagers, of a variety of different class and ethnic backgrounds, appear not to be developing masculinities based upon fatherhood.[1] The current political climate of nostalgia for, and a collective memory of, real and imagined communities is being intersected by young men's growing ambivalence towards the meaning of fatherhood. This ambivalence is emerging despite state attempts to consolidate a curriculum for fatherhood (NCC, 1990; Department for Education, 1994). At the same time, studies such as Burgess and Ruxton (1996) have suggested that fatherhood is becoming feminised. The latter argue that, historically, men's position in the family has been subject to radical change. In the nineteenth century, men held exclusive rights over their children. In the late twentieth century, women have displaced men as the key legal guardians. This has been enhanced by recent moves to give children the legal status of citizens (Collier, 1995). Most significantly, the cumulative effects of increasing deindustrialisation, feminisation of the labour market, the rise in youth unemployment, and the regulation of mass post-compulsory education and training mean that the resources that young men have traditionally drawn upon to make their gender/sexual identities are being reconstituted (Pye *et al.*, 1996).

THE REGENDERING OF WAGED LABOUR IN THE 1990S: EMERGING NEW MASCULINITIES AND FEMININITIES

Historically, rites of passage in industrial societies have tended to be rather ambiguous processes, lacking the collective rituals, structures and support found in traditional societies. However, more recently, young people collectively and individually are constructing feminine and masculine identities in a climate of rapid socio-economic change that has led to a major fracturing in the process of coming of age in England, over the last decade. For example, Willis (1985: 6) speaks of how the

young unemployed now find themselves in a new social condition of suspended animation between school and work. Many of the old transitions into work, into cultures and organisations of work, into being consumers, into independent accommodation – have been frozen or broken.

These transitions are further shaped and differentiated by sets of power relations through class, 'race', ethnicity, gender, sexuality and disability, which have contributed to a decade in which forms of material and social inequalities have greatly increased (see Brown, 1989; Mac an Ghaill, 1992). Most recently, Roberts (1995) has argued that the failure of young people's employment to re-establish itself after the recession of the 1980s and early 1990s, coupled with a national decline in training scheme participation and a rise of young people entering into further education, is creating a 'new social condition' for young people. In short, we are witnessing highly disorganised and fractured post-compulsory school transitions, with large sectors of white and black working class young people continuing to learn not to labour (Weis, 1991).

One of the key dynamics of young people's 'new social condition' is the regendering of work relations. In local economies, the disappearing 'masculine' manufacturing base is being displaced by an increase in the traditional 'feminine' service sector. As Hutton (1995: 20) has pointed out:

A quiet revolution is going on which is transforming the lives of millions of workers in Britain. The world of full-time pensionable employment is retreating before their eyes; and in its stead is emerging an insecure world of contract work, part-time jobs and casualised labour.

A large proportion of this work is being carried out by white and black working class women (Walby, 1991).

In earlier work (Mac an Ghaill, 1994a) one of us found that the emerging diverse intra-class trajectories to post-school employment were acted out in relation to such bridging mechanisms as work experience. The young men's responses might be read as a dress rehearsal for the 'real thing'. At Parnell Comprehensive School, located within the West Midlands, the disruption and accompanying restructuring of the pupils' transitions from school to waged labour, with the collapse of the local economy's manufacturing base, appeared to be creating a crisis in traditional English, white, working class forms of masculine subject positions (Department of Employment, 1994). This was of specific significance for the white, working class, low achieving boys, whose outdated mode of masculinity continued to centre around traditional manual waged labour, at a time when their traditional manual work destiny has disappeared. This is not to suggest that mass youth unemployment, the resulting racialisation of poverty and dominant state discourses of ethnic minority pathology (discourses that suggest inequalities are a natural residual of ethnic/'racialised' collectivities) were not a major critical issue for such groups as African-Caribbean and Asian boys. Nor is it to suggest that these social conditions go uncontested. However, these ethnic groups have a longer history of unemployment in racially structured local labour markets. Hence, the English, white, working class, low achieving boys tended to have more of an expectation of, and emotional investment in, local waged labour.

One of the major dangers of exploring the regendering of work, and taking masculinity as its focus, is that female experiences will be marginalised. At the present time there is much media talk proposing that the future *is* female. The main evidence cited for this is that girls are closing the achievement gap in some subject areas. At the same time, it is reported that young women are doing better in local labour markets with the increase in the traditional 'feminine' service sector and the decrease in the traditional 'masculine' manufacturing sector. It is important to stress that if the future is female, for many working class girls it is a future of low paid, part-time, non-unionised, casual work alongside continuing major responsibility for domestic labour. Earlier work on females and the labour market has conceptualised female social trajectories in terms of careers or marriage. At the present time, such a dichotomy appears no longer sufficient to make sense of the impact of the regendering of work on young female schooling experience. For example, the explosion in non-married teenage pregnancies and absent teenage fathers has created a changed material context for groups of young women in the 1990s' labour market. However, a lack of research in this area is creating a paradox. Although we can map out the changes in social and economic contexts, we can no longer be sure about what these changes mean. Unlike many media representations of the changing regendering of work, we cannot simply 'read off' meanings unproblematically.

This is illustrated in Hollands' (1990) ethnographic study of a Youth Training Scheme. He considers the way that new vocationalism impacted upon how young people understood their training allowances. For groups of young working class men, the training allowance became reconstructed as a 'wage'. Hollands points out that for males the wage is closely tied up to meanings of manual waged labour. He argues that because the young men do not have a wage, the training allowance is reconstructed as a wage, gaining a highly exaggerated importance. This fetishisation mediates itself through the traditional working class ideology of paying into the family, the 'breadwinner ethos'. However, differences between the young men meant that some viewed the allowance as less important than the job that they were doing. Others considered the allowance as agreeable, seeing the training in terms of their career prospects, arguing that the allowance represented a fair wage. Hollands argues that the development of new vocational ideologies, while reconstructing traditional assumptions of the wage, is creating new alternative understandings and challenging traditional working class values of the wage. Hollands makes a distinction between class and culture. This allows him to examine how gender, race and age interplay in the formation of a class position. His insights suggest that we can no longer predict the impact of the shifting organisation of work and the family on pupils' gender identities.

CONCLUSION

Recent work by Rudduck (1994: 9–10) on gender policy in secondary schools illustrates the shift from earlier sex role approaches to a more complex picture of gender relations and the interconnections with other social divisions. Although such an approach is not common practice in schools at the present time, she persuasively suggests a way forward. In her account, actively committed teachers

> were not exclusively about transforming the experience of girls. Charged with concern for all their pupils, they also worried about the boys. For instance, they recognised the extent to which some boys were under-achieving; they were affected by both class-bound patterns of social injustice and particular structures of masculinity prevalent in their schools or in their communities . . . In encouraging debate about gender, most teachers were anxious to avoid a crude and clumsy branding of all boys, all men as guiltily sexist. An understanding of self to broad struc-tures of socially endorsed injustice has to be carefully developed if boys are to consider the part they might and perhaps already do play in the construction of gender relations.

As suggested in the introduction, the 'boys' underachievement' thesis is an impor-tant debate that exemplifies popular theorising of gender in schooling (Moore, 1996). In this chapter, we have suggested that there is a need to develop a more theoretically adequate framework to explain gender identity formations that incor-porates studies on peer group cultures, changing family forms and changing labour markets. In so doing, we shall begin to build an alternative, coherent and progres-sive explanation which challenges current popular explanations that are informed by an anti-feminist stance. There is a real danger that the developing concern about gender and education will serve to make invisible new forms of class and racial institutional discrimination experienced by both young women and young men. We suggest that there is a need to rethink analyses that are 'overly gendered'. Instead, it is important to locate gender within other fields of social power, examining the locally situated interplay between class, sexuality, 'race'/ethnicity and age, to comprehend fully how institutional contexts produce, normalise and regulate gender.

NOTE

1 This has been carried out as part of the Leverhulme-Trust-funded project, 'Changing work and family life: developing young masculinities', ref: A94262.

REFERENCES

Aggleton, P. (1987) *Rebels without a Cause? Middle Class Youth and the Transition from School to Work*, Lewes: Falmer.

Arnot, M. (1991) 'Equality and democracy: a decade of struggle over education', *British Journal of Sociology of Education* 12(4): 447–66.

LIVERPOOL JOHN MOORES UNIVERSITY AVRIL ROBARTS LRC TEL. 0151 231 4022

Bennett, C. (1996) 'The boys with the wrong stuff', *Guardian* 6 November: 17.

Brake, M. (1980) *The Sociology of Youth Culture and Youth Sub-cultures*, London: Routledge and Kegan Paul.

Brittan, A. (1989) *Masculinity and Power*, Oxford: Blackwell.

Brown, P. (1989) 'Schooling for inequality? Ordinary kids in the school and the labour market', in B. Cosin *et al.* (eds) *School, Work and Equality*, London: Hodder & Stoughton.

Burgess, A. and Ruxton, S. (1996) *Men and the Children: Proposals for Public Policy*, London: Institute for Public Policy Research.

Butler, J. (1990) *Gender Trouble, Feminism and the Subversion of Identity*, London: Routledge.

—— (1993) *Bodies that Matter, on the Discursive Limits of 'Sex'*, London: Routledge.

Carvel, J. (1996) 'Blunkett plans to tackle "laddism"', *Guardian* 1 November: 7.

Cockburn, C.K. (1987) *Two-track Training: Sex Inequalities and the YTS*, London: Macmillan.

Collier, R. (1995) *Masculinity, Law and the Family*, Routledge: London.

Connell, R.W., Ashenden, D. J., Kessler, S. and Dowsett, G.W. (1982) *Making the Difference: School, Families and Social Divisions*, London: George Allen & Unwin.

Corrigan, P. (1979) *Schooling the Smash Street Kids*, London: Macmillan.

Davies, B. (1989) 'The discursive production of the male/female dualism in school settings', *Oxford Review of Education* 15: 229.

Department for Education (1994) *Education Act 1993: Sex Education in Schools, Circular 5/94*, London: HMSO.

Department of Employment (1994) *West Midlands Labour Market and Skill Trends 1994–95*, Birmingham: Department of Employment, West Midlands Office.

Fanon, F. (1967) *Black Skins, White Masks*, London: Paladin.

Griffin, C. (1985) *Typical Girls? Young Women from School to the Job Market*, London: Routledge and Kegan Paul.

Halson, J. (1989) 'Young women, sexual harassment and heterosexuality: violence, power relations and mixed sex schooling', in P. Abbott and C. Wallace (eds) *Gender, Power and Sexuality*, London: Macmillan.

Hammersley, M. and Woods, P. (1984) *Life in Schools: the Sociology of Pupil Culture*, Milton Keynes: Open Univeristy Press.

Harris, S., Nixon, J. and Rudduck, J. (1993) 'School work, homework and gender', *Gender and Education* 5: 1.

Haywood, C. P. (1996) 'Talking sex-sex talking: out of the curriculum', *Curriculum Studies* 4: 2.

Haywood, C.P. and Mac an Ghaill, M. (1995) 'The sexual politics of the curriculum: contesting values', *International Studies in the Sociology of Education* 5: 2 .

—— (1997) ' "A man in the making": sexual masculinities within changing training cultures', *Sociological Review* 45(4): 576–90.

Henriques, J., Hollway, W., Urwin, C., Venn, C. and Walkerdine, V. (1984) *Changing the Subject: Psychology, Social Regulation and Subjectivity*, London: Methuen.

Hollands, R.G. (1990) *The Long Transition: Class, Culture and Youth Training*, London: Macmillan.

Hutton, W. (1995) *The State We're In*, London: Jonathan Cape.

Jones, C. and Mahony, P. (eds) (1989) *Learning Our Lines: Sexuality and Social Control in Education*, London: The Women's Press.

Kehily, M. and Nayak, A. (1996) ' "Playing it straight": masculinities and homophobias and schooling', *Journal of Gender Studies* 5: (2).

Kessler, S., Ashenden, D. J., Connell, R.W. and Dowsett, G.W. (1985) 'Gender relations in secondary schooling', *Sociology of Education* 5: 34 – 48.

Lees, S. (1986) *Losing Out: Sexuality and Adolescent Girls*, London: Hutchinson.

—— (1993) *Sugar and Spice: Sexuality and Adolescence*, Harmondsworth: Penguin.

Lerman, R.L. (1986) 'Who are the young absent fathers?', *Youth and Society* 18 (1): 3–27.

Mac an Ghaill, M. (1992) 'Student perspectives on curriculum innovation and change in English secondary schools: an empirical study', *British Educational Research Journal* 18 (3): 221–34.

—— (1994a) *The Making of Men: Masculinities, Sexualities and Schooling*, Buckingham: Open University Press.

—— (1994b) '(In)visibility: sexuality, masculinity and "race" in the school context', in D. Epstein (ed.) *Challenging Lesbian and Gay Inequalities in Education*, Buckingham: Open University Press.

—— (1996) 'Sociology of education, state schooling and social class: beyond critiques of the New Right hegemony', *British Journal of Sociology of Education* 17 (2) 163–76.

McRobbie, A. (1978) 'Working class girls and the culture of femininity', in Centre for Contemporary Culture Studies, *Women Take Issue*, London: Hutchinson.

Mirza, H.S. (1992) *Young, Female and Black*, London: Routledge.

Moore, R. (1996) Back to the future: The problem of change and the possibilities of advance in the sociology of education, *British Journal of Sociology of Education*, 17 (2) 1145–61.

Morgan, D.H.J. (1992) *Discovering Men*, London: Routledge.

National Curriculum Council (1990) *Health Education: Curriculum Guidance 5*, York: NCC.

Nava, M. (1984) 'Youth service provision, social order and the question of girls', in A. McRobbie and M. Nava (eds) *Gender and Generation*, London: Macmillan.

—— (1992) *Changing Cultures: Feminism, Youth and Consumerism*, London: Sage.

OFSTED (1996) *The Gender Divide: Performance Differences between Boys and Girls'*, London: HMSO.

Pye, D., Haywood, C. and Mac an Ghaill, M. (1996) 'The training state: deindustrialisation and the production of white working class male trainee identities', *International Journal of the Sociology of Education* 5(4).

Roberts, K. (1995) *Youth and Employment in Modern Britain*, Oxford: Oxford University Press.

Robinson, P. (1988) *Do Schools Make a Difference?*, Milton Keynes: Open University Press.

Rudduck, J. (1994) *Developing a Gender Policy in Secondary Schools*, Buckingham: Open University Press.

Smart, C. (ed.) (1992) *Regulating Motherhood: Historical Essays on Marriage, Motherhood and Sexuality*, London: Routledge.

Walby, S. (1991) *Theorizing Patriarchy*, London: Basil Blackwell.

Walkerdine, V. (1991) *Feminism and Youth Culture: From 'Jackie' to 'Just Seventeen'*, London: Macmillan.

Weis, L. (1991) *Working-Class without Work*, London: Routledge.

Willis, P. (1977) *Learning to Labour: How Working Class Kids Get Working Class Jobs*, Farnborough, Hants: Saxon House.

—— (1985) *Youth Unemployment and the New Poverty: A Summary of Local Authority Review and Framework for Policy Department on Youth and Youth Unemployment*, Wolverhampton: Wolverhampton Local Authority.

Wolpe, A.M. (1988) *Within School Walls: the Role of Discipline. Sexuality and the Curriculum*, London: Routledge.

225

14

GENDER AND UNDERACHIEVEMENT

Democratic educational reform through
discourse evaluation

John Quicke

INTRODUCTION

The current interest in the so-called 'underachievement' of boys in school has to be
seen in context. For several decades now, the main focus of liberal equal opportunities policies has been 'access for girls', particularly in relation to the traditional
male preserves of science, maths and technology. Schools which took up this
challenge tried to introduce content and to develop teaching approaches which
would make these subjects more suited to girls' interests and needs. This usually
entailed intervention on a much broader front, since the problem was clearly
associated with general attitudes towards women in a male-dominated society.
Thus many schools were also concerned with positive action on sexist attitudes
and behaviours across a wide area of social interaction in schools; for example, the
deployment of gender stereotypes in the 'hidden curriculum', the exclusion of
female teachers from senior positions, boys' 'harassment' of girls.

Recently, however, there has been a distinct shift of emphasis. 'Equal opportunities' is now just as likely to be associated with boys' as with girls' achievement.
The talk is of making the curriculum more 'boy-friendly' and of encouraging boys
to be better organised and motivated as 'learners'. Although girls have for years
outperformed boys in language-based subjects (English, English literature and
modern languages) it is now evident that they have also caught up in the traditionally male-dominated subjects of science and maths and are even edging ahead
(although, as we shall see below, the situation is more complex than this). The
differences have become evident even at younger ages, with girls doing better on
reading tests and being generally more competent in language and communication
skills in all areas of the curriculum (Swann, 1992; OFSTED, 1993). It has always
been the case that more boys than girls have been labelled as having learning

difficulties and more of them have been allocated extra help in designated special needs groups or classes (Ford, *et al*. 1982).

In this chapter, I shall argue that the current emphasis on boys' underachievement is misplaced if it is defined in a way which means resources for the realisation of equal opportunities are directed away from girls towards boys. Those involved in the implementation of equal opportunities policies need to bear in mind the continuing differences in the life chances of boys and girls. Despite the changes that have taken place in recent years, inequality between the sexes is still a prevalent feature of the society in which we live. In the first part of this chapter, questions relating to gender and underachievement will be discussed in relation to the underlying social *structure* which gives rise to this pattern of inequality. In the second part the focus shifts to the possibilities for the democratic reform of education through the promotion of *agency* (capacity for autonomous action) as reflexively articulated in relation to discursive practices at the formal and informal level. It is suggested that a way forward would be for school discourses to be evaluated and recontextualised in relation to an overarching democratic discourse.

PART 1 – STRUCTURE: A PATRIARCHAL SOCIETY?

For many educationalists the lack of equal opportunities for girls reflects the male-dominated nature of the education system, which itself derives from the role of that system in the reproduction of a patriarchal society. The dominant ideology of such a society might be characterised as grounded in three main assumptions: firstly, that the separate spheres of men and women were 'natural' divisions based on biological differences; secondly, that women were inferior to men; and thirdly, that women were defined in relation to men and children rather than as individual beings (Purvis, 1981). Some would argue, however, that this ideology has been undermined in recent years by social and cultural changes, in particular those associated with the increased participation of women in the labour force, improved educational opportunities for girls and the transformation of family forms. Women now expect and achieve a greater degree of equality in the home and at work, and as traditional stereotypes of male and female are deconstructed so new gender identities are emerging.

Whilst most critics of patriarchy acknowledge the changes that have taken place, there is disagreement on the extent to which these have made any real difference to women's lives. For some, equality between the sexes has almost been secured, whilst for others the reforms of the last thirty years or so have merely scratched the surface. The position taken in this chapter is based on evidence from a number of large-scale surveys and case studies of gender segregation and social change in the 1980s and early 1990s carried out in various parts of the UK as part of the nationally funded Social Change and Economic Life Initiative (SCELI). In her summing up of the findings of these studies, Alison MacEwen Scott (1994) concludes that despite the profound economic and social changes of recent years men and women still remain highly segregated at work, and this segregation is still strongly related to inequalities in pay, career prospects and employment protection.

The surveys show that there have undoubtedly been new opportunities for women. The growth in demand for part-time work has clearly benefited women, particularly those with strong domestic commitments. The increase in the importance of formal qualifications and the break-up of traditional, male-dominated labour markets in the primary sector have also helped. But whilst some of the new jobs require highly skilled labour, many of them are low grade, poorly paid and insecure. In the professions, where women have made gains, particularly in the public sector, this has occurred at a time when 'intensification' and financial constraints have led to a deterioration in job conditions. In the 'dynamic' service industries such as building societies where there have been increased opportunities for women graduates, married women's lack of geographical mobility has often had an adverse effect on their career development.

The influence of the traditional division of labour in families is still much in evidence, as MacEwen Scott points out:

> Despite the economic changes . . . women's increased labour market participation, and changes in family structure, such as increases in divorce and single parenthood, there appears to be enormous stability in women's and men's domestic roles and the value system that underpins them.
>
> (1994: 35)

The research provides further evidence that women's long term career development is disrupted by their continuing role as the providers of primary childcare. This is reflected in the fact that career opportunities for male breadwinners increase during their lifetime and in the process their earning capacity becomes substantially greater. The primacy of the male breadwinner role continues to result in structures of employment and payment which are an expression of gender segregation based on primary or secondary earner status. In addition, the research showed

> that naturalistic beliefs about gender, embodied in notions of strength, dexterity, sensitivity and so on, play a fundamental role in the sex-typing of jobs . . . (the lack of desegregation) is mainly due to enduring inequalities in the domestic division of labour and deeply held beliefs about the nature of gender itself.
>
> (p. 35)

Boys, girls and underachievement

It is against this background, I would argue, that the gender gap in academic achievement and the dominant interpretations of this should be understood.

Not only an awareness of the existence of differences but also how differences are explained are crucial for the development of an appropriate policy response. In the past, the typical explanation for differences in achievement has been 'immaturity'. Thus, boys were usually said to need 'support' but no other measures were thought to be necessary because boys would eventually 'catch up'. However, it is clear from GCSE results that boys do not now 'catch up' in the way they did in the past. In the current period, there has been a shift of emphasis towards interpreting the 'gap' in terms of boys' 'underachievement'. In a study carried by the author of a sample of secondary schools across two LEAs, teachers explained differences in various ways but most of these were grounded in assumptions about boys' unfulfilled potential (Quicke, 1995). There are reports of schools adopting strategies for identifying underachievers and providing such pupils with extra help of one kind or another. Some have used standardised tests as predictors of GCSE results and defined underachievement as failure to realise 'potential' as suggested by such tests. Gold (1995) reports on a school in Suffolk which used scores on a reading test at 12+ to ascertain which pupils were doing worse or better than expected in the run-up to GCSEs. The majority of underachievers were boys who were then invited to work with a teacher 'mentor' once a week on study skills and examination preparation.

Explaining the 'problem' as 'boys' underachievement' carries with it a number of interrelated meanings which are often underplayed in policies involving the development of remedial strategies which target boys. To begin with it is typically associated with the assumption that girls may be 'overachieving', which itself is often related to the more general point that GCSE has become easier, particularly in the areas of maths and science (Harris *et al.* 1993). Further, it is alleged not only that the content is easier but also that methods of assessment have favoured girls. Thus, for example, the 'hardworking but not too bright' girl does better because coursework now counts for more. Despite the numerous research studies which have challenged the common sense view (see e.g. Baker and Jones, 1992), the general belief still persists that gender differences in cognitive skills are innate and that girls' achievements are often the result of 'hard work' rather than ' innate intelligence'. Thus the notion of boys' underachievement and its counterpart in girls' overachievement brings with it sexist assumptions about intellectual differences between the sexes which have a long history. It is not so much that girls overachieve in language-based subjects but that their achievements are in these 'easy', non-cognitive subjects and therefore are of less significance in the long term.

But there is no justification for discriminating between boys and girls in this way. Girls' better performance on literacy and language tests does not in itself mean that there is not as much underachievement amongst girls as boys. Girls come to school with a 'flying start' on the language and literacy front, which constitutes the 'base line' of their achievement. They may on average have more cultural and linguistic resources to draw on at the start of their education, and their future achievements must be related to these differences; that is, in current jargon, they must be seen in a value-added way. Even if we assume there is no gap between the sexes to begin with but that this emerges during the early years of schooling (for whatever reason) then for all practical purposes we are still looking at a different starting point for boys and girls. Some studies have suggested that, although there are some differences between boys and girls in the primary years, it is what happens at the secondary stage which is more crucial and that therefore the base line should be established at the end of the primary stage where attainments are not significantly different. But although the gap may widen considerably during the secondary stage, there is enough evidence to show that the differences which exist earlier are substantial (Gorman *et al.*, 1988).

We can also look at the notion of underachievement in another way. Given the position of women in society, girls need, in a sense, to achieve more than boys while they are in school. What constitutes achievement and underachievement therefore will be different for them. We can tease out some further issues here by taking a closer look at the so-called gender gap in performance in public examinations. Although, as indicated above, girls are now achieving 'better' GCSE results than boys, the picture is more complex than implied by simple comparisons of overall results. Girls are achieving success in traditional 'male' subjects (design and technology, computer studies, mathematics, chemistry and combined science) but still do relatively less well in these subjects than in others (EOC/OFSTED, 1996). In choosing options at Key Stage 4, there is still a tendency for boys and girls to make choices which reflect traditional stereotypes, with scientific and technical subjects attracting more boys, and language and arts more girls. There is also evidence that subject choice in the sixth form is heavily influenced by gender. As the authors of the EOC/OFSTED report point out, 'despite their success in these subjects at GCSE, relatively few young women are taking A-level courses which are wholly mathematical, scientific or technological, thereby denying themselves some career opportunities in science, engineering and technology' (p. 13). As far as results at 'A'-level are concerned, the pattern of performance of the sexes at GCSE level does not appear to be continued. For example, of those with GCSE point scores of sixty or more in 1992, 32 per cent of male candidates and 22 per cent of female candidates achieved 'A'-level or AS scores of thirty or more in 1994 (DFE, 1994).

Further support for these trends comes from analyses of gender differences in patterns of subject choice, standards obtained in the Scottish Certificate of Education (SCE) and post-school intentions in Scotland where Darling and Glendinning (1996) found evidence of 'gender tracks'. In their study of third- and fourth-year pupils in seven local authority schools they identified three groups: 'male-academic' orientation (group A); 'female-academic' orientation (group B); and 'non-academic' orientation (group C). The findings suggested a distinct set of interrelationships between choice and structure, like class and gender, and also between choice and career trajectories. The first two groups were divided along gender lines both in terms of character and in the actual composition of the groups (although the study also showed there was a substantial minority of girls who chose 'male subjects' and boys who chose 'female subjects'). The authors note that group

A aspired to higher status occupations than group B, thus reflecting traditional stereotyped constructions of career development. Group C ('non-academic') appeared to be less gendered at first sight but further analysis of educational and career aspirations revealed significant differences between boys and girls, with boys much more likely to consider leaving at the minimum age.

Additional support for the notion of 'gender tracks' comes from studies of pupils' own assessments of their academic abilities. The achievement of self-confidence and a positive approach to learning in the long term may not always go hand in hand with high achievement in the 'here and now' as reflected in school tests and exam results. Several researchers have found that high achieving girls do not always have a corresponding belief in their academic abilities. Teachers may unwittingly reinforce this by the way they respond to pupils in the classroom. Thus Licht and Dweck (1983) observed that teachers in the primary school have high expectations of girls but still managed to contribute to the girls' lack of confidence in their academic abilities. Girls receive fewer criticisms of their work than boys but those they do receive refer to the intellectual quality of the work. Girls tend to attribute failure in academic subjects to lack of ability and success with 'luck'. They tend to be more easily put off by failure on new tasks and to underestimate their degree of success on all tasks. Thus they tend to prefer language-related work because this is perceived as easier and there is less chance of failure. Moreover, it has been suggested that school literacy may actually be harmful for girls. For example, the reason why girls' success in school writing is not translated into achievements career-wise may be related to the fact that too many books that girls read anticipate futures where women are subservient to men. Girls are also often given the impression that creative writing is the 'best' writing, and this reinforces their disinclination to write in the non-literary genres required in science and other subjects (Millard, 1997; White, 1990).

Recent evidence of girls' success in GCSE maths and science may still not dispel notions which are deeply embedded in cultural understandings of gender identity (DES, 1989). The relatively low level of take-up of science at 'A' level by girls may well reflect their belief that the subject is too hard for them (OFSTED, 1994). In their study Darling and Glendinning (1996) found that the 'male-academic' group rated their abilities more highly than the other groups. Interestingly, pupils in their sample tended to regard their own views about their abilities as more significant than those of teachers and parents, suggesting that although pupils claimed ownership and responsibility for their choices, the latter were in fact heavily influenced by structural factors. The following quotation from the EOC/OFSTED (1996) report neatly summarises most of these concerns about gender differences in school achievement, as well as raising some important questions which will have to be addressed in the ensuing discussion.

> While girls are now achieving better academic results than boys at age 16, there is little evidence that this is leading to improved post-school opportunities in the form of training, employment, career development and

economic independence for the majority of young women. Are schools focusing on the academic achievement of girls, and neglecting the important and complementary skills of individual development and decision-making which enable young people to maximise their opportunities later on? How can schools challenge traditional expectations and roles in order to improve pupils' aspirations and strengthen their life choices and chances?

(p. 2)

PART 2 – AGENCY, DISCOURSE AND DEMOCRATIC EDUCATION

To be aware of gender as 'structure' is one thing, to be aware how gender 'works' at the level of 'practice' is quite another. If we are to challenge traditional expectations and roles in school contexts, then we need to deploy a model of teacher and pupil awareness which requires the development of an understanding of the contingent and discursive nature of identity construction. It is important for curriculum reform and teaching strategies to be formulated in the light of an understanding of the specific discursively organised contexts in which gender identities and understandings of achievement are constructed.

Discourses are characterised and defined in terms of what they make possible to say and think (including what to think about the self) and what possibilities they close off. A discourse is essentially a 'language game' associated with a particular linguistic community in a particular social context. As Peim (1993) points out, a discourse

> will have its own terminology and its own rules of expression and have rules about what kind of statements are appropriate, as well as rules about who may speak when and who may say what to whom and in what circumstances.
>
> (p. 38)

The rules of the discourse may sometimes be explicit although more often than not they are implicit. Identities are defined by the way people are 'positioned' in discourses; their sense of self is derived from how they are categorised in the language of the discourse (Davies and Harre, 1990).

School subjects have their own discourses. In addition to subject domains there are also more generalised forms of school discourse, such as classroom discourse, which has its own particular ground rules (see Edwards and Mercer, 1987). Access to these discourses may well be socially distributed (Sheeran and Barnes, 1991) reflecting the impact of other general discourses such as those of class, gender or race to which they are related. There are also the ground rules of particular pupil cultures and the specific culture of the home to consider. All social action in schools, as Walkerdine (1988) points out, takes place within the framework of discursive practices. The social context of the school, like all social contexts, is not a fixed and singular totality but a set of discursive practices which articulate in various ways. What is of interest in terms of understanding school processes is how discourses articulate in specific social, cultural and temporal/spatial locations. We may view them as having similarities or differences, as having family resemblances, as being consonant or conflicting or as having relations of dominance and subordination (Quicke, 1996a).

The notion of individual *agency* is not abandoned in this model, but redefined in terms of the self as person-in-relation with the capacity for reflexivity. Understanding the self is a process which involves working to produce a coherent narrative of the self, rather than having the aim of identifying what the 'real' nature of the self is. It is itself part of an ongoing process of self-formation, serving as a vehicle for articulating, reflecting upon and analysing the various threads of experience which we associate with ourselves. It is conceptualised from some vantage point within the existing structure of the self and its experience and understanding of the world, but this point cannot be fully articulated in advance of the process of reflection. The starting point, indeed the whole process of self-identity formation, would be negotiated within the social context of its production; that is, as, say, a school-based endeavour, it would have to take account of the educational purpose as mediated through school processes. For the educationalist presumably not all self 'becomings' would be equally 'good'. We can see many ways in which the ongoing formation of the self constituted in discourses might lead to the reinforcement or creation of representations, say of gender or race, which do not result in a 'better' self. Where this was so the educationalist would attempt to foster an awareness of the contested nature of such meanings.

The main pedagogical issue for teachers is to do with which meanings are of most relevance for the 'becoming' self of the particular students in their charge. Identity practices which are salient for particular individuals cannot be known in advance of examining the lived experience of those individuals. We might guess that in our society, discourses of class, gender, race, age and ability are still likely to be salient, but we cannot predict how they will actually impact on the psychology of a particular individual. And in any case, to understand the self purely as a formation at the intersection of these society-wide discourses (however differentiated) is not only highly reductionist (and potentially 'totalitarian') but far too crude for educational purposes. There are also usually many other discursive practices from studying science to painting pictures; from playing chess to writing poetry; from cooking to playing soccer; from making friends to making families which, though influenced by society-wide discourses, have their own specific meanings which contribute to the 'richness' of a person's identity and which are deployed by them in their reflexive self-projects (Giddens, 1991).

The articulation of discourses

In understanding the processes of gender identity construction we need to examine how key discourses in schools interact with the discourse of gender. As an example I shall use the powerful discourse of science. Interpreted as an identity constituting discourse it has been suggested that science is inherently masculinist (see also Scaife in this volume). Feminist critics have queried the whole notion of 'science' as it is conventionally understood. However, many of the points made by feminist critics echo those of others who think that the school science curriculum is in need of radical reform. As presently understood school science may be of little value to either boys or girls, even those who achieve modest success in the system. Paul Black, for example, one of the original architects of National Curriculum science and author of an OECD-sponsored report, has raised several important questions about the relevance of content, methodology and assessment for all pupils under current arrangements (see *The Times Educational Supplement*, 1995: 22 March). Although the reforms advocated by the OECD were partly motivated by the aim to secure the participation of more girls, the need for more relevance, more student-centred approaches and links with other disciplines apply equally to boys. Of course, there are likely to be gender differences in what is considered relevant or of interest, but the 'holistic' approach – one which involves connecting different experiences and includes the affective as well as the cognitive dimension – is no more 'natural' for girls than boys, and both are likely to need help in looking at science in this way.

It remains to be seen, however, whether radical curriculum reform of this kind in science can make much impact on the hidden curriculum of schooling. At the moment, I would argue, it is largely the hidden curriculum or the unacknowledged discourse of schooling which is mostly responsible for pupils' school identities, and unless this is altered then changes in the formal curriculum will make little difference to the pupils' general experience of school. Thus it could well be that science may be made more relevant to all pupils but the underlying divisions between pupils remain and the same attitudes are fostered. Regarding gender roles, girls' success in science may be incorporated into the dominant gender discourse in a way which does not threaten basic assumptions. In this analysis, it is not that science itself is masculinist but that the gender discourse articulates with the 'progressive' discourse of science in such a way that positioning in the former structures identity in the latter. It is because gender as a structuring discourse for science is itself one in which girls are positioned as inferior, marginal and less powerful than boys that its effect on science education is anti-educational and anti-democratic.

It is in the light of these considerations that attempts to look at difference as reflecting equality and diversity in approaches to learning in science have to be evaluated. For instance, in a study of gender differences in learning styles, Tolmie and Howe (1993) found that on a computer-based task in secondary school physics, both boy and girl pairs made equal progress in understanding but

234

employed markedly different styles. Males tended to take more account of the implications of 'feedback' while girls tended to explore what the problems they were investigating had in common. The authors interpreted this as reflecting how the different pairs coped with conflict. Their study supports previous findings which show that males are more inclined to assert and elaborate when faced with a conflict of opinion whereas girls typically avoid conflict and focus on what has already been agreed. Both these styles have positive and negative features from an educational viewpoint. If boys' assertiveness becomes too extreme this can then lead to outright argument which is too confrontational to be productive for learning. On the other hand, the evaluation of different ideas and rival explanations, via attention to input and feedback, is potentially a useful way to explore what should, after further consideration of the evidence, be held in common. Similarly, girls' tendency to avoid conflict could lead to their ignoring discrepant feedback and 'unsettling' ideas which, again if taken to extremes, would be dysfunctional. But their focus on commonalties provides a useful basis for seeing connections between problems.

How might these differences be understood in school science practices in a context where a conventional gender discourse is salient? The differences in interactional styles may not be interpreted as arising from 'natural differences' but can they be related to the different roles men and women play in society? If so, they are, in Madeleine Arnot's (1982) words, part of the 'symbolic separation of the sexes' that gives the oppression of girls 'the seal of approval'. Describing girls' strengths as to do with seeking commonalties and boys' as associated with assertive and conflictual behaviours seems to define them in a way which is remarkably close to those gender characteristics which supposedly are a function of the asymmetrical power relations between men and women. Girls and women grow up to be more co-operative, sensitive and caring because of the kind of role women have traditionally played in families. Boys are more assertive because they have to maintain their dominance. Tolmie and Howe recognise the difficulty in getting boys and girls to work together in mixed pairs or groups. If these divisions continue then there is every likelihood that girls' attempts to become more assertive in physics will be interpreted as having a different meaning from boys' assertiveness. For example, an expression which is defined as assertive in a boy will be seen as 'bossy' or 'impulsive' in a girl.

There is, however, another, in some ways more intractable, problem. Tolmie and Howe may overgeneralise from experiments which focus on isolated tasks carried out under special conditions. A snapshot of processes more typical of what goes on in school science is to be found in the classroom observational studies of Edwards and Mercer (1987). The emphasis in these lessons on the practical routines rather than on principled understanding of concepts attests to the practice of school physics as discriminatory and exclusive. Although certain intellectual skills are involved, it is not clear that as a school subject it is educationally 'good' for boys or girls. At the end of the day, most pupils in fact 'fail' in physics. Developments may have taken place in their capacities for dialogue in science, but how are these perceived by pupils who end up being evaluated negatively? Given these outcomes it is more likely that what is learned in school physics is not how to exchange opinions in science but how to talk to each other in ways which reproduce status differences in society. There are other discourses at work here – some 'hidden', some more overt – which influence the relationships between pupils and the way pupils see themselves. As well as discourses specific to science and gender, there are discourses of hierarchy and exclusion relating to various forms of class-based and other status differences.

Nevertheless, the 'progressive' notion of science education as outlined by Black and others is, I would argue, consonant with the values of a democratic discursive practice. It is based on a discourse of scientific endeavour which positions students as participants in scientific communities. Such communities, as Kuhn (1970) has pointed out, have different levels – from the specific to the more general – suggesting scientific practices can be seen as 'local' but also as a reflection of wider community values, like freedom and equality. The importance of the individual contribution to the construction of new meanings, the sharing of knowledge, the respect for evidence and the spirit of enquiry in genuine scientific communities are all values endemic to democratic societies, so that doing 'good' science contributes to the construction of such a society. As Miller (1973) acknowledges in his analysis of George Mead's view of creativity, it is individual *agency* and the open selves of an open society which make scientific enquiry possible. The question is: to what extent is the discursive practice of 'good' science distorted or 'corrupted' by the anti-democratic influence of gender and social class practices? As indicated above school science is problematical in this respect, but it is possible to envisage a science curriculum which recontextualises gender differences in cognitive styles and interactional characteristics and contributes to the reconstruction and production of democratic identities.

Where do we go from here?

In the first place it is evident that changes in any one area can only be a starting point for a review of how gender is constructed in the whole curriculum, at both the formal and informal level. The outcome may be that existing curriculum forms, across a range of practices, would have to be radically reformed if equality were to be realised.

The important aim of curriculum development is to build on possibilities within existing discourses. Thus, one might evaluate discourses in terms of their potential for articulating with the broader discourse of democracy and education. In relation to gender discourse this could mean a reappraisal of difference in 'strengths' and 'weaknesses' in learning capabilities, and of 'vices' as well as 'virtues' in the broader area of personality. The historical legacy of patriarchy is the sexist construction of social attitudes and personal characteristics which benefit neither sex morally and perpetuate power-influenced relations which leave girls at a disadvantage. Any talk of differences between the sexes, say in terms of cognitive or emotional development, has to bear this in mind. At the same time it is important to recognise that there have been other, more benign influences on gender relations resulting from democratic reforms which, though limited, have contributed to a reconstruction of identities where difference does not reflect inequality.

We can explore these points further by looking at interpretations of gender characteristics as expressed in the discourse of gender. Take for example the characteristics associated with female 'care' and male 'assertiveness'. The 'nurturing' or 'caring' behaviour of girls is potentially just as much a 'vice' as the aggressive and assertive behaviour of boys. Thus, whilst girls may need to be encouraged to become more assertive, they also need to examine their approaches to 'care'. If these are derived from essentialist assumptions about an emotional division of labour which is thought to spring from 'natural' characteristics, then they merely complement and legitimate uncaring behaviour in boys. Thus the notion of care has to be reviewed for girls and fostered in boys in ways which recontextualise it in democratic models of social and personal relationships. Similar points could be made about the macho behaviour of boys. From a moral perspective in patriarchal discourse this would be seen as a 'vice'. But if we go beyond reductionism and use the multiple discourse model referred to above matters are more complex. 'Macho' culture is not just about hardness, competitiveness and dominance and neither boys nor girls experience it as such. There are qualitative differences between forms of macho attitudes. All involve power *vis-a-vis* women but some may be violent, coercive and misogynist whereas others may reflect a caring (albeit patronising) view based on a perception of women as historically (thus temporarily) the 'weaker' sex. Both attitudes need to be deconstructed but they cannot be reduced to the same social meaning without oversimplifying the phenomena.

Democratic discourse and pupil culture

In developing the argument, we might now consider the question of the relationship of this analysis of discourse to curricular and pedagogical reform. We can posit the notion of *agency* in democratic relations with others as the important and overriding articulating principle of the curriculum (see Mouffe, 1993). The democratic educational community is one which enables the development of person-in-relation with the capacity for reflexivity and agency. The kind of pedagogy required is one which fosters dialogue and allows for arguments to be pursued in power-free 'ideal speech situations' (Habermas, 1971).

Following Cohen (1989) we might identify four aspects of democratic discourse:

1   Decisions must involve a deliberative approach, where participants give reasons for their proposals and are willing to subject them to criticism.
2   There must be equal opportunities to participate (see Habermas (1979) for an elaboration of this).
3   The aim is to arrive at a rationally motivated consensus.

4   There is a relational component, such that participants acknowledge one another's autonomy and mutuality.

There are others which might be added:

5   The absence of hierarchy and asymmetrical power relations.
6   An understanding of self-identity based on a view of self as morally engaged but reflexive and open to change.

This ideal discourse could be used as a criterion against which to evaluate the discourses of schooling. By way of illustration let us examine one of the informal and unofficial discourses of schooling – pupil culture. So far we have been concerned with the articulation of gender discourses with those of the formal curriculum (e.g. science), but we could also look at how gender structures practice in informal areas.

Pupils' cultural practices can be understood as consisting of a mix of contradictory elements, some more consonant with democratic educational ideals than others. According to Woods (1983) most pupil cultures, despite their variations, revolve around three common themes: *status, competence* and *relationships*. Friendships facilitate enjoyment in school, but they have the more profound purpose of fostering a sense of community and a sense of identity. They are potentially the building blocks of a democratic, autonomy enhancing school community. The theme of competence can also be interpreted in a way which is educationally positive. Pollard (1985) refers to a number of social skills which are essentially about

> how to be a member of a group of friends who can maintain and act on the shared meanings and understandings which have been constructed . . . The understanding of what a friend should be like implies a direct reciprocity of trust – sharing, playing, being with you, not showing off.
>
> (pp. 47–48)

Pupils thus not only create their own rules but create rules which are continuous with democratic educational values. But, of course, social competence also includes other skills which are of questionable value from a democratic educational viewpoint. All friendship groups are exclusive in that they have their own rules which a pupil has to understand and accept before becoming a member of the group. But some friendship groups are more open than others. Moreover, some groups are not constructed on the basis of mutual trust but on domination, as the leader exerts power over his or her followers.

In a study carried out by the author and his co-worker (Quicke and Winter, 1995) of two female 'best friends' in a secondary school, there was evidence to suggest that whether relationships were perceived and enacted democratically or hierarchically was the big point of contestation in pupil culture and, in a sense, the overarching theme in pupils' day to day cultural practices. Various forces from within and from outside the school influenced this process. Some aspects of the formal discursive practices of the school reinforced hierarchical structuring, other aspects reinforced the collaborative democratic mode. For these two aspiring working class girls, the discourses of rank, class, ability and gender were in constant interaction such that it was difficult to pinpoint which of them (i.e. the discourses) had the greatest weight in any one instance, let alone over a period of time. In all four areas the girls showed 'positive' approaches from an educational viewpoint as well as 'negative' anti-educational approaches. Examples of the former would be their understanding that 'deep down' certain pupils had 'sense', their view that they did not want to be 'identified' as 'posh' or as 'boffs', their support for girls who were the targets of sexist comments from boys and their solidarity with pupils against 'improper' behaviour of teachers. The authors argued that these views reflected attitudes which were about redressing the balance in power relations and were derived from the assumption that all pupils were of equal value.

· However, on the negative side, the girls in their day to day practices did in fact discriminate against pupils whom they perceived to be at a lower level of academic competence than themselves and took up a non-collaborative stance with regard to working relationships with most other pupils. In resisting the dominance of boys, it was not always clear that the girls approached this in a way that was educationally productive in the final analysis, since their use of determinist notions like 'immaturity' to explain boys' behaviour may have reinforced and legitimised precisely the behaviour they were resisting. Interpreting boys' sexist and non-collaborative behaviour as arising from psycho-biological features, which made boys at this age more childlike than girls, might easily be read as an aspect of anticipatory socialisation into a conventional maternal role.

CONCLUSION

Clearly, schools should examine their curriculum and pedagogy with a view to ascertaining any patterns of discrimination which are gender based. In view of present trends in achievement, particularly as reflected in GCSE results, there is probably no longer any need for positive action in favour of girls although there is need for some form of radical action; likewise for boys, further action is required but not at the expense of girls in terms of resource allocation. Schools also have to be aware of any other patterns of discrimination (e.g. like those stemming from race or class structure), which might be interacting with gender or which, in a particular instance, may even have even more significance than gender for anti-discrimination policies.

The discussion in this chapter gives an indication of a possible way forward for schools in dealing with gender issues. In the first place, it is apparent that such issues are still salient and should be addressed specifically. Secondly, rather than just developing anti-sexist policies schools should actively promote democratic gender identities through the curriculum. At the moment gender differences are usually a function of inequalities but this may not be true of all differences either in the present or the future. In conditions closer to the democratic ideal, it could be that gender ceases to be a significant category in the construction of identity in educational contexts. What gender differences continue to exist may have little social or educational significance. On the other hand such differences may be significant but no longer symptomatic of oppression. The current trend is towards an open, rapidly changing society – what Lash (1994) describes as 'reflexive modernity' – and we would anticipate further transformations in gender identities. More women may become scientists but this scientific identity itself will change as what we understand by 'doing science' and thus achievement in science changes. Female scientists may or may not 'do' the 'new' science differently from their male counterparts. Both men and women may become more 'assertive' and 'caring', and these characteristics may be the same or different for each sex.

Schools are in a difficult position in the current period mainly because of the emergence of restorationist policies which may well put the clock back in relation to equality. The uncertainties of the age in which we live and the challenges to the very notion of community in a diverse and plural world have led some to question all changes that have taken place and to advocate the need for the restoration of old structures, or in common parlance, the need to go 'back to basics'. This strategy is open to a variety of interpretations but it undoubtedly includes a focus on the family, the 'basic' nature of which may once again be construed in patriarchal terms. Teachers who seek to introduce reforms of the National Curriculum may well be blocked indirectly and directly – indirectly by the introduction by government of further 'reforms' which reduce criteria by which schools are judged to trivial measures of performance in skills considered to be 'basic'; directly by the imposition of a fundamentalist National Curriculum which treats morals as unproblematic and academic subjects as fixed entities.

All interventions in the ongoing practices of schools would have to take into account the pupils' sophisticated use of social strategies, their awareness of group dynamics, their capacities for 'political' action in their everyday relationships, and their intuitive cultural understandings of democracy and hierarchy. Teaching approaches which involved some kind of social skills training would only work if they were based on an appreciative rather than deficit view of these pupils as social actors. Encouraging a more democratic discourse could usefully build on the existing strengths of pupils' cultural practices rather than focus on their weaknesses from a democratic and educational viewpoint. The aim would be to make their understanding of the nature of democratic discourse more explicit and thus provide them with the reflective tools to refine and develop their existing practices and to be more critical of undemocratic elements.

A sensitivity to the language of discourse is one of the most crucial aspects of a reformed pedagogy. Pupils could be encouraged to reflect on how, why and to what effect they use certain words, phrases and other aspects of language (see Wilson, 1990). They could reflect on the various conversational tactics they were deploying in small group discussion. They might even address issues to do with the relationship between speaking and the different levels of power within the group (Van Dijk, 1989). How they describe themselves and explain away their own behaviour would be a useful focus for discussion. But it is important to recognise that the discursive features of democratic discourse described above are best regarded as ideals which are not fully realised even in most adult conversations in our alleged liberal democratic society. They may even be unattainable in our society, and only exist as goals to strive for rather than ones that can actually be achieved. Thus we would probably expect to find all existing discourses amongst pupils and teachers to be characterised by both democratic and undemocratic elements.

Finally, at the level of the self, the critical understanding of the 'whole self' should also be a focus for educational practices. This entails a particular emphasis on the young person's emerging capacity to reflect on the totality of their qualities and commitments and make judgements derived from reflexively interpreted accounts of what kind of person they were, who they wanted to be and what kind of life they wanted to live.

As I have argued elsewhere (Quicke, 1996b), there is a need to develop a self-reflexive curriculum as a meta-practice involving reflection upon the discourses which constitute the self, with a view to developing awareness of values or qualities and their coherence (or lack of it) in constructed narratives of the self. The discourse of this meta-practice will involve a linguistic differentiation of the 'I' and the 'me' enabling a 'way of thinking' about identity as *personal identity*, and include the imperative to understand oneself as a 'whole person' and as a continuity across practices and across space and time. It promotes a certain disengagement from commitment to a practice and enables us to review this commitment in relation to the kind of life which we perceive as the 'good life' for us. The discourse of the self-reflexive curriculum will therefore involve an ethical language which identifies the qualities or virtues across a range of discursive practices as characteristics of the person – one might say the character of the person. Crucially, what is fostered in the self-reflexive curriculum is the capacity for critical reflexivity – to deliberate about how one is constituted as a self within different discourses, and about how the way one is 'becoming' mirrors what one understands to be a 'good' life.

REFERENCES

Arnot, M. (1982) 'Male hegemony, social class and women's education', in L. Stone (ed.) (1994) *The Education Feminism Reader* (pp. 84–104), London: Routledge.

Baker, D. and Jones, D. (1992) 'Opportunity and performance: a sociological explanation for gender differences in academic mathematics', in J. Wrigley (ed.) *Education and Gender Equality*, London: Falmer.

Cohen, J. (1989) 'Deliberation and democratic legitimacy', in A. Hamlin and P. Pettit (eds) *The Good Polity* (pp. 17–34) New York: Blackwell.

Darling, J. and Glendinning, A. (1996) *Gender Matters in Schools*, London: Cassell.

Davies, B. and Harre, R. (1990) 'Positioning: the discursive production of selves', *Journal for the Theory of Social Behaviour* 20(1): 43–63.

Department for Education (1994) *GCSE and GCE A/AS Examination Results 1992–3*, London: HMSO.

Department of Education and Science (1989) *Education Observed No. 14: Girls Learning Mathematics*, London: HMSO.

Edwards, D. and Mercer, N. (1987) *Common Knowledge*, London: Routledge.

Equal Opportunities Commission (EOC)/Office for Standards in Education (OFSTED) (1996) *The Gender Divide*, London: HMSO.

Ford, J., Mongon, D. and Whelan, M. (1982) *Special Education and Social Control*, London: Routledge and Kegan Paul.

Giddens, A. (1991) *Modernity and Self Identity*, Cambridge: Polity Press.

Gold, K. (1995) 'Hard times for Britain's lost boys', *New Scientist* 145 (1963): 12–13.

Gorman, T.P., White, J., Brooks, G., Maclure, M. and Kispal, A. (1988) *Language Performance in Schools: Review of APU Language Monitoring 1979–1983*, Department of Education and Science/Department of Education for Northern Ireland/Welsh Office, London: HMSO.

Habermas, J. (1971) *Towards a Rational Society*, London: Heinemann.

—— (1979) *Communication and the Evolution of Society* (trans. T.A. McCarthy), Boston, MA: Beacon Press.

Harris, S., Nixon, J. and Rudduck, J. (1993) 'Schoolwork, homework and gender', *Gender and Education* 5(1): 3–15.

Kuhn, T.S. (1970) *The Structure of Scientific Revolutions*, Chicago: The University of Chicago Press.

Lash, S. (1994) 'Reflexivity and its doubles: students, aesthetics, community', in U. Beck *et al. Reflexive Modernization* (pp. 110–73), Cambridge: Polity Press.

Licht, B.G. and Dweck, C.S. (1983) 'Sex differences in achievement orientations: consequences for academic choices and attainments', in M. Marland (ed.) *Sex Differentiation and Schooling*, London: Heinemann.

MacEwen Scott, A. (1994) *Gender Segregation and Social Change*, Oxford: Oxford University Press.

Millard, E. (1997) *Differently Literate: Boys, Girls and the Schooling of Literacy*, London: Falmer.

Miller, D. L. (1973) *George Herbert Mead*, Chicago: The University of Chicago Press.

Mouffe, C. (1993) 'Liberal socialism and pluralism', in J. Squires (ed.) *Principled Positions* (pp. 69–78), London: Lawrence & Wishart.

OFSTED (1993) *Boys and English*, Ref: 2/93/NS, London: DFE.

—— (1994) *Science and Mathematics in Schools*, London: HMSO.

Peim, N. (1993) *Critical Theory and the English Teacher*, London: Routledge.

Pollard, A. (1985) *The Social World of the Primary School*, London: Holt Rinehart and Winston.

Purvis, J. (1981) 'Towards a history of women's education in nineteenth century Britain: a sociological analysis', *Westminster Studies in Education* 4: 45–71.

Quicke, J. (1995) 'Gender and GCSE results: what schools are doing', Paper presented to the Annual Conference of the British Educational Research Association, Bath University, September.

—— (1996a) 'Learning and context: constructing an integrated perspective', *British Journal of Sociology of Education* 17(1): 103–13.

—— (1996b) 'Self, modernity and a direction for curriculum reform', *British Journal of Educational Studies* 44(4): 364–76.

Quicke, J. and Winter, C. (1995) ' "Best Friends": a case study of girls' reaction to an intervention designed to foster collaborative group work', *Gender and Education* 7(3): 259–81.

Sheeran, Y. and Barnes, D. (1991) *School Writing*, Milton Keynes: Open University Press.

Swann, J. (1992) *Girls, Boys and Language*, Oxford: Blackwell.

Tolmie, A. and Howe, C. (1993) 'Gender and dialogue in secondary school physics', *Gender and Education* 5(2): 191–209.

Van Dijk, T.A. (1989) 'Structures of discourse and structures of power', in J.A. Anderson (ed.) *Communication Yearbook*, Vol. 12, Newbury Park, CA: Sage.

Walkerdine, V. (1988) *The Mastery of Reason*, London: Routledge.

White, J. (1990) 'Questions of choice and change', in *National Writing Project (NWP): What Are Writers Made Of?*, Walton on Thames: Nelson.

Wilson, J. (1990) *Politically Speaking*, London: Routledge.

Woods, P. (1983) *Sociology and the School*, London: Routledge.

ENDNOTE

Balancing the books: towards
a more equitable curriculum

Elaine Millard

In describing the growth of critical awareness of the role of gendered identity in school and its influence on performance in and beyond the curriculum, the contributors to this collection have made frequent references to a range of research projects completed in the late 1970s and 1980s. These established the need for equal opportunities policy in schools and focused specifically on ways of improving girls' performance. However, it appears that despite the pioneering work of feminist activists supported by equal opportunities legislation and the elaboration of ever more subtle descriptive frameworks for understanding power relations at work between the sexes, little in the balance of power in the classroom has really changed since then. Those who argue that there has been a feminist revolution in schools and that it is for this reason that boys and men are now the disadvantaged subjects will be hard pressed to provide much evidence to show that the conditions for learning, identified in the earlier reports, have been 'remedied'. Though girls have the advantage over their brothers in terms of academic success it is not predominantly because gender reforms have widely prevailed.

Those of us who make frequent visits to secondary classrooms, in the role of researcher, supervisor or inspector, are given constant reminders of rigid divisions in classroom organisation that create a version of gender apartheid in most mixed-sex classes. Observations of who does what in class show that boys continue to dominate intellectual space, particularly in whole class discussions, and to monopolise prime physical areas of the school, such as the main corridors and playgrounds and, significantly, the best positions in the classroom such as at the front of the laboratory for demonstration periods. Moreover, when small working groups are left to form without active teacher direction, they are constructed predominantly of single-sex units, with a few mixed friendship groups, thereby reinforcing the differences in the working patterns of boys and girls described by Davies in Chapter 1. In mixed schools, in areas of the curriculum where subject choice is made available, boys continue to choose differently from girls, more frequently absenting themselves in spirit from subjects, such as modern foreign languages, as Clark has described in Chapter 2, when their participation is compelled by statutory requirements. This kind of gendered subject choice, as Staples (1990) has shown, is less marked in single-sex schools. Further, in most mixed classes, girls' disaffection is expressed less vociferously than that of their male classmates, although increasingly, changes in the curriculum are creating more female resistance amongst the less successful students, notably those from lower socio-economic groups.

Analysing a similar picture of difference in the uptake of particular subjects in the Australian system in *Who wins at school? Girls and boys in Australian secondary education*, Teese *et al.* (1995) have commented on a long tradition of devaluing the humanities, in both secondary schools and universities. Specifically, they point out that girls and boys still select subjects along traditional lines. Girls continue to be overrepresented in modern languages, the humanities and biology, while boys dominate high level maths and the physical sciences. Moreover, the science subjects, particularly the 'hard' sciences like physics and chemistry, often carry more academic status. In response to this imbalance, Teese argues that both secondary and tertiary sectors need to provide humanities courses which are far more structured, so that they will gain academic prestige and therefore attract more boys' participation. In Australia, however, the whole emphasis has been on encouraging girls into maths and technology, further enhancing a hierarchy of knowledge that places these subjects on a higher level than those in which girls have traditionally succeeded. The problem is not that the girls who do not choose maths and science are limiting their options – it is the very fact that the choices remain gendered and reinforce traditional patterns of success and failure. Teese *et al.* stress that boys' comparative weakness in the humanities is a very good reason for boosting the prestige of these subject areas.

In the UK, the Equal Opportunities Commission points to the improved performance of girls in GCSE examinations to support its claim that current differences in performance result from girls' increasing success. This is marked in the improved performances of girls in maths and science, but as Opie and Scaife have shown in this collection, differences of choice and opportunity at 16+ still leave girls significantly less well qualified in science and technological subjects. Further, they are at a numerical disadvantage when applying for suitable courses in the tertiary section of education where the humanities subjects, which they continue to prefer, are more oversubscribed than technology, engineering and computer science courses, favoured by young men. Moreover, as Brine has shown in Chapter 11, EU legislation, which had as its intention the extension of opportunities for women, has been interpreted in a way that often achieves the opposite, excluding them from career development and promotion opportunities within their existing traditional patterns of employment. The message continues to suggest that it is girls who must adapt their career options rather than tackling the low status of work in traditional female occupations such as childcare or textiles. Indeed, as Quicke comments in Chapter 14, in terms of careers, even in professions with large numbers of highly qualified female members, men seem able to commandeer a greater proportion of the senior, highly paid posts. In relation to men's advantage at higher levels of employment Acker (1994) cites Lortie's findings on male teachers' career aspirations in American first schools, which showed that of the small number of male teachers in his sample, most had low motivation and low interest in their work, but all expected to become principals within five years. The Australian data cited above likewise shows that despite girls' increasing overall success in school work, certain boys still continue to lead in subjects granted the highest status and remain at the top in their future careers as a result (Teese *et al.* 1995: 108). They conclude that girls' subject choices are often less coherent, less vocational and less mutually supporting than those of the group Teese *et al.* name the 'elite' boys, who appear to be more directed towards stronger vocational pathways.

WHY HAS SO LITTLE CHANGED?

We need therefore to consider why there have been so few changes in the gendered nature of schooling, despite the copious evidence of its effects on subject choice, achievement and access to continuing education. Firstly, we need to restate that gender is deeply rooted both in the minds and behaviour of individuals and within the cultural patterns and practices of schools as institutions where it is particularly impervious to change. Secondly the chapters in this volume have shown how schools work to reinforce particular versions of gendered identity and constrain individuals rather than helping to redress educational and social inequalities. Indeed, elsewhere, Mac an Ghaill (1994) has argued that schools in themselves are largely masculinising institutions and are complicit in producing inequalities both in gender processes and power relations. However, in addition to these semi-permanent structural conditions, a further contemporary contingent factor is to be found in the massive upheaval which has resulted from the imposition of a National Curriculum on schools in the 1990s. This National Curriculum has narrowed the prevailing conception of the purposes of education by restoring a view of it as largely the transmission and reception of narrowly defined areas of knowledge and culture, rather than encouraging a more critical concern for the conditions under which effective learning can take place. It has become increasingly unfashionable to differentiate pupils in ways other than by attainment, measured simplistically through their performance recorded in league tables, and in consequence only simple solutions to remedy 'failure' are sought, without questioning the structures of the curriculum itself. Teachers have been deflected from searching for a better understanding of the social relations within and beyond school which influence pupils' attitudes and motivation to what they learn.

The restitution of a neo-conservative programme in curriculum planning has been manifested as the insistence on 'back to basics' and a restatement of formal and traditional subject content. This has worked towards a closure of possible meanings and constrained teachers' creative response and openness to curriculum change. There has also been a decreased choice of content and therefore more limited opportunities for pupils to question what they are being asked to learn, which has at the same time prevented their teachers from discussions of the relevance of the curriculum to educational objectives. Standards, with an accompanying assumption of a 'drop' in levels of literacy, are evoked as if there have always been measurable 'products' from education from which comparisons can be drawn.

Furthermore, curriculum development which explores the interrelationship between gender and education, an area which has always been a subordinate discourse in school, has been made to 'disappear' by a governmental preoccupation with individualised performance aimed at identifying 'failing' schools. An emphasis on individual performance has shifted an interest in gender from an analytic and productive methodology for change, to a descriptive category which institutes difference as biologically determined. Using governmental criteria of academic performance, schools can always be shown to have 'failed' some of their pupils and the numbers of such 'failures' include both boys and girls. However, it is the differing patterns of failure that ought to concern educationalists as it is the meaning drawn from the patterns which will provide a sound rationale for intervention. As John Quicke has suggested in Chapter 14, there is a pressing need to interrogate the prior discourses which construct curriculum knowledge in order to avoid producing oversimplified definitions of winners and losers and to work towards a curriculum that will better empower all learners. In following up boys' seeming disadvantage in language-based areas of the curriculum it is important to avoid slipping into old patterns of biological determinism that suggest all boys suffer a similar disadvantage while all girls succeed.

A similar open-mindedness is required when examining interests outside school where patterns of different access to the curriculum are mirrored in opportunities presented to boys and girls, to pursue their interests beyond the confines of the school gates. Wellington's chapter has identified patterns of imbalance in the access given to what is supposedly our 'national game'. Interestingly, the pseudo-scientific, biological arguments which were used for over a century to 'explain' female inferiority in maths, science and technology have now been mobilised to undermine or ridicule girls' participation in extracurricular activities such as soccer. Indeed, the whole area of school-based PE or games, as Skelton has shown in Chapter 6, has been subject to government policies, which have reinstated patriarchal competitive values and which therefore work to exclude large numbers of pupils from full participation in physical activity.

THE PROBLEM OF THEORISING GENDER DIFFERENCES IN EDUCATIONAL TERMS

Post-modernist researchers' more sophisticated analysis of social and cultural pluralism has worked to make gender theorists uneasy about oversimplified categorisations of male and female which carry within them traces of a 'grand theory' or biological determinism. Feminists have identified a tendency in their earlier theorising to overgeneralisation and a consequent drift towards the same kind of biological determinism, used initially to limit girls' access to education, through an analysis which privileged discussion of patriarchal systems in so far as they limited women's opportunities and development. A new awareness of the effect of gender, drawn from research on men and masculinities, has an important part to play as part of feminist approaches to education. At a period when boys' relative 'underachievement' is being highlighted it is necessary to understand how different forms of masculinity and femininities are negotiated and taken up by individuals in order to avoid simplistic definitions of 'victim' and oppressor. In Chapter 13 of this volume Mac an Ghaill and Haywood argue that gender is actively produced within different contexts and this in itself works to destabilise the centrality of the curriculum. Similarly, the editors of the special issue of *Gender and Education*, 'Masculinities in education', suggest that 'an interest in gender differences has been, if not replaced, then complemented by research on gender *as* difference, and a concern with how gender, femininities and masculinities are "done" in different educational contexts' (Griffin and Lees, 1997: 6). Such an emphasis should avoid the pit-falls of previous gender initiatives that have often reinforced, rather than deconstructed, existing hierarchies of knowledge by privileging certain disciplines, notably science, technology and mathematical thinking, over others (see Quicke and Scaife on science education in this volume).

In the light of both these issues, that is school curriculum development and theoretical concerns related to gender and identity, this collection of essays has identified key areas of concern for both teachers and researchers engaged in creating a more equitable and democratic access to education. The evidence currently being amassed about boys' and girls' performance suggests that there are already sufficiently compelling arguments for taking steps to balance the gender equation within the existing curriculum. However, it is important to stress that those concerned with implementing programmes to remedy 'underachievement' should avoid reading the various contributory factors in the context of the identification of 'competing victims'. The effect of such a focus has been most clearly described in relation to the experience of Australian anti-sexist programmes in which the interests of boys and girls were seen to be constantly in competition for attention and remedy (Alloway and Gilbert, 1997). In Australia, this led to a backlash against what has been described by some commentators as the feminisation of schooling. This oversimplification of the effect of gender reforms is well illustrated by the response of Dr Ken Rowe, who described problems identified in boys' school attainment as the result of too much 'oestrogen' in the curriculum (Williams, 1996). The 'oestrogen' in question is identified by Rowe as verbal reasoning and an increase in the need for literacy, aspects of knowledge which most teachers would assume are important for all pupils' learning. It is important, therefore, to avoid such simple attributions of particular gender biases if we are to equalise opportunities for all to achieve their full potential within the education system we construct for them. It also means we need to acknowledge difference and diversity as positive rather than negative attributes of learning, while ensuring access for all to the most powerful discourses of the culture. To do this effectively it is therefore important to understand how gender, social class membership and ethnicity are interwoven in the system into complex patterns of powerlessness, disadvantage and difference. Equally important is a sense of the specific histories and the complexities of the competing discourses that contribute to shaping the disparate elements of the school curriculum. Most significantly, gender studies have begun to emphasise the need to deconstruct our implicit notions of what it is to be successful by challenging dominant narratives and allowing a wider range of voices to be heard.

Until very recently, despite a pervasive rhetoric that valued literacy, creativity and the various subjects of the humanities as academic and cultural accomplishments, these attributes had not been accorded equal status in the workplace. 'Being good at reading and writing has not necessarily led to careers in language-based professions – or even well-paid jobs' (White, 1986; Alloway and Gilbert, 1997). School literacies have therefore been undervalued by both boys and young men, but have not always delivered everything they might seem to promise in the way of access to high achievement after school to the successful schoolgirl. However, it is only with the decay of a traditional industrial base and the emergence of an information-led economy that the possession of weaker literacy skills in large numbers of young males has been understood as a positive disadvantage.

In the past thirty years the conventional transition from school to full-time paid labour has broken down. Traditional understandings of the nature of work and the masculine signifiers that it generates retain little currency. Types, such as the building worker, the rigger, the steel erector, the miner, are redundant in contemporary social and economic conditions, so that many young people have abandoned the ideal type of the manual labourer as sites of identification, precisely because they no longer correspond to any realisable aspiration.

Within this socio-economic framework, as Millard has argued in Chapter 3 it is insufficient to focus exclusively on school performance without considering the social and cultural practices that create opportunities for other, newer forms of literacy to emerge and be developed outside formal teaching contexts. Conversely, a post-modern emphasis on negotiated 'identity' difference and the complexities of socio-economic power relations can act to paralyse any practical course of intervention in school. Discussing the problems of a post-modern perspective on knowledge for education, Carr (1997) in a paper addressing the relation of philosophy to educational research has warned that

> educational researchers who are now organising their inquiries around such fashionable postmodern concepts as 'difference', 'identity', 'diversity' and the like have locked themselves into an exclusive and excluding subculture in which the value of intellectual inquiry is no longer judged by the extent to which it contributes to progressive educational change,

but simply to the extent to which it displays ironic detachment and aesthetic sophistication.

Carr give his emphasis to the need for educational theory that contributes to informed and principled action. Too frequently, post-modernist analysis of social and cultural complexity has contributed much to academic debate, but too little to practice.

On the other hand, in an analysis of the economic and cultural imperatives operative in the USA, which bear marked similarities to our own, Michael Apple (1996) cautions against precipitate action based on the 'common sense' school of argument, which, among other things, both in the USA and the UK has suggested that a National Curriculum can create social cohesion by measuring all schools and their pupils against 'objective criteria'. He asserts that given the existing differences in resources and in class and race segregation, the measures will achieve exactly the opposite and 'legitimise inequality': 'The "same treatment" by sex, race and ethnicity, or class is not the same at all' (1996: 33). Further, he suggests that the achievement of 'really equal treatment' can only come about through a curriculum based 'on a recognition of those differences that empower and depower our students in identifiable ways' (p. 33).

However, because 'academic' success in the core subjects at 16+ is still the means by which pupils are most frequently rated within and beyond school it remains essential to gain a better understanding of who gains what in the current distribution of curriculum honours. We need to know more accurately which boys and which girls are the likely winners or losers, rather than veering from a concentration on either boys' or girls' interests at any one time. The current danger is that boys' so-called 'underachievement' will be used to overturn the kind of support given to girls which has improved their educational opportunities. In these essays, Jesson's chapter gives an account of a more sophisticated way of analysing the measurable components of the curriculum through the notion of 'value-added' school variables, which provides different questions to be asked of current league tables. Jesson's statistical analysis allows the identification of objective data which as a by-product allows access to believable accounts of where efforts to improve performance have been less gender-unfriendly. Issues are addressed through the analysis of instances where performance differentials have been reduced by enhancing the performance of boys without limiting that of girls, statistics which are of vital importance in helping to recognise aspects of current practice that can empower the full range of students' learning.

In the UK, the imposition of the National Curriculum has resulted in a subsequent loss of teacher autonomy and a reluctance on the part of most institutions to engage with what are now seen as distracting social and cultural issues. The curriculum has been to all intents and purposes 'frozen' and the important work of attending to the constantly shifting relations of teachers and taught and the complexities of social and technological change, which affect the quality of the lives of contemporary young people, ignored. Teachers feel constrained by bureaucratic demands to concentrate exclusively on what is required by a prescribed curriculum and its processes of accounting so that a majority of recent in-service courses have focused on implementation, monitoring and assessment, rather than on curriculum development and change.

WHAT ARE THE WAYS FORWARD?

Yet, there is still an urgent need to enter into debate about what should be taught and how teaching translates into learning. Further, gender remains an important category related to such curriculum choices through which it works either to empower or disadvantage significant groups of pupils within the current system. For many western cultures, the focus for concern as we approach the millennium is the problem perceived to stem from the disaffection of a growing number of boys from much of mainstream schooling and school-based literacy practices in particular. This, coupled to a rapidly changing infrastructure, which in most areas has replaced traditional heavy industrial work with more feminised, and literacy-dependent forms of employment, has driven some institutions to look for quick fixes in targeting groups of older boys for preferential mentoring, in effect penalising today's girls for their sisters' past records of academic success.

We now know something about the effects of gender on aspects of school social organisation and academic performance, but far less about its interaction with ethnicity and social class and even less about the most effective ways of addressing the issues raised. For this reason, some of the contributors to this volume such as Clark, Davies, Povey and Millard have suggested specific classroom strategies for approaching key aspects of unequal performance. In doing this, however, they lay stress on the importance of the needs for teachers and students of both sexes to arrive at a better understanding of the specific contexts in which gender differentiation occurs. We can also learn much from the documented experiences of Australia, where, following the publication of *Girls, School and Society* (Commonwealth Schools Commission, 1975), the first Australian national report on the education of girls, there have been strong top-down gender reform policies at state and federal level, combined with bottom-up grass roots feminist activism in schools. A tightening of government controls and the retreat from social justice policies also occurred much later in Australia than in the UK, and there has therefore been more opportunity to evaluate processes of reform and the effectiveness of a wide range of anti-sexist initiatives (Yates, 1993; Gilbert, 1996).

The Australian experience has shown that gender reform policies work best within an institutional framework that allows students to take charge of their own processes of deconstructing meaning and which reflect the processes of gender redefinition and uncertainty which have occurred over the past two decades. Gender reform was best seen as a form of discursive practice in which meanings surrounding concepts of success, power and responsibility were opened up to questioning and where received opinions and central 'truths' about knowledge could be contested by both students and staff. Counterproductive was the imposition by a school staff of outdated understandings of gendered relations, coupled with simplistic views of how to remedy such disadvantages. Young people were found to be less tolerant of top-down pronouncements about the nature of sexism than they had been twenty years ago and needed to be given sufficient space to construct their own responses and resistance to dominant narratives in the light of local circumstances (Kenway and Willis, 1997).

The essays in this volume, by focusing on gender issues specific to individual subject areas of the secondary school curriculum, as well as those contingent on social relations beyond schooling, aim to broaden other teachers' and researchers' understanding, firstly of their own practice and secondly of the curriculum as a whole in relation to the gendered nature of its outcomes. There have been many examples given in this collection where classroom practice has worked against the development of a curriculum which could enable all pupils to achieve. Ultimately, it is hoped that identifying key areas where pupils are disadvantaged will encourage further investigation into the effects of intervention and refocus attention on the pressing need for a curriculum which can be made more relevant to young people who will live most of their lives in a new century. Such a curriculum, idealistic in intention, but practical in its solutions, would reflect a commitment on the part of teachers of every discipline to increasing educational opportunity for both sexes and would aim primarily to grant them a more potent voice in articulating their own intellectual and social development.

REFERENCES

Acker, S. (1994) *Gendered Education*, Buckingham: Open University Press.

Alloway, N. and Gilbert, P. (1997) 'Boys and literacy: lessons from Australia, *Gender and Education*, 9: 49–58.

Apple, M. (1996) *Cultural Politics and Education*, Buckingham: Open University Press.

Carr, W. (1997) 'Philosophy and method in educational research', *Cambridge Journal of Education*, Special Issue: Philosophy and Educational Research.

Commonwealth Schools Commission (1975) *Girls, School and Society*, Report by study group to the Schools Commission, November 1975, Canberra.

Gilbert, P. (1996) 'Talking about gender: terminology used in the education of girls policy area and implications for policy, priorities and programs', Australian Government Publishing Service, Canberra, Australia.

Griffin, C. and Lees, S. (1997) 'Editorial', *Gender and Education* 9(1): 49–58.

Kenway, J. and Willis, S. (1997) *Contesting Gender: Girls, Boys and Teachers*, London: Routledge.

Mac an Ghaill, M. (1994) *The Making of Men: Masculinities, Sexualities and Schooling*, Buckingham: Open University Press.

Staples, A. (1990) 'Differences between pupils from mixed and single sex schools in their enjoyment of school subjects and in their attitudes to science and to school', *The Educational Review* 42: 221–30.

Teese, R., Davies, M., Charlton, M. and Polesel, J. (1995) *Who Wins at School? Girls and Boys in*

Australian Secondary Education, Department of Education Policy and Management, The University of Melbourne, Australia.

White, J. (1986) 'The writing on the wall: beginning or end of a girl's career?, *Women's Studies International Forum* 9: 561–74.

Williams, E. (1996) 'Male brain rattled by curriculum oestrogen', *News & Opinion*, TES 15 March.

Yates, L. (1993) 'The education of girls: policy, research and the question of gender', Australian Centre for Educational Research', Hawthorn, Australia.

INDEX